Entitlement and Complaint

Entitlement and Complaint

Ending Careers and Reviewing Lives in Post-Revolutionary France

DAVID G. TROYANSKY

OXFORD
UNIVERSITY PRESS

Oxford University Press is a department of the University of Oxford. It furthers
the University's objective of excellence in research, scholarship, and education
by publishing worldwide. Oxford is a registered trade mark of Oxford University
Press in the UK and certain other countries.

Published in the United States of America by Oxford University Press
198 Madison Avenue, New York, NY 10016, United States of America.

© Oxford University Press 2023

All rights reserved. No part of this publication may be reproduced, stored in
a retrieval system, or transmitted, in any form or by any means, without the
prior permission in writing of Oxford University Press, or as expressly permitted
by law, by license, or under terms agreed with the appropriate reproduction
rights organization. Inquiries concerning reproduction outside the scope of the
above should be sent to the Rights Department, Oxford University Press, at the
address above.

You must not circulate this work in any other form
and you must impose this same condition on any acquirer.

Library of Congress Cataloging-in-Publication Data
Names: Troyansky, David G., author.
Title: Entitlement and complaint : ending careers and reviewing lives
in post-Revolutionary France / David G. Troyansky.
Description: New York, NY : Oxford University Press, [2023] |
Includes bibliographical references and index.
Identifiers: LCCN 2023012255 (print) | LCCN 2023012256 (ebook) |
ISBN 9780197638750 (hardback) | ISBN 9780197638774 (epub)
Subjects: LCSH: Pensions—Government policy—France—History. |
Retirees—France—History. | Social security—France—History. |
Public welfare—France—History. | France—History—1789-1900.
Classification: LCC HD7105.45.F8 T76 2023 (print) | LCC HD7105.45.F8 (ebook) |
DDC 331.25/20944—dc23/eng/20230323
LC record available at https://lccn.loc.gov/2023012255
LC ebook record available at https://lccn.loc.gov/2023012256

DOI: 10.1093/oso/9780197638750.001.0001

Printed by Integrated Books International, United States of America

For Amy, as ever

Contents

Preface ix

Introduction: Rights, Careers, and the History of Aging 1

PART I: CAREER AND RETIREMENT

1. Pensions as Favor and Pensions as Right 17
2. Careering across the Revolutionary and Napoleonic Divide 28
3. Setting Rules from Old Regime to Midcentury 54
4. Restoration, Revolution, and Retirement: Ending Careers, 1814–53 75

PART II: THE LANGUAGE OF RETIREMENT

5. Entitlement and Complaint: Creating a Rhetoric of Retirement 119
6. Changing Content and Expectations 144
7. Gender, Widowhood, and the Limits of Entitlement 160

Conclusion: Right and Memory in the Shadow of Revolution 183

Notes 189
Bibliography 217
Index 229

Preface

This project has been with me a long time. I was already familiar with the archival sources more than twenty years ago, when I first saw their potential significance. As I gathered more and more material, I found I had something to say about a range of issues in French history. I had begun with a few ideas about age and retirement. My dialogue with the sources—it often felt like a conversation, but the only noise came from typing a little too heavily on a series of laptops—allowed me to say something about the shaping of the modern life course, the emergence of particular constructions of self and career, and the role of the magistracy in the development of ideas of public service and entitlement. I gave papers, published some of them in obscure places, and looked forward to completing a monograph about ten years ago, by which time I had indeed written much of a draft. Then it sat. I wrote another book and coedited two more. I organized conferences. I changed jobs, took on administrative tasks, dealt with some usual and some not so usual challenges. The project still beckoned. And I discovered the great advantage of having taken so long.

Not only did I understand more about the passage of time and the making of a career—I never believed that really mattered when in my younger days I began writing on old age—but by observing changing trends in historical writing I was able to approach the task in new ways. What I initially wrote grew out of an enthusiastic response to the archival sources. It also came about through discussion with gerontologists and others in the humanities and social sciences who had an interest in aging. Sometimes I shared my work with other historians; sometimes I was the only historian in the room. Both kinds of audiences convinced me that I had very rich material, begging to be "written up." Of course, sources don't simply "speak for themselves." There was a scholarly framework. It concerned the development of state institutions on the one hand and uses of those institutions by a large group of relatively privileged individuals on the other. Within that framework, I reported on people who made careers in an extremely turbulent time, who tried to make sense retrospectively of their experiences, and who made themselves both heroes and victims on the French historical stage. I was interested in the workings of a new bureaucracy that encouraged the creation of dossiers and an accounting of professional lives, but I was also interested in individuals' self-presentation and, by accumulation of evidence, the self-presentation of entire cohorts of individuals.

That might have been enough. I did produce those articles and chapters in collective works. I wrote much of that draft. But as time passed, the historical literature developed in ways that led me to think differently about my own material. No one else was doing precisely what I was doing, but historians in a number of related areas were beginning to think about issues that I had been describing in what had sometimes felt like great isolation. Regional studies of magistrates and *fonctionnaires* were beginning to appear and to provide new empirical evidence about change and continuity, social origins and professionalization, and the intersection of national politics and local experience. I never felt I had waited so long that I was being scooped. My initial findings were already out there, and I knew I had much more to say. But while that early draft made easy reference to scholarly literature about ideas of right, of social debt, of life course and self, I now found people theorizing about things that in a naive way seemed fairly obvious from close reading of my archival sources but that had resisted analysis and were not really obvious at all. These included the history of the legal profession and the judiciary, the history of bureaucracy, the history of emotion, the notion of memoir and its particular form in the first half of the nineteenth century, the character of the political weathervane (*girouette*) at times of regime change, the deployment of strategy in writing public institutions, and, yes, there was even an analysis of requests for pensions by historians Jean-Luc Chappey and Antoine Lilti. Those requests came from writers, not government officials, but the process was comparable. They were part of the same historical universe.[1]

That additional scholarly literature confirmed for me the salience of the project and allowed me to connect the already compelling stories of a large group of individuals, as well as an analysis of their career patterns and their rhetoric, to all those other things that I now saw made the post-revolutionary half-century such an extraordinary era. It was almost as if the framework I was using owed so much to the gerontological literature and the rules of the bureaucracy under study that I was losing sight of the narrative arc. The historical literature helped me find it.

In large part, the historical literature has necessarily been about regime change. Magistrates, like so many others, had to negotiate historical transitions. Social and political reconstruction were on virtually everyone's agenda. How would the republic be reimagined after the drama of 1793–94? How would the French overcome trauma and bury their dead? How would the Napoleonic era build upon both Old Regime and revolutionary pasts? What would the Bourbon Restoration restore? What would it try to forget? How would "Romantic Catholics" or nineteenth-century liberals make sense of the passage of time.[2] And so on, as we move to July Monarchy, Second Republic, and Second Empire.

Historical actors who made those transitions imagined lives for themselves and their families that cut across multiple regimes. The civil servants whom Sarah Maza has opposed to the imagined or mythic bourgeoisie of the post-revolutionary era and the families of Vannes that Christopher Johnson identified as provincial bourgeois, with their combined familial and economic strategies, were all involved in crossing period divides.[3] How they understood themselves was hardly limited by any one regime or a political seesaw of revolution and reaction. They had their own stories to tell and to build on. They could take advantage of political or financial opportunities or keep their heads down. And they could guard their private stories for themselves.

Pension demands also told stories of public and private life, and a work that appeared as I was putting finishing touches on this book, Emma Rothschild's *An Infinite History*, resurrected even more varied stories, as families made their way across time, their private lives, careers, and investments intersecting with big or small public events.[4] Even those who appeared fleetingly on the public stage had their own concerns. How they balanced it all in networks barely visible to posterity was central to Rothschild's reconstruction. Making lives and contributions visible at least to state officials was a goal of "my" characters. I cannot know what they might have thought about becoming visible to twenty-first-century readers.

Over the years I have tried to incorporate social history with cultural history. In this case, cultural history refers especially to the use of language. But in no other work have I attempted so thoroughly to communicate the taste of the archives and the tone of the sources. As social scientists historians test hypotheses, count, and argue. As humanists we seek out meanings. But even in pursuing the history of the self or the history of emotion, we may reconnect with the fundamental historical work of exploring the past and communicating what comes from longtime immersion in its material remains. In all that I have learned from theory-minded gerontologists whose works appear in my notes, I have never lost sight of the archival sources that lie at the heart of the process and of the historians whose books communicate the taste of the archives.

None of this would have been possible without institutional support. A Fulbright Research Fellowship, a two-week fellowship at the Institute for Advanced Study at the University of Iowa, and a couple of Faculty Development Leaves from Texas Tech University were important in the early stages. Along the way I tried out my ideas at seminars at the Université de Lyon and the École des Hautes Études en Sciences Sociales (Paris) and as keynote speaker at a conference at Ithaca College and a meeting of the Society for French History in Newcastle (UK). I thank the organizers and participants of those events for their responses and suggestions.

A sabbatical from Brooklyn College in 2014–15 afforded me more time in the archives but also allowed me to delve into that new French scholarly literature that helped me reframe or at least tweak the project. Pierre Serna's seminar at the Sorbonne was a useful and welcoming place for reconnecting with current practices of French history across the eighteenth and nineteenth centuries. The café in the Bibliothèque nationale de France was another.

Sessions of the Society for French Historical Studies, the Western Society for French History, and the Consortium on the Revolutionary Era as well as informal discussions during those events were useful for trying out the ideas in this book. I also presented pieces of the manuscript at two events at Columbia University: a combined "Eighteenth-Century" and "Law and Politics" seminar and a 2018 gathering of eighteenth-century French specialists. I thank Paula Fichtner and Isser Woloch in particular for their responses at that first event. I thank Jeff Freedman for organizing the second, where friends' and colleagues' suggestions essentially set my agenda for the next-to-last revisions. For advice that resulted in the draft I submitted to Oxford University Press, I thank Jeff Horn and John Merriman. Their page-by-page reading strengthened the manuscript in innumerable ways. They helped me articulate what the book is really about, and I'm grateful that they demonstrated how I could make large cuts to individual stories without weakening the argument. Having such friends in the profession has been a real joy. John's death, before this book appeared, came as a shock, a major loss to the field and to his many friends.

I have explained the idea of the book to several groups of students at Texas Tech, Brooklyn College, and the Graduate Center of the City University of New York. I am grateful for their fresh perspectives. They may not have been aware of their contributions, but every time I tried to explain eighteenth- and nineteenth-century France I was keen to have their reactions, which in turn helped me think about how to reach a serious, nonspecialist readership. Thanks to former and current graduate students who have listened to me explain one part or another of the project: Megan Brown, Kyle Francis, Emmy Hammond, Andrew Kotick, Thomas Schellhammer, Sophie Tunney, and Ben Tyner; and the Graduate Center students who discussed a chapter as I was finishing: Dourayeb Ben Moussa, Jack Devine, Ben Diehl, Tom Discepola, Rachel Dixon, Kay Healy, and Thierry Nda.

Thanks to colleagues in Texas: Jim Brink, Howard Curzer, Stefano D'Amico, Dan Flores, George Flynn, Hafid Gafaïti, John Howe, Allan Kuethe, Patricia Lorcin, M. Catherine Miller, Danny Nathan, Patricia Pelley, the late Ron Rainger, Walt Schaller, Ed Steinhart, and Aliza Wong; colleagues in Brooklyn: Swapna Banerjee, the late Ted Burrows, Chris Ebert, Phil Napoli, Steve Remy, and Gunja SenGupta; and colleagues at the Graduate Center: Tim Alborn, Joel Allen, Manu Baghavan, Dagmar Herzog, Ben Hett, Cliff Rosenberg, and Helena Rosenblatt. Members of the eighteenth-century group—Basile Baudez, David Bell, Andrew Clark, Charly Coleman, Madeleine Dobie, Thomas Dodman, Lynn Festa, Jeff Freedman, Jeff Horn, Lucien Nouis, Thierry Rigogne, and Joanna Stalnaker—offered particularly trenchant criticisms but also sustained my thinking about the period. Discussions among colleagues in the NY Area French History Group kept me apprised of scholarship that was adjacent to my own.

Thanks to friends and colleagues scattered throughout the world (and in several cases no longer with us) who have helped one way or another, whether suggesting alternative ideas and readings, providing lodgings, sharing meals, or just talking: W. Andrew Achenbaum, Robert Aldrich, Rick and Jane Andrias, Jean-Pierre Bardet, Jean-Paul Barrière, Rafe Blaufarb, Patrice Bourdelais, Michel Cassan, Jean-Luc Chappey, Aline Charles, Tom Cole, Christoph Conrad, Françoise Cribier, Sophie Cribier, Denis Crouzet, Babette Crouzet-Pavan, Paul D'Hollander, Dominique Delande, Robert Descimon, Elise Feller, Corinne Field, Anne Fuchs, Pierre Guillaume, Peter Herman, Julia Langbein, Pavel and Jacqueline Macek, Teresa Mangum, Margaret Morganroth-Gullette, Fred Ohles, Desmond O'Neill, Sarah Ottaway, Tim Parkin, Janet Polasky, Pierre Serna, Monsieur et Madame Edmond De Sèze, Kavita Sivaramakrishnan, Margery Vibe Skagen, Ronen Steinberg, Tyler Stovall, Pat Thane, Michèle Vialatte, Michel Vovelle, Carl Weiner, and Wiley and Susannah Wood. A special thank-you to Nancy Toff, my editor at Oxford University Press, who saw something in a proposal of a book already largely written but nonetheless helped me improve upon it, to Sean Decker and Madison Zickgraf, project editors, who shepherded it through the production process, and to the press's external reviewers, who "got" the project and made suggestions for improvement. And thanks to Christopher Little for making some last-minute high-resolution scans of documents.

This book shows, among other things, how institutional and familial concerns can blur. But in some ways they are separate areas. On the domestic front, research for this book began when Anna and Aaron were still at home. Now they have their own lives, and Anna and Mike Dow have their own children. Someday Lillian and Russell will read their names in print. As ever, I thank Amy Anderson Troyansky for accompanying me all along the path, for sustaining me in numerous ways, and for always demonstrating the importance of finding *le mot juste*. I dedicate this book to her.

Introduction

Rights, Careers, and the History of Aging

"Claim you have a right. You'll get something. It's the French way." France is the home of human rights, but the colleague with whom I was lunching in the faculty and staff dining room at the University of Limoges was holding forth on a somewhat less elevated subject: ways of obtaining discounts on public transportation. I may not remember the conversation exactly—it was a long time ago—but, in a mock-serious way, he was conflating concrete entitlements with abstract human rights. *Droits* come in many guises, from the fundamental rights of man celebrated worldwide in the bicentennial of the French Revolution to the particular privileges possessed by individuals and groups. Sometimes the French speak of *acquis*, those things that had been obtained by struggle and negotiation. In the kind of linear history that one might imagine running from the French Revolution to the welfare state and beyond, what had been acquired could not be given up.

Living through the last decades of the twentieth century and the first ones of the twenty-first in the United States or Western Europe, however, one was aware of shifts in thinking about entitlements and rights. Americans revisited the New Deal legacy, and Europeans rethought the operations of the welfare state, but criticizing the institutions that had developed since the nineteenth century, and most rapidly since the middle of the twentieth, did not mean abandoning them completely. It did mean a selective defense. For some in the United States, "entitlements" sounded secure, but others associated them with selfishness or "special interests." Confusion over the logic of Social Security led to neoliberal ideas of individuals' rights to their own contributions. The real functioning of transfer payments from one generation to another, with its associated idea of intergenerational solidarity, was obscured, as was the process by which rights had been obtained.

An American living in France is easily struck by the passion with which people defend hard-won rights and seek to extend them. Late twentieth-century French rhetoric on social policy displayed little of the intergenerational conflict that contemporary Social Security politics prompted in the United States. I remember sitting in the reading room of the Archives Nationales, perusing early nineteenth-century pension demands, while outside French truckers struck successfully for a retirement age of fifty-five. The French public sympathized easily with the *camionneurs*, put up with blocked autoroutes and temporary fuel shortages, and accepted as natural the desire for a comfortable retirement.

And the 2019–2023 strike wave against Emmanuel Macron's plan for pension reform revealed an important continuity in French political life. French culture had long made room for the notion of a good retirement for at least some members of society. Comparative study of late nineteenth-century and early twentieth-century French and German press accounts of pension programs makes that point eloquently. The Bismarck pensions were about disability more than old age, but the French emphasized the latter.[1] Their notion of a good old age, at least as an ideal, went back to the eighteenth century, when a traditional culture of mockery of the old gave way to one of respect and sentimentality. By the era of the French Revolution, many proposals anticipated modern demands for social security and pensions.[2] A good old age, which might include retirement, could already be understood as the reward of citizenship. But it did not apply to many people, so the historical literature on old age in the more modern period generally leaps over much of the nineteenth century and emphasizes the constitution of social problems, including the association of old age with poverty, and the emergence of debates about workers' pensions at the end of the century.

Unlike most histories of retirement, this one takes seriously developments in the early nineteenth century, when particular groups in the public sector led the way. It focuses on the retirement of magistrates. My principal archival sources are letters and supporting documents addressed to the Ministry of Justice. They claimed entitlement to pensions, and they revealed an associated right to complain. The acquisition of a right brought with it the need to defend it and to elaborate upon it. Anyone who felt unjustly denied became an interpreter of the law, and individuals associated their arguments with the abstract talk of rights deriving from the French Revolution.

Claims of entitlement were couched in terms of those rights. They referred to law, precedent, and equity. They expressed a desire for justice that only the state might satisfy. But they were hardly limited to the dry language of bureaucratic correspondence. Individuals cried for help, recounted their life histories, laid bare their ailments and miseries, and exposed their personal circumstances to scrutiny. Magistrates had a sense of belonging to a corps of public servants who had lived through a remarkable period of history. Some associated themselves with particular regimes and tendencies in French politics. Others saw themselves as contributing to an undifferentiated public embodied in the nation. A few appealed directly to that public.

At a time when creative writers were developing modern ideas of the self, magistrates too were constructing selves for others' scrutiny.[3] They made sense retrospectively of a turbulent history and linked their own fortunes with those of the nation. They made precise claims based upon particular forms of service, and they seemed to be searching for meaning in their life experiences. Surely, they thought, their actions and decisions as well as their misfortunes added up to something worth recounting and rewarding. The search for meaning and identity has been a theme of the "new cultural history," which has emphasized construction of identity along axes of language, race, nation, ethnicity, class, and gender. Often missing is age, and I was discovering material that would allow access to people's sense of their experience of aging.[4] There was something remarkably modern about that material, posing a connection between aging and retirement, a connection that lies at the heart of much social scientific literature on the life course.[5]

A sociological historical literature has often assumed a fairly straightforward connection between demographic aging and the emergence of retirement. After all, the most dramatic relevant demographic changes and the generalization of retirement have both occurred since the late nineteenth century. For many historians, the important development in the twentieth-century West was that a majority achieved the expectation of a work-free old age and that transfer payments replaced or supplemented individual savings or investments. Yet it has become clear that the idea of demographic aging was itself loaded with political meaning, that the welfare state emerged out of contested notions of the social contract, and that other forms of retirement have existed. Older practices of withdrawal from the workplace provide models that still inspire retirees. They include religious retreat, which, in a secularized version, has become the "life review" that is virtually normative in gerontology, and the "stepping down," often accompanied by intergenerational exchange, seen already in peasant and artisanal life. Both models can also be found in the early modern retirement of the officeholder, even under absolutist regimes. The post-revolutionary French setting, however, provides a rich laboratory for the study of early forms of retirement because of both new demands made of a once-and-future revolutionary state and the search for security by civil servants jumping from regime to regime or joining the public sector somewhere along its Tocquevillean way. In the French case, a world of venality gave way to a world of service, careerism, and entitlement.

A parallel development is visible in the history of Jacobinism from the French Revolution to the present. What had begun as a revolutionary way of thinking and acting became an expression of adherence to the centralized state, which would serve as guarantor of civil servants' entitlements and citizens' equality and social security.[6] The life course of the modern French citizen has its origins in revolution as well as an evolving notion of social contract.

Social gerontology and modern social history have emphasized the shaping of the life course into three periods: training, work, and retirement. The German sociologist Martin Kohli has tried to accommodate aging in the world of social theory and described retirement as a particular way of managing old age.[7] By his account the aged are one of two groups (children being the other) who do not work in a work-oriented society. His analysis of the institutionalization of the life course has been quite influential, and it parallels the work of others who see the aged as essentially marginalized and experiencing a "social death."[8] Kohli's own view is not necessarily so pessimistic, but his approach encourages a twentieth-century focus. Peter Laslett famously argued for the unprecedented nature of twentieth-century developments.[9] But a closer look suggests that there is no automatic connection between demographic aging and retirement. Consider those French truckers in the 1990s or the citizens taking to the streets in 2019–2023. As people in the Western world have retired at ever younger ages, aging and retirement have become increasingly separable. Confronted with such evidence, French gerontologist Anne-Marie Guillemard has written of the deinstitutionalization of old age as retirement.[10] The world that Kohli explained has evidently broken down. In the late twentieth and early twenty-first centuries gerontologists spoke increasingly of a fourth age (the old old) and often painted a positive picture of "successful aging."[11]

Scholars who address the institutionalization of old age as retirement can, therefore, see a number of ends to the story. This book concerns the beginning, when the histories of aging and retirement began to coincide. That coincidence was a result of the fixing of rules and the demands of individuals. And the context was one of transition from a society of orders and privilege to one of careers and bureaucratization. It is a particularly French story, but it has something in common with the rest of the Western world. It traverses a great historical divide in which an Old Regime gave way to a new one, and it bridges the gap between social and cultural history.

The general tensions between social and cultural history are visible in the literature on the history of old age and the aged. Peter Stearns, who had made important contributions to the social history of old age in the late 1970s and early 1980s, returned to the topic in 1991 with a long review of Georges Minois's culturally oriented survey of the history of old age from the ancient world to the sixteenth century.[12] High culture predominated in that book, and, while Minois played with ideas of the relative security of the aged based upon their percentage of the total population, Stearns took him to task for generalizing about attitudes toward the elderly based upon literary, philosophical, and artistic representations as opposed to more social-historical and quantitative sources.

More narrowly defined cultural history offered glimpses of past representations of the life course, some of which built upon medieval models.[13] The stereotypical *degrés des âges* or *Lebenstreppe*, so common in the Renaissance and early modern periods, took the form of a ladder ascending by decade to fifty and descending to one hundred. Such images hardly conformed to typical human experience; they rendered the life course allegorically and urged adherence to prescribed roles and attention to the omnipresence of death. In the sixteenth and seventeenth centuries, flames of hell beneath the stepladder warned of the punishment for straying. In the eighteenth, the images turned secular. Other sources suggest a very old tradition of seeing sixty, sixty-five, or seventy as the threshold of old age. Some historians have asked when people began to see each other as old, placing the emphasis on physical appearance, and some suggest the menopause as a female threshold.[14] Institutions such as hospitals and hospices often settled on sixty or seventy, but labor and environmental conditions presumably resulted in more "premature" aging. Overall, the elderly have been identified more in terms of physical and mental condition, household authority, and cultural status than numerical age.

Religious, philosophical, and scientific texts provided prescriptions for aging well; often they had to do with related themes of vanity, honor, and preparation for death. Religious retreat and humanist retirement to the study were among the recommended options for the fortunate minority, but there was no formal marker of entry into a new life stage. Literary and artistic materials offered descriptions of experience but tended to repeat traditional tropes and images among representations of the elderly. As a category, old age was constructed in moral ways to laud and censure forms of behavior deemed appropriate and inappropriate. Graphic representations of youth and age enforced social and sexual norms.[15] Cultural historians recognized the predominance of certain images from the ridiculous, lascivious graybeard or crone to the dignified wise man or woman. The Protestant Reformation, as described in Peter Borscheid's work on early modern Germany, stimulated the emergence of patriarchal power, encouraged even more in the political construction of centralized states after the Thirty Years' War.[16] The Enlightenment has been associated with a softening of the image of the patriarch and a process of de-Christianization that focused new attention on the last years of earthly existence and harmony between old and young.[17] Nineteenth-century middle-class culture further developed eighteenth-century sentimentality, announcing the great era of grandparenthood, and also produced a powerful image of the indigent elderly.[18] In all those periods, one found nostalgic evocation of a time in the past when elders were respected.

By contrast, as Paul Johnson has explained, social historians have favored the themes of participation, well-being, and status, and addressed them in studies of employment, political activity, property ownership, health, and the transmission of household authority.[19] Social historical investigations have revealed different patterns of "stepping down," the emergence of institutions dedicated to the care of the elderly, and the impact on older Europeans of particular regimes of marriage, remarriage, and inheritance.[20] The earliest efforts tended to follow an already creaky "modernization" scheme. For some, the modern world rendered the elderly marginal. For others, it was premodern society that had no use for them and modernity that invented them as a group.

Such simple choices proved unsatisfactory. The history of old age would not be contained in a one-directional master narrative of progress or decline.[21] But knowledge about particular aspects of social experience in particular contexts was possible. Studies examined the age structure of populations, the shape of households, entries to and exits from hospitals, age consciousness in official records, the development of social policies concerning old age and retirement, and the creation of demographic methods for studying aging.[22] A common theme was the medicalization of old age. But no overarching model has emerged.

Social histories provided the background for understanding the development of policy. Thus, Josef Ehmer's social history of old age concerns social policy, demands by organized labor, conditions in working-class households, and the coming of the welfare state.[23] Similarly, Christoph Conrad surveys changes in the status of German elders, examining how working-class elders in the Rhineland cobbled together an existence from the era of the Bismarck pensions until 1930.[24] He, like some American economic historians, rejects the idea that social policies were simply designed to meet real needs.[25]

In France, Guy Thuillier has studied the history of French pension legislation, and Gilles Pollet and Bruno Dumons have explored the implementation of pension programs and the emergence of modern retirement.[26] Dumons has traced the retirement experiences of civil servants in the region of Lyon, examining where they went, how long they lived, and what material resources they possessed. In the absence of comparative data, the work remains a rich regional description. Pollet's thesis suggests that the idea of retirement emerging from the Enlightenment and the development of the public sector provided a new model for the life course. What we lack is a study of how individuals created and lived that model. The familiar part of the story is that of how the state left its mark on society; less familiar is the story of how people used the state and created a sense of their own lives as coherent and meaningful, in effect establishing new norms.

Investigations into the history of pensions and social welfare explore how society was imagined. Peter Baldwin has called into question the laborist explanation of the origins of the welfare state, according to which workers demanded security and got it, and Susan Pedersen has shown how debates were shaped by notions of motherhood, childhood, and a gendered social contract.[27] Americanists have been considering the roles of the military and motherhood as well as of workforce participation by age groups.[28] Social historical approaches have seen retirement as part of the development of capitalism.[29] Different models of aging and retirement have been seen in different social classes.[30] For labor leaders, retirement was a diversion; for workers in the nineteenth century, it was barely a possibility. For businessmen, it permitted a new kind of management of the workforce and consumption in a leisure society. John Macnicol examines all those players in the emergence of state pensions within the British political economy.[31] Again, the tendency has been to focus on the period when retirement became conceivable for large numbers of people; we have missed the story of how particular groups became eligible for formal retirement in advance of the rest and set a pattern that others followed.

We have also ignored the cultural component to the social history of old age and retirement. After all, one must ask what retirement means: forced inactivity in a society that values work, freedom for self-expression, a choice, a reward, a buyout, a function of the labor market? Should it be understood within the context of the history of leisure as a new opportunity for consumption or within the context of the history of unemployment as an early surprise? To take a very social view, does retirement call into being new kinds of social relationships? Does it mean new forms of help with children and grandchildren, intimacy or bother with spouses, advice or meddling with successors, risk or security with the state, cohort solidarity or continued difference with other retirees?[32]

Some social scientists have explored the cultural component implicit in their work. Conrad's study recognizes different ways of being old. Françoise Cribier has demonstrated different ways of retiring in two different cohorts of Parisians.[33] The difference is both social and cultural. She describes a process of acculturation as workers learn to anticipate and enjoy retirement. They migrate between the capital and the countryside. One of her students, Elise Feller, studied careers ending between the world wars in the public transport industry of Paris and more generally in France. It was a study based upon quantitative analysis of careers and life-course events and a close reading of letters explaining the meaning of work and retirement.[34] Her Parisian workers describe the intersection between careers, family histories, and such events as the First World War and the Great Depression. She has found some useful correspondence between pensioners or their relatives and pension administrators. Similarly, Thomas Sokoll, working on English pauper letters, shows how the marginally literate in the early nineteenth century fashioned an identity and presented themselves in old age to local authorities.[35]

More elaborate self-presentation emerges among the subjects of this book, as relatively privileged folk negotiated with the French state and revealed their expectations. Take the judge François David, for example, who worked for fifty-six years, more than thirty since the outbreak of the French Revolution. He admits, in a letter of January 1, 1821, "that the ever increasing weight of years would soon force me to renounce labors superior to my strength," and his doctor reports that he "is stricken with a permanent catarrh that keeps him in his room for a part of the winter; that he is also subject to periodic attacks of gout and pain in his thighs, which render walking wearisome . . . moreover that he is overwhelmed with the infirmities that are the result of his great age (79 years)." But as condition of his resignation, he asks to be replaced by his son, a favor he solicits "as the consolation of my old age and the most flattering recompense of my long services." If not, his demand ought to be ignored.[36] In the Old Regime, officeholders might actually have their sons perform tasks that would only later fall to them officially. Even in the Restoration, some individuals attempted to follow that old pattern. Separation of public and private spheres of operation took a long time.

By reading demands of officials, we gain a sense of how they viewed their careers and their ideas of proper aging and retirement. I am not calling simply for a history of external representations but also self-images (recognizing the considerable interaction between them). The sources permit a look at subjective experience of aging and retirement in the past. The self-portraits of postulants demanding pensions use the stock of representations described in cultural historical studies, but they involve appropriations for individual purposes, especially the desire to convince the ministry to part with money. What did people want, expect, and get out of late life? The documents reveal cultural meanings even in the paper generated by a developing modern bureaucracy. They were keen to debate issues of entitlement and distributive justice and to talk about themselves. Letters to bureaucrats can be explored as a kind of autobiographical writing. Literary scholars have made the point that first-person writing depends upon models, that it should not be taken as some pure form of personal expression, and they have even begun to look closely at the impact of bureaucratic thinking.[37] If we learn something from them and explore the functioning of bureaucracies, we may discover the mutual influences among dominant cultural discourses, self-consciousness, and individual behavior.[38] If modern youth was invented in the Romantic culture of the early nineteenth century, then some aspect of modern age was invented in the bureaucratic culture of the same period. The same generation that aspired in youth to a Romantic heroism contributed to an age of the bureaucratic self.

This book grows partly out of the logic of the historical literature, partly out of a fortuitous archival discovery. The gap between the Old Regime and revolutionary materials I had exploited in my book on old age and the late nineteenth-century sources that other historians were mining for the history of retirement led me to investigate social groups who sought and obtained retirement pensions in the nineteenth century. I set to work in the Archives Nationales and, having read the minimal materials concerning pensions for teachers and police, I discovered the extraordinarily rich cartons of pension dossiers of the Ministry of Justice. The documents themselves convinced me of the potential for a focus on magistrates. The fact that an archivist was creating a very useful inventory meant that it would be possible to use the cartons of pension dossiers in a new way. An alphabetical list of names includes birthdate, birthplace, date of initial pension demand, and last position. A geographical index permits effective sampling of the materials.[39]

The dossiers themselves were created because royal edicts of 1814 and 1815, building upon Old Regime, revolutionary, and Napoleonic precedents, established a system of retirement pensions for judges and other employees of the Ministry of Justice.[40] The state set rules and created norms. Thirty years of service at sixty years of age or older earned an absolute right. Ten years of service and infirmity earned a potential right. Widows and orphans had a need-based claim. When demanding pensions, postulants told stories that conformed to the ministry's norms but also described individual life experiences in greater detail than I have found for any comparable group in French society. After studying the first three hundred dossiers, I decided to follow all demands made in six departments of France until 1853, when the system became unified with others in the public sector. By then the documents had become much more formulaic and much less revealing. In order to achieve some geographic and political diversity, I selected the departments of Bas-Rhin, Bouches-du-Rhône, Calvados, Haute-Vienne, Rhône, and Somme. Major provincial cities fall within the sample, but rural areas are certainly in the mix. Later I worked my way back to demands of the Napoleonic era that predated the royal edicts and read those twenty-one cartons in their entirety.[41]

When I began the project, I had little interest in magistrates per se. I knew that the research would take many years, and I hardly thought of men of the law as exciting, amusing, or even interesting individuals. Professionally they should appear solid, respectable, and maybe a bit boring. It came as something of a shock to discover their ability to sing their own praises, to dramatize their experiences, to recount their physical ailments, and to complain. Historians need not like their subjects, but they must have the confidence that it is worthwhile spending a good deal of time in their company. Aging magistrates' search for sympathy and claims of entitlement humanized them. Their culture of complaint grew out of a privilege that has become widely shared in the contemporary world. Indeed, it is no longer a privilege, but a right that a minority claimed in the nineteenth century and that we now take for granted. The materials themselves call out for attention. They exist because of a desire for bureaucratic attention, but they gripped me as a reader and as a historian. I may have occasionally identified with them. I often identified with the ministerial officials who received claims, organized dossiers, and responded. I found myself regaling colleagues in the lobby of the archives with tales of adventure, disappointment, and pathos. "Let me tell you about the one who fought brigands in the south... about the regicide who claimed to be a friend of the Bourbons... about the old man who lost almost all his children in the Napoleonic Wars... about the widow who begged for support."

The stories themselves led me to think about the so-called return to narrative in historical writing, but no single story seized my attention. Rather, I began thinking about multiple stories and their patterns and of ways of speaking of rights and of telling life stories in time of revolution. Along the way, I recognized that scholars in disparate fields were addressing similar issues. Natalie Davis's pardon tales were examples of self-justification, other historians paid increasing attention to matters of memory, both individual and collective, literary scholars explored autobiography and narrativity, and gerontologists like Jay Gubrium moved away from overarching theories and expert points of view and began to appreciate how ordinary people recount their lives.[42]

The language of my sources gripped me, but stories have contexts, and I came to appreciate how I might use them to probe a particular milieu and write a history that fuses the social, the cultural, and the political. No particular group can represent everyone, but in France public employees have played a central role in politics and society. Magistrates are not the sorts of people to take to the barricades, but they are public functionaries, and they have already been appreciated by historians for their take on Old Regime and Revolution. Lawyers were primary actors in the national drama.[43] They also had a great deal to say about themselves, and their early experience of retirement served as a model for other groups, first in the public sector, then in French society at large.

Between the early modern history of cultural representations and the modern history of policy, this book studies meanings of retirement as well as continuities and interruptions in individual career patterns. It charts such quantifiable things as duration of career and years from retirement to death, but it also confronts more qualitative issues. Demands of officials indicate how they viewed their careers, their situation vis-à-vis other generations, and their expectations of aging and retirement. They combine political, professional, and familial concerns. Historians have created important specialized literatures on political culture, the legal profession, and the family, but here they intersect.

The retirement dossiers of French judges permit a study of the retrospective construction of lives and anticipations of retirement among public officials over the long term. Their pleas indicate the evolution of French notions of right and citizenship, studied often at a high level of intellectual history by students of political culture.[44] Here right descends from those heights and joins autobiography and entitlement. Assertions of right that had been made for humanity in the revolutionary era are made for civil servants in the Restoration and after. They range from high-ranking officials to modest *juges de paix*. Some of the postulants have already in effect retired. Others speak of their hopes and goals. One finds retirees who work informally, people who claim to be in desperate need of aid, people who insist that the title of honorary judge is important for a good retirement, more important than financial aid, especially in provincial society. Many explain how they intend to spend their retirement, writing history or poetry, devoting themselves to family, and so on. They present themselves as having lived through a coherent career, reconstruct events, and justify past decisions. If there are several demands, the story may change from one version to another, especially as one passes from Restoration to July Monarchy; sometimes confidential information is given by local officials, often former colleagues. Activities during the revolutionary turmoil are recounted with pride or with excuses. Reports are submitted about the hopes of candidates during the Hundred Days. Monarchists claim a lifetime of service—even several generations' or centuries' service—to the crown. The administrators consider time of service, as the law specifies, but also political, professional, and personal behavior, and medical and financial need. Familial heritage, political experience, and professional training and accomplishment all mattered.

The world of "my" magistrates moved away from the system of venality of office to one of individual merit, but it still valued state service and professional independence. Within that world pensions evolved from recompense at all ages to reward at a particular stage of the life course, from favor and privilege to equity and right, foreshadowing modern social questions and the development of ideas of citizenship and entitlement. That evolution is visible in life histories running from the Old Regime to the Restoration, as multiple careers bridged the revolutionary and Napoleonic divide. Individuals juxtaposed national history and their own experiences, as they sought stability in time of revolution and war, and they pushed the ministry into responding to their demands. Looking at multiple narratives reveals how claimants patterned their life histories, presenting the corps as intermediary between individual and nation, and engaging in a process of self-fashioning and life review. Lives that were often rooted in Old Regime values crossed the Revolution and Napoleonic interlude to take shape in the Restoration.

Rules for retirement emerged from some Old Regime precedents and developed through a history of legislation from Revolution to Restoration and the consequent structuring of a system that rewarded public contributions, publicized heroism, and normalized honor. Particularly important were the *ordonnances* of 1814 and 1815 and their aftermath in the building of bureaucratic structures, the debate on forced retirement in 1824 and the 1850s, and the conflict between life tenure (*inamovibilité*) and the removal of the superannuated.

Rules tell us part of the story, but a focus on how individual careers ended throughout the first half of the nineteenth century reveals the emergence of a reward structure and the normalization of careers in constitutional and bureaucratic regimes. Revolutions begin to resemble restorations, and a close look at retirement dossiers themselves, including letters and increasingly standardized forms, offers a new perspective on continuity and change in the period. Examination of a famously turbulent period reveals characteristics of remarkable continuity, considering holdovers from the Old Regime, old revolutionaries, and others contributing to the development of careerism. Bureaucracy and autobiography intersected. Within a new civic order, issues of entitlement, citizenship, and bureaucracy arose, as magistrates justified lives and pioneered new territory.[45] They were acutely aware of changes in political regime, but they could build on long experience, and in late life they constructed their worlds out of elements of diverse regimes.

A rhetoric of male retirement emerged, as magistrates evoked themes ranging from poverty and disease to honor and family. They blended private and public narratives and learned to deploy a style that included elements of pathos and melodramatic complaint as well as prosaic accounting and formulaic claims of professional dignity. A moral language of honor and merit combined with a practical language of need, as life-course events and historical circumstances prompted individual demands. Meanwhile, institutional demands encouraged greater self-consciousness and representation of careers according to expected norms. Late life became medicalized, as magistrates and their physicians employed a medical discourse concerning diseases of the sedentary life. The language of retiring magistrates looks ahead to a range of gerontological models: disengagement, decline, activity, creativity, and narcissism.

Magistrates were men, but the gendered aspect of retirement emerges from widows' letters and the limits of entitlement. A comparison of male and female writing about work, family, and public life reveals gendered themes and rhetoric and different modes of complaint. The study of widows' demands also raises questions of degrees of entitlement, considering questions of right, culture, and need. The gendered comparison even permits reflection on different temporalities over the life course.

The study of nineteenth-century French magistrates opens a window onto the political and cultural origins of modern retirement and the eventual democratization of a particular way of growing old. The state and its servants played a central role, and rights to retire and complain derived from particular relations to the state. Magistrates may well have learned something in listening to others' excuses and complaints; moreover, they had access to a language of honor, service, and heroism, and they knew how to make the language work for them. Their stories contribute to a long-term history of aging, retirement, the individual, and the state; they reveal how fortunate and unfortunate individuals alike cobbled together a post-revolutionary world.

PART I
CAREER AND RETIREMENT

1
Pensions as Favor and Pensions as Right

In some important ways, retirement pensions symbolize modernity. In Europe, they have remained almost sacred even as welfare states have entered a period of retrenchment. They support the lengthening last stage(s) in the modern life course, and their expectation over the last hundred years has increasingly disciplined careers. Modern social histories see their acquisition as representing the triumph of rights and social protection in the emergence of the welfare state. In the twentieth century they contributed significantly to people's incomes, and their administration fell to large bureaucratic structures.

The historiography of pensions describes a shift from private arrangements to public programs. In theoretical terms it explores issues of right. In practical terms it examines ways of dealing with accident, sickness, and retirement. The earliest historical works focused on political parties and interest groups in the framing of legislation and on the growth and extension of benefits. They explored debates concerning contributory programs, preferred by liberal politicians, businessmen, and civil servants, and universal systems, the eventual preference of the majority of citizens. More recent studies elucidate the functioning of pensions both institutionally and individually, balancing policy and individual desire.

In the literature on the European welfare state and the history of retirement, the obligatory Bismarck pensions in Germany (1889) have pride of place. They have come to symbolize the modern state that uses benefits to gain legitimacy. They represented a conservative reformism in co-opting a potential issue of the workers' movement, and they tied the German public to a paternalist and bureaucratic state. The primary actors were Bismarck, state bureaucrats, big industrialists, and the Reichstag. One notable student of German social entitlement, Greg Eghigian, accepts this traditional description, but he asks why insurance should have been the preferred solution to problems of social conflict. He ties it to a long history whose roots lay in the early modern "police state" and in nineteenth-century social administrative thought that dealt with matters of risk and security and the creation of nonpolitical social affinity.[1]

For all of the originality of German legislation, however, parallel histories exist in Europe. The discovery of old age as a social problem and debates over the creation of pension systems took place on a European-wide stage. As Christoph Conrad has demonstrated, programs for particular occupations and businesses developed between the middle of the nineteenth century and 1890. Skilled workers had already organized friendly societies or mutual aid societies and administered their own emergency funds, which were geared primarily for disability but could function for retirement. Some salaried industrial workers, particularly miners and railroad workers, received pensions in the second half of the nineteenth century. National retirement laws emerged in Europe between 1889 and the First World War, and social insurance legislation was passed in Britain in 1908 and in France in 1910. Germany covered white-collar workers, Britain focused on the poor, and France included farmers in their system. Thus, Germany was not alone, and in each country the historical actors, whether activists or beneficiaries, were multiple.[2]

The historical literature has typically sought to explain the coming of social security by asking what groups pushed for legislation. Although pensions were not very high on the socialist agenda, workers' organizations were eventually drawn to the idea, and European labor eventually claimed some responsibility for the achievement of old-age security. Social welfare systems financed by general revenues are commonly assumed to have been most highly developed in Scandinavian countries as a result of social democratic activism in the 1930s; however, Peter Baldwin has claimed a major role for the relatively conservative Danish and Swedish agrarian middle classes making demands for universal and solidaristic social legislation in the late nineteenth century.[3] A politics of retirement emerged in late nineteenth-century England, according to John Macnicol, because of structural labor market changes. Aging workers were replaced by younger ones, trained to perform new tasks, and traditional forms of relief were insufficient to meet the challenge. Interest groups and political parties debated the wisdom of public pensions when ideologies of liberal individualism and worker control of savings blocked ideas of reform.[4] Pat Thane has less faith in Macnicol's materialist explanation, but a consensus has emerged that in much of Europe retirement became a way of managing old age at the turn of the twentieth century.

Gilles Pollet and Bruno Dumons have described the emergence of a new social fact in the era preceding the French law of 1910:

> Through the concept of retirement, its becoming widespread and routine, and the debates, polemics, and institutions that it prompted, the national community recognized a new social fact: a great part of the management of the "social question" rested on the capacity of the nation to ensure an honorable old age to the whole of its workers and fellow citizens.
>
> This social acculturation of the French people played a role in the advent of a new democratic space. Thus, the "retirement phenomenon" would seem to put itself at the heart of a complex democratic process, characteristic of European industrial societies of the beginning of the twentieth century, that we will try to describe, analyze, and understand.[5]

They tell a story of a convergence of attitudes around the idea of state-supported, obligatory retirement pensions. It was not easily accomplished, as it involved the overcoming of two sorts of opposition: classic liberal opposition to an intrusive state and suspicion of the Third Republic from both left and right. Some liberals remained opposed to obligatory participation in a retirement system because they saw the principle of obligation as interfering with individual responsibility for providing for one's own security.[6] At the extremes, integral Catholics and monarchists were as opposed to projects of the bourgeois state as socialists, anarchists, and syndicalists. Debates over retirement legislation paralleled other debates over the proper role of the Third Republic. The Radical emphasis on national solidarity and public interest and mutualist concern for social protection provided the ground for eventual compromise. Liberalism itself evolved through the actions of "opportunists" of the 1880s and *progressistes* between the 1890s and the First World War, and socialism took a reformist turn.

Legislation was part of the story. At the same time, retirement emerged as an increasingly common life-course phenomenon. Retirement was a right to which more people had access, for both political and demographic reasons. Although it took the better part of a century for most French people to take advantage effectively of that right—Elise Feller sees the critical turning point in the period between the world wars—some were already living the life of the *retraité* at the turn of the century.[7] Dumons has examined pension dossiers of municipal employees of Lyon from 1875 to 1918 in order to see where they went and how they lived, and he used electoral lists to find people identifying themselves as retired. He concludes that more and more workers were aspiring to "a peaceful life of a small property owner on his native soil" and living primarily in rural France and in small provincial towns.[8]

For all of the novelty of the late nineteenth and early twentieth centuries, it is clear that the age of pensions and retirement stretches back in time. Private pensions have a very uneven history; they depended upon employers' paternalism or workers' foundation of mutual aid societies. More important over the long run were public pensions, which evolved in individual areas of public service. They became standardized and centralized in France in 1853, Great Britain in 1859, and the German Empire in the 1870s and 1880s, but government ministries had been running individual systems since much earlier in the century.

A series of publications by Guy Thuillier has revealed a history of pensions for civil servants in France going back to the eighteenth century. Thuillier has traced the accumulation of programs for servants of the state and debates concerning their mode of operation across the nineteenth century. The sheer amount of state activity was impressive. At a time when classical liberalism argued in favor of individual responsibility for savings, employees of the state belonged in a different category. They enjoyed a kind of security that their contemporaries did not, but served as a model for all other salaried workers later in the century. Pioneering they were, but the exact nature of the history is only understood in outline form. The law of June 8, 1853, tried to create order and coherence in an administrative universe characterized by diverse practices and theoretical uncertainty. Different government ministries had created pension funds since the Napoleonic period. Some required thirty years of service in order to receive a pension at any age. Others demanded a minimum of age sixty. The percentage of salary withheld varied, and so did the return. For some, the pension could not exceed half the active salary; for others, it could. Thuillier suggested several areas in which research ought to be undertaken. We do not know exactly what pensions cost the government in the nineteenth century. We have little knowledge of the length of pensioners' lives, age at retirement, the circumstances that normally led to retirement, or the handling of pension funds themselves.

Thuillier is a useful guide through debates concerning *capitalisation* and *répartition*, the creation of funds and their functioning, the property claim that came with withholding, and the budgetary problem raised by contributions by the state. Ministries created their own funds and were responsible for their maintenance. But periodic infusions of government money led many to conclude that a contract had been drawn up between the state and its *fonctionnaires*. Whether it had was not completely clear, nor was the idea of a social debt universally accepted. Withholding and the formation of a ministry fund did not translate into social debt in the way that a budget obligation did. Thuillier also traces debates concerning rights of widows and orphans, and the literature of reform. As much as anyone else, he has reminded social historians of the importance of the state and politics in their own domain of historical research.[9] His reprinting of legislation, reports, and regulations concerning pensions for employees of the internal customs service, fiscal officers, diplomats, hospice employees, academic administrators, the national press, police, and others makes clear that a remarkable number of people, especially when including dependents, were involved in the evolution of retirement and bureaucracy.[10]

The Napoleonic period emerges as crucial in the development of public pensions because of the widespread practice of withholding portions of salaries to accumulate pension funds. Different schemes were developed for employees of the Ponts-et-Chaussées, Mines, Relations Extérieures, Préfecture de Police, and Ministère du Commerce. In all cases, Napoleon sought ways of ensuring loyalty, and pensions were promises of future reward as well as payment of what civil servants considered their property.

Nonetheless, as in so many other areas, Napoleonic policy was derived from French revolutionary legislation; it effectively codified and developed ideas of the 1790s. In turn, revolutionary ideas denigrated Old Regime pensions as personal and corrupt, and revolutionaries worked out a variety of public arrangements and recognized a right to pensions in legislation of August 3–22, 1790. The revolutionary Comité des Pensions, which examined Old Regime practices for abuses and excessive expenditures, painted a picture of frivolous pensions for Old Regime favorites. It proclaimed a right to a reward for a variety of services to the nation and some security in old age. Mass mobilization for war left soldiers' dependents in difficult circumstances and made military pensions more important than ever. Aging veterans and their widows had already posed a challenge in the Old Regime.[11] The revolutionary and Napoleonic periods only added to the problem, and more and more people began speaking a language of social right. This required them to go beyond the Old Regime notion of a pension as an individual favor. It also meant an abandonment of the idea of state office as property. People who owned their offices, as was often the practice in the Old Regime, could simply sell them.[12]

Some Old Regime pensions were based upon need and merit, but there was certainly some degree of truth in the revolutionary characterization of them as rooted in personal favor and, therefore, wasteful.[13] Revolutionary pensions were to be different. They were to be public rewards for exceptional service to France. They would go to inventors, artists, and others who made sacrifices for France, to dependents of soldiers, and to the worthy poor. At first, they had little to do with careers. But soon enough, bureaucratic systems were set up within government ministries. Thus, what was presented as extraordinary and important public service was transformed into the norm.

New norms emerged most tellingly as state employees negotiated the shift from a society of privilege to a nation of citizens, but they experienced more than one shift, as no regime lasted very long. Several recent studies demonstrate how the French built upon revolutionary foundations and how people made careers within the state. They trace the development of a new civic order, processes of professionalization, the emergence of notions of honor associated with public service, and the working out of bureaucratic rules, civil service status, and expectations of full career and retirement.[14]

Was the revolutionary break fundamental? Certainly advocates of modern social welfare have thought so. In the nineteenth and twentieth centuries, those who sought pensions and social welfare spoke of a promise made in the Revolution but never fully redeemed.[15] Yet some scholars discount the novelty of revolutionary pensions and develop Tocqueville's idea that revolutionary invention built upon ten generations of work or see even in Old Regime ministries' practices examples of what sociologist Georges Gurvitch called an "intuitive right" that operated before being assured in law. In this light, revolutionary legislation can be seen as reforming and rationalizing rather than innovating.[16] Still, Thuillier and Vida Azimi point to what they claim was the innovative bureaucracy of the *fermiers-généraux* (tax farmers), who were in many ways quintessential characters of the Old Regime. They embodied the private nature of the state, and could easily be portrayed in the Revolution as representing the corruption of the Old Regime. And yet tax farmers became innovative "civil servants" in a reforming monarchy, and all those who spoke of reforming pensions could point to that experience. Withholding was practiced on more than twenty thousand employees as early as 1768. Thuillier sees that as the real origin of the French social security system.[17]

That example leads us to modify notions of revolutionary innovation, but over the long term it is probably fair to say that the history of pensions in

France is the story of a transition from an early modern culture of royal favor and venality of office to a modern world of entitlement and citizenship. Old Regime pensions were dispensed at all stages of the life course as recompense for service and tools for ensuring loyalty. But such assurance was limited, as the sale of offices alienated little bits of the state. Magistrates were particularly involved in the legal trafficking in state offices and, therefore, viewed them as property. The French Revolution formally outlawed venality and attempted to eliminate costly pensions, but it created a new civic order that included public service as a career and pensions as support in retirement. When pensions evolved into awards granted at the end of careers, they still carried with them an association with personal favor and an odor of venality. Bringing about new ideas of career and retirement, however, involved the creation of new institutions that made new demands.

The institutional demand to review careers and life-histories of those claiming pensions parallels a new form of self-consciousness and representation of the career. Retiring public servants, and magistrates among them, claimed a right to an honorable retirement, supported and symbolized by a pension. This element in the history of rights was generally ignored in a French revolutionary bicentennial that emphasized human rights. Some of the bicentennial literature was very theoretical. But this was a practical claim of a right to something very tangible. The Revolution of human rights was also the Revolution of rights to material benefits or entitlements. Such an interpretation was not common in 1989, when entitlement had begun to be seen as a bad thing.[18] Yet part of what happened two hundred years ago was the transformation of human rights into group entitlements. For all of the novelty, this did not represent a complete break with the past, as we have seen. It also involved the survival of older ideas of favor, venality, and honor.

Magistrates had something in common with bureaucratic employees, but their sense of being derived also from belonging to what has been described as a "themistocracy," an aristocracy of lawyers deserving of their own order separate from the classic three estates, and from the historical experience of making careers in an increasingly bureaucratic world.[19] As men of the law, they spoke the revolutionary language of human rights and the careerist language of entitlement. Their values were formed in both Old Regime and Revolution. Their pension demands referred to the appropriate legislation and revealed personal expectations. As "themistocratic" professionals, they presented themselves as respectable and honorable; as postulants, they dramatized their life experiences and pleaded for sympathy.[20] In other words, their self-fashioning extended beyond their own professional group to their status as human beings, but professional structures and identities mattered.

In order to understand the magistracy of the late eighteenth and early nineteenth centuries, it is necessary to appreciate the historiography of justice. The scholarly literature explores judicial structures from seigneurial and royal courts of the Old Regime through the more accessible public courts of the revolutionary and Napoleonic eras. Some of the historical literature concentrates on the mechanisms of dispute and resolution, whether in formal court proceedings or informal arrangements. Social historians have used criminal court cases to understand crime and punishment and the values of Old Regime society. Some of the literature focuses on the politics of justice.

While recent historical scholarship on lawyers, magistrates, and *fonctionnaires* in the nineteenth century has not done much with the theme of retirement, it has offered portraits of professional groups, including their social origins, collective identities, political tendencies, and career trajectories. Robert Allen and Emmanuel Berger emphasize the novelty of the revolutionary era, but at least one scholar, Hervé Leuwers, sees lawyers and judges in the postrevolutionary period as trying to reconstitute some sense of belonging to a corporate body.[21] Those who have tried to follow lawyers and magistrates across the nineteenth century have often narrowed the geographic focus to particular regions, where over the long run those working in the legal profession found opportunities in particular regimes and dodged challenges in others but generally established themselves as part of a new elite. A study of magistrates around Poitiers emphasizes continuity, with some change resulting from the March 1, 1852, decree on obligatory retirement. A parallel study around Angers illustrates a shift from a magistracy dominated by local elites to a more open, national, and republican profession.[22]

Even before the Revolution, men of the law were talking about justice as the province of the nation as well as the king, a central element of French society. The *cahiers de doléances* often mentioned the desire for easier access to the justice system. Law was at the center of Enlightenment reform, and lawyers played key roles in the runup to the Revolution and the events of the Revolution itself.[23] But studies of justice have also paid a great deal of attention to matters of personnel and practice. Much of the literature concerns matters of social status, the relative roles of aristocrats and nonaristocratic lawyers. That literature reveals a great marketplace of offices and a thirst for honors.[24] Obtaining office meant dealing with the current holder (or his heirs) as well as the Chancellory. "Office" itself was both a public function and a piece of private property.[25]

Judges in the Old Regime did not expect to live on their salaries. They were expected to have wealth and honor. As Jean-Pierre Royer puts it, "The good judge is the one whom virtue designates to everyone. He is that public man whose quality deploys itself in the four cardinal virtues of *prudence* (wisdom, science, knowledge of the true), of *justice* (equity, righteousness, impartiality, integrity, probity), of *courage* (strength, firmness of soul and of body), and of *temperance* (moderation, measure, honor, dignity)."[26] The ideal type of the judge shared a number of characteristics with the self-image of the lawyer. Lucien Karpik's study of French lawyers over many centuries takes the self-image seriously as something more than ideological cover for self-interested professionals. They both identified with the state and challenged it. Such people had engaged in the great debates between king and *parlements*; they focused on constitutional issues that would continue to attract attention throughout the nineteenth century.[27]

One of the key issues about justice, at least on the theoretical plain, was that of free access (*gratuité*) by the public and not just the wealthy or privileged. It was raised in the Maupeou reforms of 1771, and it was enshrined in the August 1789 decree suppressing venality of office. Karpik finds lawyers before the second half of the twentieth century keeping their distance from the marketplace. Magistrates and lawyers viewed themselves as engaged in public service. That access to courts of law was such an important goal in the French Revolution indicates that Enlightenment-era ideals had not yet been realized.

Magistrates of the Old Regime made careers by investing in offices, by owning a piece of the state. Revolutionary changes included the institution of elections to office and a reduction in the requirements for service. Some of the revolutionary-era debates harkened back to conflicts between judges and lawyers in the Old Regime. Old Regime values survived even as revolutionary justice was characterized both by extraordinary activism, especially in the Terror, and by efforts to achieve equity and stability, the major ideal of the Napoleonic era. The revolutionary interlude saw election to limited judicial terms. In the Constitution of the Year VIII, Napoleon created a system in which the idea of career made sense. Nomination was combined with the principle of lifetime tenure. The First Consul (later emperor and king) would name magistrates, who would then enjoy independence.

The personnel was quite mixed, whether in terms of political leaning or social origins. As much as anywhere else in French society, Napoleon sought to combine remnants of the old aristocracy, the newer professional classes, and some more popular elements, who had snuck in by election, particularly as justices of the peace. Napoleon continued to work on the problem of stability and purity. He introduced the idea of a five-year provisional period to be followed by *inamovibilité* (life tenure). But that meant an opportunity for purging the system. Thus, on March 24, 1808, he fired sixty-eight magistrates and demanded the resignation of ninety-four others. Another purge came in 1810.

An important factor in personnel changes in the revolutionary and Napoleonic magistracy was the changing fate of the French military. Wherever France ruled, magistrates were named; wherever France lost territory, magistrates found themselves without responsibilities and perhaps on the run. But the biggest purge of the early nineteenth century came in the Second Restoration of the Bourbons, who had been more tolerant of difference in the First Restoration and were now desirous of punishing those who had rallied to Napoleon during the Hundred Days.

Independence was a supposed characteristic of French justice going back to the Middle Ages, and it was a favorite ideal of lawyers in general in the Old Regime. For them, independence was related to honor and more important (in theory) than wealth. Moderation and equity were great ideals, and the men of the bar could claim to be defending the public good against both the state and the market. Karpik reprints a line quoted by Sarah Maza from the judicial writings of Falconnet in the 1770s: "What is the judge? The voice of the king. What is the lawyer? The voice of the nation."[28] Magistrates could actually claim to be both, appointed by the sovereign and speaking for the nation. It had to do with their experience in each regime. Honor and merit transcended regime.

Of course, all this is to say that magistrates were a special case. But they were a special case that used themes of honor and justice and equity to play a role in a new administrative world. Their ideals may have transcended regimes to some extent, but they were also appropriate to their time. They spoke of their careers and shaped them according to current demands. Thus, they could speak the language of the new civic order and claim entitlements in an increasingly bureaucratic world.

Honor meant protecting reputations. The magistrates compared themselves to colleagues and worried how they would be viewed by the community and by their children. As Bessejon de la Chassagne noted in 1815, "Without fortune and without retirement, persons who have not followed my long career think doubtfully of the manner in which I have conducted myself. I am myself confused by my plight, and don't know how to explain it. The lowliest clerk in the most minor administration is better treated than I."[29] Every magistrate kept track of his colleagues' progress. Such tracking had begun in school, and continued throughout their careers, but it was most poignant at the end. In a world increasingly governed by public opinion, aging involved a certain amount of narcissism. It involved honor and, to use the language of the time, emulation.

Magistrates compared their plights not only to those of colleagues but to what they imagined to be the model career, partly rooted in the past and partly emerging as the norm. The characteristics that appear over and over in discussions of magistrates—probity, experience, assiduity, and good judgment come to mind—are generally associated with age. The most important characteristic of the judiciary in French history, and more generally in the Western tradition, is independence. Thus, age and independence were key, but the time came when independence was threatened. Underlying every discussion of justice from the late Middle Ages into the nineteenth century is the belief that an independent magistracy must be protected by the principle of *inamovibilité*. Despite the turbulence of the era, magistrates thought of themselves as permanent fixtures; yet they were pioneers in the history of retirement pensions. On the one hand, older histories of the French judiciary claim that judges remained active as long as they were physically and mentally able (and longer), but on the other hand, magistrates wrote more about their right to retirement than any other group I have investigated, and they did retire. Hence the thousands of dossiers in the Archives Nationales.

French state bureaucracies were collecting information on thousands of individuals. Paper was necessary to make sense of the new civic order and to sort out entitlements. Magistrates were not the neediest, but they spoke the language of justice, justified their lives, and pioneered an aspect of life that has become normative. Many of them composed autobiographical apologies. They were seeking security and making claims for individual service. Their narratives recounted both individual careers and an emerging national history.

2
Careering across the Revolutionary and Napoleonic Divide

On July 19, 1810, a sixty-nine-year-old judge named Thouvenel wrote the French minister of justice to explain, "His great age and his infirmities no longer permitting him to continue his functions as judge of the tribunal of Sarrebourg, he dares hope that by your acting as intermediary, he will obtain from his majesty the emperor and king [Napoleon Bonaparte] a retirement pension that will permit him to arrive honestly at the end of his career."[1] It was a call for help that grew out of a new recognition of what a career ought to look like. It was prompted by an awareness of disability, a combination of weakened eyesight and compromised attention and memory. The latter may have been the result of aging, but the ophthalmia, he claimed, was occasioned by overwork in studying the new laws of France. The job itself, performed in particular historical circumstances of evolving legal codes from Old Regime through revolution and empire, rendered him less and less fit to attend to the public good.

The pension he demanded was to be "proportional to the munificence of the emperor" but also to the "length of his services, which in every era merited him public consideration." Was a retirement pension a favor, dependent upon the generosity of the ruler? Or was it a reward or right? The language is ambiguous. He merited favor but had earned a reward. Moreover, as rules developed, reward became right. In many contemporary demands, postulants claimed the right to demand favor. Over time, favor would become entitlement—state pension systems and eventually social security depended upon it—but clarification of the two principles occurred gradually. Nobles in the Old Regime were already speaking a language of merit while not abandoning privileges of birth, and civil servants long after the French Revolution often employed a language of favor and personal connection.[2] Only later would citizenship rights themselves confer old-age security. Even then, rights would be rooted in time of service, a fusion of abstract human rights and reward for years of activity. A look at the past of a country whose

Entitlement and Complaint. David G. Troyansky, Oxford University Press. © Oxford University Press 2023.
DOI: 10.1093/oso/9780197638750.003.0003

social security system would eventually be among the world's most fully developed and "sacred" reminds us of the contingency of entitlements and the fragility of public protection, even for aging public servants.

Formulas for the spelling out of entitlements developed over time, but early nineteenth-century demands were characterized by the elaborate use of rhetorical strategies for justifying the granting of pensions. The tone of their narratives ranged from the heroic to the pathetic, as they recounted their roles in the great events of the revolutionary and Napoleonic eras and told tales of physical decline. Their narratives were designed to win the approval of government bureaucrats and officials. Ultimately, entitlements were claimed by relatively privileged individuals, who learned how to employ a language of rights and to cast their narratives in institutionally acceptable form. In reading account after account, often multiple demands by the same man, one can almost hear the old man telling of the greatest adventure of his life. Some narratives reached back a century or two, expressing remarkable continuity across many generations. Others began with their own educations. Some presented the Old Regime as a paradise lost; others recognized how their destinies were linked to the Revolution. Turning points sometimes corresponded to the critical moments in traditional historical narratives.

Letters from claimants resemble the life review that psychologically inclined gerontologists treat ahistorically, but these letters depended upon precise historical circumstances, and they were motivated by specific desires.[3] Gerontologists have debated whether the life review is universal. Some even question its desirability, for it may encourage a self-satisfied nostalgia as much as it permits an integration of the personality or development of wisdom.[4] Historically it resembles a secularized version of the religious confession. In recent years, gerontologists have paid close attention to narratives constructed by aging individuals.[5]

Thouvenel was one of many magistrates who juxtaposed personal narratives with French political and institutional history. He described his various services since long before the French Revolution. He had served in religious and royal institutions since 1771. During the Revolution, he performed judicial functions under a succession of regimes. In late life, he expressed the desire to be rewarded for all his labors. His professional life provided the continuity that had been broken in both public and private spheres by political events. Moreover, in order to accentuate familial continuity, he remarked upon more than three centuries of judicial service from father to son.

Thouvenel was contemplating an end to his career even as institutional procedures for negotiating that end were evolving. Before the French Revolution, magistrates owned their positions and had the right to pass them on to heirs. Pensions were irregular rewards for services or loyalty, sometimes understood as pieces of an investment portfolio, not necessarily linked to late life and inactivity. The French Revolution, with its new notion of public service and citizenship, moved France away from the private ownership of public office. However, in the early years, questions of appointment took precedence over questions of retirement.

A system for dealing with the right to retirement would be elaborated later in the Bourbon Restoration (1814/15–30), but the problem was already arising in the Napoleonic period (1799–1814/15). Napoleonic offices were filled by a diverse group, ranging from Old Regime officials to creatures of the Revolution.[6] Many individuals served in some capacity in every regime. Those whose careers began before 1789 were reaching maturity and old age. Structural and personnel changes in the 1790s and Napoleon's periodic purges and institutional reforms, moreover, left some magistrates out of work. Individuals might find themselves without posts for political, institutional, or medical reasons. Loss of territory in a period of international warfare also meant loss of office. Therefore, by 1806 and 1807, the government addressed the need to work out rules for retirement. A decree of September 13, 1806, spelled out eligibility requirements of thirty years of service and sixty years of age.[7] A decree of October 2, 1807, addressed problems of blindness, deafness, and other serious infirmities.[8] The granting of pensions would be determined on a case-by-case basis.

Individual cases required bureaucratic judgment and encouraged advocacy. Local superiors of people like Thouvenel provided information that would confirm or contradict the claimant's narrative. The chief prosecutor in the Appeals Court of Nancy, Demetz, appreciated Thouvenel's medical condition. He wrote on August 4, 1810, that Thouvenel had told him a year earlier of his plan to retire but that he had counseled him to stay on as long as possible so as not to suffer so dramatic a reduction in income. Now Thouvenel could no longer read, and Demetz claimed that the pension could not be refused. He evoked Thouvenel's dignity and his poverty, and he appealed to the minister's humanity for a pension proportional to Thouvenel's needs. Another local judge, Henry, provided further details. The assignats, paper money of the revolutionary era, had ruined Thouvenel financially. During his service in Sarrebourg, his wife lived with her daughter and son-in-law, a small grocer in Nancy. Thouvenel had just joined them there. Henry mentioned two sons in the military who could be no help. Thus, the ex-colleagues spoke of work, favor, and need.

At the same time, the government itself sought justification for forcing some employees to retire. The Napoleonic legislation spelled out a method for informing on magistrates who were no longer up to the job. The chief prosecutor in the Appeals Court of Liège, Danthine, had written the ministry in April 1809 that one Collignon, age seventy-three or seventy-four, a judge of the tribunal of first instance at Dinant in French-occupied Belgium, was barely alive and needed to be retired. Danthine also proposed to the judge himself that he ask for the pension.[9] However, when his health improved, Collignon resisted the call to retirement. The ministry, nonetheless, proceeded on January 13, 1810, to announce to Collignon that it had been informed "that your great age and your habitual infirmities have made you incapable of fulfilling your functions. If your situation is such as is announced to me, the imperial decree of October 2, 1807, makes it a duty for you to ask for your retirement." Some of Collignon's colleagues claimed that he was "not inaccessible to corruption in the exercise of his functions," but the facts were very uncertain and vague, as others claimed that he performed his tasks with integrity and probity. Still, according to Danthine, the judge's capacity was declining daily, his legal knowledge was outdated, and his infirmities led him to pass his work on to a clerk rather than attend court himself. Danthine recommended a pension. Collignon responded within a week that the informants were wrong, that despite his age he enjoyed good health and was assiduous at fulfilling his obligations. A more favorable report, from the presiding judge of the Appeals Court of Liège, Dandrimont, confirmed on March 3, 1810, that Collignon could still do the job. Dandrimont forwarded a letter from a colleague in the tribunal of first instance, De Lautremange, that "although of a very advanced age, Sr Collignon has followed the procedures of the court with great assiduity and has never stopped fulfilling his functions. He has suffered from a long and violent cold, along with severe gout, so that it is understandable that he was thought incapable of continuing the exercise of his functions, but he currently enjoys good health and lacks neither zeal nor devotion." De Lautremange identified a judge who was even more infirm, but Collignon's name disappeared from the roster of the tribunal in 1811 (*Almanach Impérial*).

Those who asked for retirement pensions paid attention to historical circumstances. A clerk in the occupied states of Parma, Jean-Antoine Vignali, for example, timed his request to correspond to the triumphal return of Napoleon to Paris. He wrote, "The happy circumstance of the return to Paris of his imperial and royal majesty our august sovereign from the camps of victory and of glory encourages me to reiterate" a demand for aid, a position, or a pension.[10]

The continuity of family service to the state that many tried to establish even extended into hopes for the future. Long after the practice had supposedly been eliminated, some magistrates tried to hand posts on to their heirs. Thus, Nicolas Acher, judge in the Appeals Court of Lyon, wanted to retire and have his son appointed to his position in May 1810. He wrote, "After having exercised since 1771 useful functions for the state in different administrations and since the Year VIII those of appeals judge of Amiens and now of Lyon, I might hope to be included in the composition of the imperial courts; but I am in my eighties and I would willingly resign my place in favor of my son . . . if a retirement pension proportional to the length of my services were accorded me."[11] In a subsequent letter, Acher described his literary work, which would continue after his retirement. He also hedged his position, saying that he could still do the job and that his resignation was only contingent on the son's getting the job. He announced that in the next year he would be completing the fourth and final volume of his *Digest of Plutarch's Lives*.[12] His doctor's note usefully but contradictorily supported both scenarios of retirement and continued work. In one letter, Acher himself mentioned that his age was his principal infirmity, but that it only caused seasonal disability. Thus, the narrative might end with succession and professional inheritance or continued activity.

In the period before the organization of the system by royal ordinance in 1814–15 individuals offered their life histories as essential elements of their demands. They often tried to link their individual narratives to the developing national narrative. The working out of the system led to a more formulaic narrative, but it took time to evolve, and the narratives that survive reveal uncertainty and indecision. Did Acher see the narrative ending with succession by his son or by indefinite service on his part? Would retirement involve being rewarded by a stable regime?

Some cases juxtaposed personal narratives with word-pictures of current misery. A magistrate named Cudenet, protesting the meager pension that had been offered him, based his complaint both on his service and on the misfortunes of his family. In a memorandum of over eight pages, he narrated his legal career of fifty years.[13] He remarked upon his lack of wealth but touted an important heritage of virtue received from his ancestors. He evoked his hard work and the expense of raising children. The Revolution ended the old judicial system, but the creation of justices of the peace in 1790 was an occasion to be called again to service and to sacrifice for the public good. After a brief period of private activity, he acceded to the wishes of his community of Saint-Malo, emphasizing the honorable but nonlucrative nature of his duties: "All I had to meet the needs of my spouse, and of twelve children almost all quite young, was a salary . . . paid me in paper of little value. I resolved to quit and to return to my profession. But the insistence of my fellow citizens, the unanimous suffrage of ten thousand inhabitants, reversed my view and changed my resolution." How, he asked, could he resist such public confidence? "I stayed at my post, and I occupied it until the moment when Representative of the People Carpentier, on mission in the departments of the west, judged it convenient to get rid of me. They accused me of moderation and turned a virtue repressing all excess into a crime." Thus, he presented himself as a victim of excess, a defender of virtue. He linked the story of his life to the critical junctures in the emerging French historical narrative. Reinstated after Robespierre's fall on 9 Thermidor, he had been reelected and appointed (as the system changed) ever since. Only accidentally over the course of twenty-one years was he divested of his role as judge.

He then summarized the narrative and explained it in terms of self-sacrifice and a standard of living that required his wife's commercial activities, which suffered setbacks from the capture of Louisbourg in 1758 and the end of the 1802 Treaty of Amiens in 1803. Family setbacks continued. "A kind of fatality seems to print its iron fingers on my entire family: my children, my two sons-in-law, all have been struck by the hand of misfortune." He described the failed business ventures and wartime captivity experienced by the next generation, and then focused attention upon himself, now the object of the minister's gaze:

> In order to paint the final stroke of this picture of my situation, it remains for me to speak of myself, Sir.
> May Your Excellency deign for one moment to imagine transporting himself to an apartment devoid of its furniture: the first object that strikes his vision is an old man—languishing on a bed without covers: despair is on

his brow, worry in his eyes, and the muscles of his face seem contracted by sadness. At this moving spectacle, Your Excellency, moved by a secret compassion, would not fail to inform himself of the age of the old man, of his physical and moral pain, of which everything announces he is the prey; of his state, and of his means of existence.

The voice shifts yet again:

His worthy wife, her face lined by sorrows even more than by the hand of time, would respond that her husband is reaching the end of his seventy-second year; that for the last six years infirmities of all sorts undermine and consume his fragile existence; that he can barely walk, that he can only take a step with the support of a cane and held up on the arm of one of his daughters, that, despite so many ills, he sits at court at the rank of judge, whose functions he has exercised over a period of twenty years; that a harsh necessity imposes its rule upon him, having only his salary to meet his expenses, those of his wife, of two of his daughters and of four of his grandchildren gathered around him because of the plague of war; that his salary is used up the very day it is received; that often her husband suffers needs that she cannot satisfy; that these needs will become more pressing every day, because soon he will cease to be active, and an imperial decree reduces his resources to a retirement pension whose amount is fixed at the sum of five hundred francs; a decree which for him, for her, and for his unhappy family will be a sentence of death and dispersion.

Then he returned to the first person to make a final plea.

Pardon, My Lord, the frankness of this exposé. I exaggerate neither my misfortunes nor the consequences of the imperial decree, if it were maintained without augmentation of the pension. . . . But everything presages for me a soothing of my fate, and I regard as a pleasure putting beneath the eyes of the August Chief of the Empire the sad situation in which I find myself: the most just of princes as well as the wisest of men, the one who carries in his heart all the charitable virtues, will never allow a magistrate in his seventies to lack the basic needs, the prime necessities of life.

If Your Excellency deigns to be my spokesman before His Majesty the emperor and king, if you place at his feet the record of my services and of my misfortunes, of which His Majesty is not yet aware, a happy future will open before me, and I will end my days in peace in the bosom of my family.

A postscript listed notables who could vouch for the veracity of his account and concluded that "if there is in the empire an active judge older than I, there is none more infirm or more unfortunate." He wrote again and again, but I have found no record of a change in the pension. The narratives corresponded to the sentimentality of late eighteenth- and early nineteenth-century fiction. The verbal self-portrait of the old man on the bed even calls to mind the sentimentally moralizing genre paintings of Jean-Baptiste Greuze, who routinely depicted families in moments of emotional crisis.

Complaint was the mode of another ailing judge. The sixty-five-year-old Cartault wrote on November 30, 1807, complaining of the deleterious climate of Fontainebleau.[14] He could imagine three alternative ends to his career. One would be an assignment in his birthplace of Paris, whose more moderate air, his physician claimed, would better suit him. Another would be an appropriate and honorable retirement pension with the decoration of the Legion of Honor. The third, remaining at Fontainebleau while suffering from catarrh and spitting blood, would mean certain death. He wrote of his five sons, two of whom served in the military, one having died in Prussia, the other posted to a naval artillery regiment in Brest. "I am neither deaf nor blind, but, besides my bad chest whose dangers augment every day, my frequent nervous crises often prevent me from writing because of trembling that I cannot control." Recognition of the minister's busy schedule kept him from demanding a personal audience. "But this letter and the important papers that I take the liberty of handing over to you say everything."

An earlier account, written on July 1, 1807, linked his declining health to the political narrative of the Revolution, but he began by recounting his Old Regime service as lawyer, notary, and *secrétaire du Roi*. The suppression of that post in 1790 led him to leave Paris for his property of Boissette near Melun. Three months later he was named justice of the peace; more important judicial positions followed.

I can assure you, My Lord, that for the more than forty years that I have worked at the study and practice of the law, no one has had the slightest reproach to make of me. Justice of the peace during the Terror, I have by my firmness and often at the peril of my life maintained the people of my jurisdiction. I prevented the pillaging of the city of Melun and of the farmers.

I alone forced more than two thousand seditious people to put down their arms.

However, his great exertion had dire consequences.

A vessel burst in my chest, and since that time, that is, since 1793, I spit blood from time to time when this too full vessel opens again. That doesn't prevent me from always being very exact in my functions, except for the moments when I sense a hemorrhage coming on. I would like to remain a judge for three years to complete my twenty years, but I fear that I won't be able to make it that long.

Cartault called again for help by writing the prosecutor of the Appeals Court of Paris on September 9, 1808; this time he even complained about the demands of his family, who wanted him to work another two years. "But if the process of my retirement is done and accepted, with the honorary title and pension that I demanded, it is Providence that will have decided my fate and I will have at least the consolation of having put an interval of repose between life and death." In a postscript, Cartault suggested that the state might provide support to old or infirm judges by naming them members of the Legion of Honor and granting them the appropriate pension.

Honor rooted in personal dignity and public service was an important component in magistrates' self-images, and their narratives aimed at honorable conclusions. A former judge in the Appeals Court of Aix-en-Provence, Pierre-Toussaint Durand-Maillane, began anticipating retirement in January 1806, when he wrote both of his great age of seventy-seven years and the distance between the court and his family residence.[15] He thought he should step aside for someone younger, but worried that a proper retirement would require him to look to his finances, political situation, and honor:

Uniquely occupied with the public interest in the entire length of my legislative service, I returned to Paris as poor and poorer than I was in April 1789 when I went to Versailles for the Estates General; I needed, I say it to you before God, my stipend (2,400F) in order to live, in order to meet my domestic expenses.

After having long been on the main stage of the Revolution, after having played a very active part there, the prudence that I here call political forbids that I fall suddenly to the parterre in a denouement that exposes me to the insults of all parties; because, My Lord, it is necessary to be in the departments and above all the departments of the south to be completely convinced whether these parties are now contained by the wise institutions of this government.

Finally, my honor, not that honor which relates to personal feelings, but that which opinion renders very important in society, rightly makes me fear a scorn of which I am not worthy if, after having fulfilled my duties without

Pierre-Toussaint Durand-Maillane, a former judge in Aix-en-Provence, wrote of legislative and judicial service during the revolutionary and Napoleonic eras, with emphasis on honor, infirmity, and the need to reward retired magistrates much in the way that military veterans had been in the past.

Augustin Challamel and Désiré Lacroix, *Album du centenaire: Grands hommes et grands faits de la Révolution française (1789–1804)* (Paris: Furne, Jouvet & Cie, 1889)

reproach in all positions I have occupied in the Revolution, I retire without any sign without any trace of the esteem of the government to which I have been devoted.

His life story merited an honorable end, but it had to be confirmed by the government. To win support, he placed his current situation in a classical context.

Cicero teaches us that in Rome they made it a duty for citizens to respect those who had held major positions in the republic, and in our Old Regime they honored veterans. Without speaking of my publications, which had some success before the Revolution, I was a deputy to the Estates General, by unanimous vote in the *bailliage* assembly of Arles. During this first assembly, they elected me first judge in the tribunal of my district of Tarascon, which elected me in 1792 deputy to the National Convention; after which I was returned to the Council of Elders by vote of a great number of departments.

He went on to discuss his service, his infirmities, and the need to reward old magistrates as much as war veterans.

However, the moment was not right in the narrative of the nation for this particular petitioner to win retirement benefits. A former colleague warned that he would be doing a disservice to the public by retiring and that as long as his moral and physical powers permitted, he owed it to his country to continue. Durand's own letter of March 24, 1808, mentions that in 1806 a purge was underway; other colleagues advised that retirement at that moment might compromise his reputation. Therefore, he had stayed. But now physical impairments drove him to retire. His doctors wrote of irregular urinary flow and pain in the kidneys and urinary tract. This time, he provided a much more laconic review of his life, little more than a list of appointments and elections, but it still offered his hopes and some of the twists and turns in his career. He suggested that some of his Old Regime publications on canon law and church property, which had appeared in multiple editions, might enjoy a comeback after Napoleon's concordat with the Catholic church, and he mentioned having prevented homicides in the south, saving at least one hundred prisoners who were going to be thrown in the Rhône River. Some people had wished him ill, and that made it more necessary to receive official honors. The pension was granted. The end of the story came in April 1814, when Napoleon was first deposed. Durand wrote on April 24 that he had read in the newspapers that military pensions would be continued but that there had been no word about civil pensions. It is not clear that he ever received a response. By August, he was dead.

Before the overthrow of Napoleon, policy changes and financial constraints caused by military expenditures limited the full development of a pension program, and the instability of the regime limited the development of a stable historical narrative. One out-of-work, aging magistrate evoked melodramatically the horrors of the Napoleonic Wars: "My older son of twenty-three years, having returned crippled in the Grande Armée... overcome with sorrow at seeing himself without a position, and his unhappy father also, and having nothing to exist on, threw himself in the water."[16] Another had obviously thought about how a magistrate should end up: "In a situation so different from that in which I was raised... the mediocrity of my fortune has even forced me to retire to the country whose genre of life suits poorly a man grown old in the functions of the *magistrature*."[17] However, there were others who welcomed a rural retreat, modeled after classical and Enlightenment notions of the good old age.

Some retirements began as leaves of absence. Some were second choices when senior magistrates were not offered plum positions. Some demands demonstrated clear material need and offered the bureaucrats a spectacle of the unfortunate magistrate and his family. At the very least, many postulants asked to be named honorary judges in their former jurisdictions. Thus, they maintained a certain status, expressed both in a formal role in civic functions and in still being listed in the imperial or royal almanac.

Such magistrates depicted themselves as the heroes of their time. "I saved a great number of émigrés and refractory priests, slowing things down, asking for interpretation of existing laws, prolonging investigations, delaying judgments until a gentler regime permitted me to free them."[18] Such heroism deserved another outcome. Many of those who wrote of material need pretended that poverty itself brought no personal shame because losing wealth while serving the public suggested virtuous behavior, but they described a shame that might redound to the magistracy and public service should their misery be widely known. Personal and family honor were tied to the honor of the magistracy and to a magistrate's own last days.

The language of honor was second nature to the magistracy. Humanist education had formed them, and classical texts would even speak to matters of late life, shifting in emphasis from Augustinian to Ciceronian ideas. It should come as no surprise that judges describing their aging had recourse to Cicero's apologetic *De Senectute*. Magistrates and others pursuing public service were precisely the kinds of individuals who fit Cicero's Roman model of aging and civic virtue. For example, Gilles Joseph Deligné, an octogenarian judge in Rennes who found himself without a post after a reorganization of the courts, headed his first demand for a new post on September 5, 1810, with a Latin quotation from *De Senectute* with French translation in a footnote. "Good sense, reason, and prudence reside in old men. Without them there would be neither cities nor societies."[19] He used Cicero to argue that despite his age he still had "all the zeal and all the intellectual and moral means of continuing the functions of judge," and identified his handwriting as proof that he had not fallen into decrepitude. After observing that "one does not die because one is old, but because one is a man," he returned to Cicero for an observation on the importance of continued activity and adding to Cicero's examples of active old men his own cohort of magistrates who had begun their judicial careers in the Parlement de Bretagne under the Old Regime. He then asked a rhetorical question:

> Why should old age, healthy in body and mind, which in all centuries, even among savages, has always obtained marks of veneration, become among the most humane and enlightened people in the universe (the French) an object of rejection and inconsiderateness? Isn't old age, on the contrary, the surest guarantor of maturity of judgment, of a long experience, and the most solid morality[?] I add that if there exists a passion in an honest and upright old man, it is that of dying at the post he has occupied for many years, and in which his hair has whitened. I avow that such is and will always be the dearest wish of my heart.

While Deligné's first wish was for a new post, he expressed a secondary desire to receive a retirement pension. An honorable retirement would save him from the shame and humiliation of being thought to have been fired and from the recrimination of families against whom he had rendered judgment. He fell back on a second line of argument that admitted some physical decline and the increasing difficulty of attending court for long hours and engaging in tiring legal argument that required "young and vigorous lungs." Two days later Deligné wrote again, describing a bad debt he had not been able to recover and apologizing that his busy schedule did not leave him time to write more briefly, in a less diffuse fashion, or in a hand that, while not

In a passage that includes quotations from Cicero's *De Senectute*, the most influential of classical texts on old age and one that was mentioned in many magistrates' demands, Gilles Joseph Deligné, a judge in Rennes, writes to the Duc de Massa, the minister of justice, on September 5, 1810, requesting a new post or, if that proves impossible, a retirement pension. He asks why old age had become "an object of rejection" in France and asserts, "One does not die because one is old, but because one is a man."

AN BB25 5

noticeably different to my eyes from that of the previous demand (where it was proof of competence), he characterized as clumsy and resembling that of a schoolboy. If, he concluded, he received neither a new post nor an honorable retirement, and were isolated and abandoned by the government, he would quickly die.

Three months later, having received neither a new post nor a retirement pension, Deligné tried another strategy, emphasizing an infirmity that dated back twenty-one years. Recognizing that physical disability might result in an entitlement, he told a story of an icy New Year's Day 1789 in Rennes, when he fell and broke his right leg, the setting of which resulted in the loss of two and a half inches of bone and a need for crutches. But this was not just any break. It was occasioned by patriotic activity. For while he had left his house in the morning to attend mass, mention of which probably neither helped nor hurt, he braved the weather at 6:00 p.m. to observe a secret "antipatriotic" meeting of deputies of the Third Estate. "It is evidently to my patriotic zeal for the success of our revolution that ... I owe the unfortunate fracture of my leg." Refusal of a pension would constitute another misfortune. He ended the letter with an accounting of his income, his dependence upon his wife, and the fact that his son-in-law had received a military pension.

The document revives a particular moment's rhetoric of patriotism and revolution and moves between arguments for continued service and repose. When a new list of judicial appointments drawn up on April 14, 1811, did not include Deligné's name, he wrote again on the twenty-third, invoking personal connections in the magistracy and seeking sympathy for his great age and poverty. When speaking of his diet as being reduced to bread and water, he added in parentheses that this was the truth. Perhaps Deligné understood that readers of such demands were bombarded with claims, or maybe he recognized that since his last post had been a temporary one, he did not have the absolute right that some of his colleagues did. Moreover, he was writing in the Napoleonic period, when the system was still uncertain, and funding for such matters was often in short supply.

Repetition of the narrative, whether written or oral, gave the author a chance to shape it into compelling form. It constituted more than a cry for help, for it accompanied that cry with a sense of a long career, following a centuries-old model, veering off course, and meeting new expectations, punctuated by moments of drama and emergency. Deligné's series of memoirs covers the range that characterized a great many postulants' demands. It is difficult to separate their themes, for they were interrelated, but time and again demands featured three: professional service, with its moral, economic, and domestic components; participation in formal politics; and the aging of the body. Memories of the Revolution itself and the negotiation between magistrates and the ministry over interpreting the law provided a kind of narrative punch.[20]

Judges demanding help revealed expectations that derived as much from memories of the Old Regime as from awareness of recent legislation and practice. They described work undertaken in every regime and presented the qualities of a good magistrate, exactitude, zeal, and impartiality, as transcending political and constitutional changes. The ministry had to determine what functions in the Old Regime constituted national service, not a simple matter. Magistrates and *fonctionnaires* had sworn oaths to various regimes. They had purchased Old Regime offices and been appointed or elected since. Loyalties multiplied as they aged. Continuity in their reconstructed careers came from identification with the magistracy itself, with an evolving idea of the state, and with single- or multigenerational narratives. People who had purchased offices in the Old Regime argued that they had never been properly reimbursed during the Revolution, and habits of thinking of the magistracy as inherited property died hard.

For magistrates whose careers began in the Old Regime, post-revolutionary memories expressed nostalgia and sometimes resentment. They rooted individual narratives in family, regional, and national histories. They wrote of multiple generations of public service, encompassing both royal and republican regimes. For some, the Revolution was a great interruption; for others, it provided new challenges and continued service. For some, particular events stand out and provide the drama of a lifetime; for others, events flatten out. Some began their accounts generations back; others began with their own educations. They applied different rhetorical modes: heroism, pathos, simple expectation, special pleading. Some presented the Old Regime nostalgically; others recognized how their destinies were linked to the Revolution.[21] In interesting ways, they juxtaposed individual experiences and public events. Arguments about justice, paternal kindness, right, equity, welfare, humanity, and need depended upon a subjective understanding of the historical moment, but much depended also upon the circumstances of retirement. Was it forced? Was it the result of warfare, institutional in-fighting, political conflict, purge, personal enmities, or cutbacks in the ministry? Was it the result of physical or mental decline? Was it desired or resisted? In some cases, judges presented the decision to retire as part of a plan for the rest of their lives. Some described decisions resulting from months or even years of planning. Others described emergencies.

Political events offered some of the more memorable emergencies. In the life of Louis-Alexandre Devérité, a civil judge from the northern city of Abbeville, the political might involve the keeping of the peace in his town when three wagons loaded with wheat passed through during a time of scarcity in November 1791, causing a great commotion. But it could also mean taking a moderate position in the sentencing of Louis XVI in the National Convention.[22] He recounts his exchange with Robespierre, who chastised him: "One does not accept a place as representative when one does not have the courage to fill it." The reply: "You will see that I will have that courage; because I am going to vote the appeal to the people, beside you, and despite your lesson." He writes, "And I did it."[23]

When the Bourbon Restoration came in 1814–15 (with the one-hundred-day Napoleonic interlude), it became practical to present oneself as counterrevolutionary and more dangerous to emphasize revolutionary service. Thus, Jacques Alexis Thuriot de la Rosière, regicide, sometime member of the Committee of Public Safety, and one of the men who presided over the Convention on 9 Thermidor, tried to claim that he had been maligned and was really a defender of the royal family.[24] His letter of March 6, 1815, right before the Hundred Days threw things into uncertainty, responded to an ordinance of February 15 concerning his eligibility for a retirement pension. He launched into his life history: born in Sézanne, Marne, May 1, 1753, lawyer in the Parlement de Paris since July 9, 1778, judge in the district tribunal, service in the Legislative Assembly, Convention, and so on. Laws and ordinances, he claimed, assured him a pension. He also explained that his property had been devastated by the allies' invasion of France. He claimed his intention was to reside in the country but that he would have to return to Paris to support his wife and son. In 1814, he had received assurances that the new king, Louis XVI's brother, would not hold a grudge, but was still sent into exile in 1816.

Then came his great exercise in self-fashioning. In January 1824, at age seventy-one and in ill health in Liège, he wrote King Louis XVIII, himself eight months from death: "Justice is the principal attribute of Royalty, the right of claiming it is sacred and inviolable." He recalled saving the riches housed in the Tuileries during the great insurrection of August 10, 1792, which overthrew the monarchy. He headed a deputation of the Legislative Assembly that faced the Paris crowd in the courtyard of the Tuileries.

The scenes were frightful, the crowd was enormous, the most horrible vociferations made themselves heard, everything was braved by the deputation.

By force of perseverance I managed to make myself heard and to make them promise to respect the two palaces and the riches that were there.

He went on to recall his protecting the queen by advising her through the intermediary of a tall, brown-haired employee of the royal household, his attempting to delay a December 16, 1792, decree banishing members of the royal family from France, and his arguing for the queen in the Committee of Public Safety in July 1793. For all this, he said, he was denounced. Furthermore, he recovered some royal property and participated in the downfall of Robespierre, an event he narrated in great detail, painting a portrait of the horrors he had prevented. He claimed to have protected the king's daughter, saved the National Library, and negotiated the safety of six fellow magistrates who had been members of the Convention. The last two pages focused on the pension itself, his claim that his right to it was "incontestable," and his desire to return to France.

His memories of 1792-94 were vivid, his self-presentation that of the moderate squeezed from both extremes. His old age was one of remembering and interpreting. The shape of that memory depended in part on his perception of the law and current political circumstances, but he could always claim it was a patriotic memory.

Even a man who had offered to serve as a spy for the English—we only know this in retrospect and from other sources—turned himself into a patriot. His public face was similar to that of Thuriot, whom we just met, but he spoke in a sense for an entire generation. François Joseph Gamon justified his pension demand by recounting his services and explained his decision to retire by saying that he could not help it that he came of age during the Revolution and reached old age in a very different era.[25] Born April 6, 1767, in the Ardèche, he served as a youthful legislator in the National Convention. He had opposed the execution of the king, and he was proscribed with the Girondins and denounced by Marat, fled the country, and returned after the fall of Robespierre. He recounted the "deluge of maledictions" and "violent murmurs" that accompanied his moderate proposals in the Convention. He explained his desire to retreat from public life. He was tired of political battles, suffering from "this fatigue of the soul that one suffers when one has known the men and profound perversity of our century." He deserved a pension,

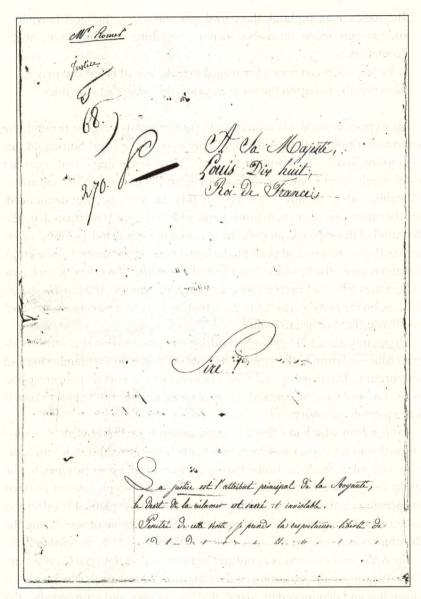

Jacques Alexis Thuriot de la Rosière, a regicide, remakes himself as a protector of the royal family in a letter to King Louis XVIII claiming pension rights for his service. The letter leaves much space on the opening page in a way that accentuates the salutation: "Sire."
AN BB25 36

he said, because of twenty-four years of legislative, judicial, and administrative service, the mediocrity of his fortune, and "because if a fatal destiny has thrown me onto a theater of crimes and revolutions, I have resisted the torrent of public corruption, and I braved death, I dare say, to save the life of the king, and also to save France from anarchy: nevertheless, I was one of the youngest among the passengers embarked on the vessel of the revolution."

Gamon's sense of historical time and his political memory forged his identity:

> I am French: and if I have the regret that in the time I have lived, all my services were rendered to the *patrie*, and not at the same time to the Bourbons, the illustrious head of that family will recognize that having come, so to say, into the world in 1791, being born in the cradle of the republic, I had to be by force of circumstances as well as by my principles one of the defenders of this republic that declared itself the enemy of the Bourbons, that this separation of France and her former kings was from the origin of the Revolution the will of my century, and that to obey the general will was my duty.

Like Thuriot, he suffered exile, but his return was authorized in 1818, and, like Thuriot, he was a man caught in the middle; as he told it, he was persecuted by revolutionaries for being a royalist and by royalists for being a revolutionary. His clandestine service to England through the network of the comte d'Antraigues during the Directory only compounded the complication of his identity.[26]

The revolutionary divide plainly had a fundamental impact on individual lives and careers, but aging magistrates looked back and tried to create coherence. When Augustin Loubers (de Cordes) discovered in August 1810 that his position was going to be eliminated, he began his letter to the ministry by recounting his calling to the law, both by birth and by taste, his teaching in the law faculty of Toulouse before the Revolution, and his service in a series of judicial posts ever since. In principle he would have preferred staying active, "But his advanced age and the infirmities he has contracted in the painful exercise of his functions put him (to his great regret) out of condition to continue his services."[27] Loubers remembered a particular case in the winter of 1805 (Pluviôse, Year XIII), when he had to travel to the town of Grenade, in the arrondissement of Toulouse, to track a criminal. He fell, hurting his right leg severely and forcing him to stay in bed for twenty months. The pain and the remedies applied deprived him of the greater part of his "physical and moral faculties," so that he could not undertake another career. The immediate cause of Loubers's inactivity was the suppression of his post. As he told it, however, in his demand for support, it was his life story, not an institutional reform, that merited attention. In his narrative, destiny had shaped his career until the combination of accident and aging brought it to an end.

The end of Pierre Chiniac's career was more political.[28] He had made serious enemies during the Terror. A cover letter of January 24, 1811, accompanied a twenty-four-page printed justification of his political behavior and a four-page handwritten plea, which began: "When I asked your Excellency's permission last year to go to the waters for the reestablishment of my health, I took the liberty of saying that if my infirmities would no longer permit me to exercise my functions, I would hope that out of his goodness he would procure for me an honorable retirement. I see with pain that my forces diminish each day, that there remains for me very little time to live and that it is time to put an interval between life and death." He then went on to present "the picture of my life" and his works as a man of letters and as a magistrate.

"I was born May 5, 1741, of a family that for more than three centuries occupied places in the *magistrature* at the Sénéchaussée Présidiale of Périgueux." He recounted his studies at the University of Paris, his reception to the bar by the Paris Parlement, and his naming in the Limousin town of Uzerches to major offices, which he held until the Revolution. Then, as he told it, he was "forced" by the inhabitants of the city of Uzerches to accept the command of the National Guard "to maintain among them good order and union" and, in January 1790, was unanimously elected mayor of the city. Administrative and judicial appointments and elections followed. Thus, he presented his political life as honorable service forced upon him. Selfless performance became part of the remembered self.

By the fall of 1793, Chiniac had moved to Agen and married, but people he described as "disorganizers of society" denounced him as an "enemy of the people." Political persecution constituted part of his life story, literary ambition another. He wrote on the Gallican Church, the Celts, moral philosophy, and tolerance, and both the political and literary components of his life took a toll: "These literary works and what I have suffered in the Revolution, especially during the year 1794 when I was in irons, have altered my health, which was very robust. I have had an attack of paralysis, and its effects warn me every day that I have little time to live. My fortune was reduced almost to zero by the diverse losses that I suffered in the Revolution and the expenses that they've occasioned." He claimed it would pain "the generous heart of his Imperial and Royal Majesty" to let him suffer at seventy years of age, and asserted, "I have so little time to live that the payment which his Majesty will deign to give me cannot be a charge for the state." He asked also for the title of honorary counselor at the imperial court of Agen, a decoration of honor, and a stipend to protect him from need in his old age.

The printed memoir included a more detailed discussion of Chiniac's political career and an assortment of documents demonstrating his political and moral virtues. It recounted cruelties and kindnesses during his ordeal. In describing his arrest and transfer from Toulouse to Agen, he recalled the cruelty of the authorities who would not allow his wife to ride with him, forcing her to hire another coach. When the committee of the commune of Agen planned to take him north to Brive, he feared he would be killed, but he had a happy memory of the officers who escorted him and allowed him to spend the night at home, giving his wife a chance to launch a successful appeal.

The handwritten account used some of that material but weaved together a political, professional, and medical history. It constituted a demand and a memoir, which featured the high and low points of his career and how it had ended up. The French Revolution might have set precedent in the history of civil service, the magistracy, and public pensions, but it was also an occasion for heroic activity that avoided the "excesses" of the Revolution or for painful loss of property. Memory of that activity formed a kind of life review.

Another magistrate who supplied a political self-portrait was Joseph-François-Ignace Roussel-Bouret, who wrote the minister of justice on June 16, 1810.[29] Roussel-Bouret claimed to have been owed a pension that dated back to the Old Regime. His letter referred to more than fifty years of public service, "as much in the old as in the new regime."[30] He lamented his destiny, wondering how it could be that after a "life devoted to so many works as useful as they were painful," after a youth of ease and then so much misfortune, described in his self-portrait, "would it be my fatal destiny that I end my days in the greatest distress, in poverty, in the denial of the things most necessary in old age?" He evoked the themes of justice, equity, welfare, and humanity, and interjected that the minister had invited him personally to write.

Roussel-Bouret's next written demand came in August and began with a physical accounting, including colic and fever that prevented him from pleading in person. Claiming he had been the victim of calumny and quoting the Bible, Richelieu, and La Fontaine about how good men always have their detractors, he signed off as "the very humble, very devoted and very obedient servant Roussel-Bouret, more than octogenarian, former magistrate of the

Pierre Chiniac writes to the minister of justice, the Duc de Massa, to justify his political choices. He squeezed much into four manuscript pages, presenting himself as a man of letters and magistrate, but he also submitted a twenty-four-page printed memoir that he had addressed to his fellow citizens.
AN BB2 10

sovereign courts, as much before as since the Revolution, pensioner of the state, originally of 2,000 livres, now reduced to 166 francs!!" Another letter repeated the essentials in January 1811. It added a comparison with the success of mere copyists in obtaining greater pensions, and it complained that the printing of his political life cost more than three years of his little pension. He repeated the minister's own words, that "you can count on my justice," that "the intention of the Emperor is to accord to public functionaries pensions proportioned to the importance and duration of their services." How to interpret the law became part of the story.

Storytelling was a feature of the demand of Richard François Chaix d'Estanges, a prosecutor who found himself without a position when his court was suppressed.[31] The dossier remarked that he was guilty of some sort of "immorality," but his own testimony suggested he was in trouble only because he was a married former priest. Whatever the truth, he recounted several events in which he had distinguished himself in local history and found himself at odds with religious officials.

The combination of present misery and historic service is obvious in the dossier of François Anne Louis-Phelippes de Coatgoureden de Tronjolly, a judge in Brittany, former president of the Revolutionary Tribunal of Nantes and opponent of Jean-Baptiste Carrier, who recounted his sacrifices for France and the defense of humanity, and complained that "the air of Napoléonville [Pontivy] is killing me and that 1,250 francs, which comprises my salary, are insufficient to support me in this city even alone." He described his family's discomfort in Rennes.[32] Born in 1751, and thus fifty-seven years old when he tried to obtain a new post or a pension, he wrote about thirty-five manuscript letters, including one across which he scrawled, "I await justice!" He assured the minister that he was neither mad nor infirm, but that the region's climate was killing him and that he did not understand the local language. He said he had been happier imprisoned in the Conciergerie of Paris during the Terror. In one of numerous printed justifications, he wrote in the third person, "Yes, SIRE, his sorrows and his name belong to history; he will declare until death, his wife and children will claim, when he is no longer, he sacrificed his fortune for the state."

Tronjolly claimed to have rendered thirty-six years of service, following in a five-hundred-year, fourteen-generation tradition of his family in Brittany. He saw himself as performing on an even bigger stage, however. "Christopher Columbus was treated as a visionary and as a madman, after having rendered great services for the Spanish and posterity: he had discovered America."

Putting himself in such world-historical company, he lamented: "But, SIRE, what haven't I done for the French?" recalling the drownings, shootings, and brigandage of the Terror in the Loire region, and declaring himself an avenger on a Europe-wide stage. In other words, at the time of the greatest internal conflict in revolutionary France, he saved the country. And he placed himself in a long tradition of magistrates, citing a 1711 *Mercuriale* of d'Aguesseau that both praised the magistrate who settles conflicts and explored the career and dignified old age and retirement of a recently deceased colleague, M. Le Pelletier.[33] Thinking ahead to posterity, he even printed verses, written ostensibly by someone else, to be placed beneath his portrait. A note suggests that they were not intended for the eyes of Napoleon or his ministers, but somehow they found their way into his dossier:

> Magistrat éclairé, juge intègre et sévère,
> Courageux ennemi des ennemis des lois,
> Son zèle, quarante ans, soutint contre eux la guerre
> Et du faible opprimé fit triompher les droits.
>   Pendant ces jours de deuil, où la France avilie
> Gémissait sous le joug, en proie à des brigands;
> Quand l'horrible terreur par mille arrêts sanglans,
> D'un règne monstrueux prolongeait la folie,
> Que l'espoir était mort, la vertu sans vigueur
> Et tous les coeurs saisis d'une lâche stupeur,
> Le premier il osa, par un élan sublime,
> Concevoir le projet de détrôner le crime,
> Et s'offrant à la mort, ce nouveau Curtius,
> Par un trait immortel, couronna ses vertus.

> Enlightened magistrate, honest and stern judge,
> Courageous enemy of the enemies of the laws,
> His zeal, for forty years, waged war against them
> And rendered triumphant the rights of the weak oppressed.
>   During these days of mourning, when degraded France
> Groaned under the yoke, plagued by brigands;
> When the horrible terror by a thousand bloody orders
> Of a monstrous reign prolonged the madness,
> That hope was dead, virtue without vigor
> And all hearts overcome with a cowardly stupor,

> First he dared with sublime energy
> To conceive the project of dethroning crime,
> And, offering himself to death, this new Curtius,
> By an immortal stroke, crowned his virtues.

Tronjolly had been memorializing himself for years. In a 1789 pamphlet, he had spoken critically of the exercise of arbitrary authority in the ancien régime and declared his having defended humanity and liberty, deploying language of *salut public*, *honneur*, and *devoir*. He claimed to have opposed ministerial despotism in the early 1780s, working against arbitrary imprisonment, protested the distribution of bad tobacco by the *fermiers généraux*, and saved the lives of hospitalized children.[34] When he wrote Napoleon on September 29, 1807, he referred to "the happy government under which we live," but in an 1814 pamphlet seeking government aid he supported monarchy, claiming to have opposed the factionalism of the Year II, anarchy of the Directory, and tyranny of Napoleon. The pamphlet itself says he has been demanding an indemnity and recompense for more than thirty years.[35]

Tronjolly was obviously capable of changing with the political winds, but he also saw himself following in a long magisterial tradition. Ideals whose French origins went back to at least the sixteenth century formed the basis for values that were still held in high regard. Such continuity lay at the heart of his 1829 book on judicial eloquence.[36] He gave voice to a corporate and increasingly national sense of style, accomplishment, and professional identity. Magistrates who shared such values clung to them even as they negotiated the politics of the revolutionary era.

The pattern for many magistrates was to recount memories of resisting radicals at the height of the Revolution. Others expressed considerable pride in their revolutionary contributions and credentials. Napoleonic magistrates, like politicians of the era, came from virtually all ideological backgrounds, but they naturally attempted to refashion themselves. Seeking stability in time of revolution and war, they constructed life histories and expressed a civic identity that built upon a remembered corporate one. Their often modest stories were important in themselves, but their experiences gave the Revolution itself meaning and became reconfigured as regime gave way to regime. As they bombarded the ministry, colleagues, and political leaders with their tales, they contributed to a new state system and an emerging collective memory.

3
Setting Rules from Old Regime to Midcentury

The Ministry of Justice was one of many public institutions that dealt with retirement issues in the nineteenth century. Until the Napoleonic era, retirement had not been high on the national agenda. Old Regime retirement was largely a private or individual affair. Professionals often passed their roles on to heirs against some form of payment. Guilds saw to emergency needs more than long-term retirement. The idea of a restful old age certainly existed, as a Ciceronian old age had become an ideal in the second half of the eighteenth century, but, aside from the army and *fermiers-généraux*, formal institutional procedures were not common. Magistrates owned their offices and could arrange succession or sale of office to support an inactive or semiactive old age. Looking back at the pre-revolutionary world, Restoration-era magistrates recalled that colleagues and families convinced infirm judges that it was time to step aside, for they would have had no material interest in holding on. They could consider themselves honorably retired, and some had created an association to aid those magistrates who had fallen on hard times. During the Revolution, pensions arose for consideration, but it was more important to deal with elections, appointments, and the working out of new political and judicial institutions with more uniform *départements* replacing traditional provinces, than to think about how to end careers in the magistracy.

The story of social welfare in the revolutionary period was one of uneven implementation of Enlightenment humanitarianism and the idea of social right, as revolutionary *bienfaisance* sought to replace traditional charity. The early years of the Revolution, which were characterized by the creation of uniform administrative and tax structures, saw a serious examination of social problems, including old-age poverty. A far-reaching pension proposal in the Year II addressed the needs of aged farmers and artisans, rural mothers, and widows with children. The law of 8 Messidor proposed semiannual payments of 160 livres to such a population. It called for documentation of work and need by the commune and of infirmity by two surgeons. Nevertheless, social welfare legislation for the aged poor failed to live up to expectations throughout the 1790s, as military demands soaked up resources, economic crisis reduced the money available, Thermidorean politicians seeking to stabilize a political system riven by ideological tensions (civil war, international war, and Terror) lacked the will of their predecessors, and revolutionary administration proved inconsistent.[1]

When administrative institutions achieved greater maturity and had greater resources under Napoleon, it became clear that only civil servants, not the poor in general, would benefit in a systematic way from state pensions. A decree of 1806 set out a new system, with withholding from salaries and some budgeted money to create a pension fund. But the revolutionary Jacobin idea of social right continued to play a role well into the twentieth century. Political and internal administrative discussions of pension policy in the Ministry of Justice went back to revolutionary precedent. Indeed, they referred to legislation of 1790 and 1791 as fundamental. A look back at that activity will provide important background to what would develop well past the Revolution.

Indicative of that evolution was an internal manuscript: "Notes on the bases to follow for the liquidation of pensions given at the start of the Year XII by the Bureaux du Conseiller d'Etat Directeur Général de la liquidation." The report began with general laws of 1790 and 1791.[2] The needs of civil servants had already been addressed in the general law of August 22, 1790, which awarded one-fourth of the salary for thirty years of service, plus one-twentieth of the remaining three-fourths for each year beyond thirty. Thus, a pension could reach the level of the salary after fifty years, but it could not exceed ten thousand livres. Other state service, military or civil, should count, but military service of twenty-five years would be the equivalent of thirty years on the civilian side, and service in wartime would count double. For civil service, the pension would be based upon the salary one had in the last post as long as it was occupied for three full years. Those whose wounds or ailments forced them to retire before thirty years would receive a pension "determined by the nature and duration of his services, the type of wounds, and the state of his infirmities." Widows of midcareer functionaries were to receive a subsistence-level pension, and their children's education would be paid by the state.

The proclamation of the August 22, 1790, law outlined what should happen among a "free people," discovering its rights and responsibilities. Serving the state was considered a duty of every citizen, but the proclamation also spoke of recompensing particular services and providing support in "the age of infirmities." At the most basic level, the state ought to recompense services to "the body social, when their importance and their duration merit this mark of recognition." The nation owed citizens reimbursement of sacrifices made for "public utility." Thus, the proclamation singled out services that concerned "the entire society." Such rewards would publicize the heroic service of individuals and, over time, make honor the norm.

The state was interested in providing such rewards but recognized the potential cost of its largesse. It refused to permit a "clause of reversibility," the principle that shifted the beneficiary to widow or orphan, but it would help on the basis of need. It promised ten million livres for pensions and another two million for other rewards or assistance. If money ran short, pensions would be distributed by order of age and service. Except for those wounded or having contracted infirmities while exercising public functions, no one would be able to obtain a pension who had not worked for thirty years or had not attained the age of fifty.

A law of July 20, 1791, building upon a decree of the National Assembly of July 2, addressed former pensioners who had been given some support in 1790 but also judges and other officials of the judicial system who had worked for at least twenty years and had been receiving pensions. Those pensions would be limited to eighteen hundred livres for those in their sixties, twenty-four hundred livres for those aged seventy to seventy-five. The law singled out nonnative magistrates and officials who had served in Corsica, where all they needed was ten years of service.

The manuscript notes referred to more specialized legislation from 1791 through the Year III, and found models for awarding support to widows of civil servants in a 1793 decree for widows of military servicemen and a law from the Year IV covering civilian employees within the navy. The "Notes" described what kinds of official documents should be required of retirees and then turned to the treatment of demands, which would be divided between those of individuals who were already at least in their sixties and those who were not. And in each group one should proceed from the oldest to the youngest. But age was one factor among many, including importance of service, infirmity, financial need, the loss of a support or care giver, and so on. Finally, it would not be permitted to receive a pension while still collecting a state salary.

Laws and edicts did more than deal with individual problems that arose. They contributed to shaping careers and structuring society. Legislation in the Consulate delved again into the matter of pensions. An *arrêté* of 15 Floréal, Year XI described a two-stage procedure, from admission to retirement to awarding of pension. Oversight was granted to the *directeur général de la liquidation*. Pension demands for services that ended before January 1, 1792, would not be admissible. Each ministry would rule on service since that date. The *conseil général de la liquidation* would continue paying pensions granted, in accordance with laws of June 19, 1793, and 9 Vendémiaire, Year VI. A three-year limit was placed on payments in arrears. And a pension law of 15 Germinal, Year XI placed a limit of six thousand francs on pensions. Other decrees referred to particular groups of individuals: those owed pensions from the Dutch government, superintendents of drawbridges, their widows, and orphans, hospital pharmacists, actors and employees of the Théâtre Français. The diversity indicates the practical importance of pensions and grassroots concerns.

The Ministry of Justice under Napoleon received hundreds of demands for pensions. Although we do not have a complete picture of its operations, a few surviving documents indicate that the ministry granted some support. The September 13, 1806, decree addressed the procedure for developing a pension system, but it did not override systems that had already been set up within individual ministries and had already withheld a percentage of the salary. It put into action the law of 15 Germinal, Year XI (April 5, 1803). Each applicant for a pension sent his demand and official documentation (*pièces justificatives*) to the head of his administration, who forwarded everything to the appropriate minister. Each ministry kept a register of demands organized by date and number. The formula was less generous than that spelled out in previous legislation. The thirty-year rule was maintained, but the minimum age for the healthy retiree was raised to sixty. The pension was paid at one-sixth of the salary of the last four years of service. Each year above thirty was augmented by a thirtieth of the remaining five-sixths. The decree also tried to limit amounts paid. Thus, pensions were not to exceed two-thirds of the salary, and an absolute limit was set at six thousand francs.

Looking back on his accomplishments, Napoleon described the importance of retirement accounts for civil servants: "One's future will no longer be an object of solicitation, a favor; it will be a right, a true property."[3] Such accounts dated to April 23, 1800, in the Ministry of Foreign Affairs, 1804 in the Corps of Engineers (Ponts et Chaussées), April 1810 for the employees of the state stables, November 18, 1810, for the mining engineers, October 23, 1808, for the employees of the prefecture of police. A common fund for pensions for civil personnel, based upon 2 percent withholding, was proposed in the Council of State on March 5, 1811. Individual security contributed to institutional coherence and loyalty.

Anticipating situations in which aged magistrates would not be able to continue their activities, the Napoleonic regime issued a decree on October 2, 1807, that court officers suffering from blindness, deafness, or other serious infirmities be granted retirement. When such individuals neglected to ask to retire, presiding judges and prosecutors were to inform on them to the minister of justice (*Grand Juge-Ministre de la Justice*), who asked the judge or officer in question for his own observations. The minister of justice then reported to the emperor.

The decree was packaged in positive language: "Law concerning judicial officers to whom infirmities give the right to a retirement pension." Retirees had a positive right. Even when legislators in the 1820s criticized the decree, they appreciated the notion that right and honor were served. Retired court officials retained honorary titles, continued to be listed in official records, and attended public ceremonies. They were accorded pensions fixed in each individual case by the emperor's orders. But criticize it they did, for they viewed the decree as increasing the power of the government at the expense of the magistracy. The emperor ("*L'Usurpateur*" to his detractors) and his minister of justice could intervene and purge the courts, using as an excuse the alleged infirmity of a judge.

From the perspective of the Bourbon Restoration, Napoleon's decree had destroyed the *inamovibilité* of the magistracy. Retirement, if forced, was an attack on an individual's liberty and an institution's integrity. Napoleon could still claim he was improving public service and aiding the infirm, but ten days later, in the Sénatus-Consulte of October 12, 1807, he focused on the other end of the judge's career and proved his critics right, placing a limit on *inamovibilité* itself. The act proclaimed that in order to ensure the talent, knowledge, and morality of the magistracy, only after a probationary period of five years would life tenure be awarded.

Reorganization was also a threat to life tenure and could prompt retirements. An imperial decree of July 6, 1810, concerned the organization and service of "imperial, assize, and special courts." Thirty years were required for *présidens* and *conseillers* to retire with honorary title. But the order had to be given by the emperor. They would retain their honors and privileges and even be able to deliberate in court proceedings. And they would be eligible for other marks of esteem. Three years after the death of an especially worthy magistrate, his portrait might be displayed in a courtroom.

Through some of the surviving documents, it is possible to attach names to what sometimes appeared to be theoretical situations. And they concern employees as well as magistrates. One former bureaucrat, *ex-chef de bureau* François-Jean-Baptiste-Louis Cuissot was receiving 250 francs a month in 1808, and Marie-Jeanne-Cecile Duvanel, widow Chatizel, was receiving 12.5 francs a month. When Duvanel died in March 1809, Cuissot was the only retired employee receiving a pension until another widow, Marie-Anne-Françoise-Elizabeth Merigot, widow Leloup, received 13.88 francs a month beginning in May 1810. By December seven Parisians received pensions. In September 1811, twenty-nine Parisians and two provincials were recipients. Of the twenty-eight Parisians being paid in November 1812, twenty were lower-level employees, and eight were widows. The lowest monthly payments were 15.5 francs for men and 5.32 francs for women; the highest were 389.58 for men, 109.63 for women. The ministry was spending 2,239.87 francs per month.[4]

By 1814, payments seem to have been made quarterly rather than monthly, and they were evidently need-based. There were thirty-three names on the list for the third quarter, fifty-nine in the fourth.[5] The administrator who would long remain in charge of pensions for the ministry, Nicolas-Joseph Romer, wrote the Garde des Sceaux on October 5, 1815, to say that the individuals on his list were mostly "in extreme need." He had not included those who had taken up service during Napoleon's Hundred Days. The source of the funds came from vacant posts and the 2 percent withheld from salaries.[6] The numbers of recipients inched up. In the second quarter of 1816, sixty-four Parisians, including nine widows, received annual pensions ranging from 128 to 7,000 francs; thirty-seven non-Parisians, including seven widows, received pensions from 130 to 2,700 francs per year.[7] By the third quarter of 1817, 94 names appeared on the Paris list, 268 on the provincial one.[8]

Whether those lists were complete is unknown. Some documents from 1811 indicate that the numbers may have been significantly higher. A letter from the Ministry of the Treasury, bureau of pensions, to Minister of Justice Claude-Ambroise Régnier, Duc de Massa, on March 28, 1811, concerned pensions accorded twelve officials of the courts of appeals of Metz and Nancy. The Treasury needed to know when their successors had been installed. A June 22 letter complained that birth certificates were needed and that even when they were provided, the names did not always match the pension decrees. That same spring, a table provided dates when seventy individuals stopped work. And in August 1812, an official in the Netherlands, Goget, explained in a letter to the Duc de Massa the difficulties of continuing payments to Dutch pensioners and of adding even more functionaries and employees. Demands were pouring in. Goget warned that the work could not remain hidden from former functionaries in other departments. He claimed that most of the former functionaries—he provided seventy-five names— were dying of hunger, without lodging or clothing. Many "are after long and faithful services reduced to begging for their bread; their age, infirmity, their complete lack of understanding of the French language render them incapable of beginning a new career."[9]

As in the Netherlands, so too in other lands under Napoleon's control, the judiciary saw reorganization and conflict.[10] A multinational French empire had responsibility in 1811 for the support of seven magistrates in Turin, nine in Genoa, sixteen in Brussels. But all over France more and more magistrates acquired retirement pensions: six in Pau, seven in Nîmes, thirteen in Montpellier, nine in Limoges, eight in Besançon, nine in Poitiers, and so on. The ten in the area of the court of Amiens were owed pensions ranging from four hundred to six hundred francs for judges of smaller tribunals of first instance, six hundred to eight hundred for prosecutors in those tribunals, and one thousand to three thousand for judges or prosecutors in the appeals court itself.[11]

Bureaucrats in the Ministry of Justice had an eye not only on calculating the service of individual magistrates but also on the changing fortunes of France. For all the attempts to create a functioning bureaucracy, the ministry had to deal with lists of individuals in need and jurisdictions that were either eliminated or joined to others. And procedural details needed to be worked out.

The principal legislation came in 1814 and 1815 under the Bourbon Restoration, which, in the Constitutional Charter, restored the principle of *inamovibilité* of the magistracy. Debate about *inamovibilité* came up in the weeks preceding the September 1814 *ordonnance*. Thus, M. Dumolard spoke in the Chamber of Deputies on August 30, 1814, to support the principle. He began by presenting it as almost self-evident, particularly in a monarchy. He granted the king's right to name judges as the source of justice and honors, but he claimed such appointment needed to be for life in order to guarantee "their independence and the uniformity of their decisions." Such an arrangement was "one of the distinctive characteristics of monarchy. Destroy it: you have a republic or despotism."

Claude-Ambroise Régnier, Duc de Massa, the longest serving minister of justice under Napoleon, received pension demands from across Europe.
Musée Militaire Vaudois, Château de Morges (Switzerland)

Dumolard went on to review the process by which Napoleon had turned himself into an emperor. He purged the judicial system, named judges, and promised life tenure only after five years of exercise. The result was "five years of arbitrary government." Only "people without experience of men or things" would see it as raising the standard of justice. For Dumolard, only stability and immediate life-tenure would have improved the judiciary. "Changes, retirements and the fatal order of nature would have brought by themselves the necessary purges. The most estimable families would have seen for their children, in this noble career, an assured state, and the people would have resumed the habit of supporting them with its confidence and its respect."[12] His view was disputed by Laborde, who claimed there was a strong enough statement of life-tenure in the Charter, article 37.

The Charter represented a significant break. However, as we have seen, the Bourbon regime also built upon revolutionary and Napoleonic precedent, and it set forth a system that functioned until the Second Republic. The *ordonnance* of September 23, 1814, based upon a report by Chancellor Dambray, called for funds to be combined from vacant posts and the money withheld from salaries. The principle of thirty years of public service was reaffirmed, including ten years in the magistracy itself. Without thirty years, it was still possible to receive a pension if accident or infirmity made it impossible to remain active or if the post itself were eliminated, but ten years of work were required. Legislative, judicial, and administrative service would all count as long as they involved the government. Indeed, as the bureaucracy developed, forms identified in a separate column each of those three types of service. The pension after thirty years amounted to half salary, increasing by a twentieth of that half for each additional year. A pension granted before thirty years amounted to a sixth of the salary for ten years' service, with an additional sixtieth for each year over ten, but the pension could not exceed what would have been awarded for the full thirty years. The amount of the pension was based upon the average of the salary for the last three years, with an assured minimum of two hundred francs and a maximum two-thirds of the salary of six thousand francs, whatever the salary.

Widows and orphans of officials and employees who died in activity after ten years of service or having been awarded a retirement pension could obtain a pension or aid in cases of financial need. Healthy children were supported until age eighteen or until they were supported in a state-supported establishment. Widow and orphan pensions could never exceed two-thirds of the pension that the husband or father would have received.

Firing or resignation took away any right to a pension. Legitimate candidates for retirement had to ask for their pensions. Accumulating pensions was forbidden, as was combining a pension with a salary.

Funds were invested and earned 4 percent interest. A pension was considered void if a pensioner did not collect it for three years. The Chancellory kept itself informed of pensioners' deaths. Pensions were to be paid every three months.

The *ordonnance* of September 23, 1814, was supplemented by one of January 9, 1815. Its need had arisen because of doubts about the original's application to certain individuals and financial need of the Restoration regime. Moreover, some magistrates had offered to augment the fund with further withholding, and equitable division among contributors was desired. Only those who were employed at the time of the original *ordonnance* would have those particular pension rights. Those who had ceased to work before September 23, 1814, fell under the decree of October 2, 1807, and, so far as possible, following the outlines of that of September 13, 1806. Someone not owed a pension might be accorded a provisional salary not to exceed four thousand francs. It would be paid for one year and reconsidered later. Borrowing again from Napoleonic practice, the *ordonnance* called for 2 percent withholding on the salaries of judges and other court officers, combined with the proceeds of vacant positions, to form the pension fund. Withholding would begin January 1, 1815. Pensions would be paid only up to nine-tenths of the available funds.

The system of retirement pensions that evolved from Old Regime, revolutionary, and Napoleonic precursors into royal *ordonnances* of 1814 and 1815 underwent some periodic refinement until midcentury. Tracing that evolution requires a look at further legislation and challenges launched by individual magistrates. First, the return of Napoleon led to a modification. A decree of April 14, 1815, removed the first two articles of the *ordonnance* of January 9, 1815. Thus, it eliminated the distinction between those still active on September 23, 1814, and others. Things went the other way in the Second Restoration, but not immediately. First there was some purging. Then, an *ordonnance* of January 2, 1817, modified the 1814 and 1815 *ordonnances*. Only those magistrates who were active in 1814 or who were not because of suppression of their posts or because their place of assignment no longer belonged to France would receive a pension. Anyone else would be rejected.

The pension system grew significantly during the Restoration. Pensions financed by withholding and vacancies in the Ministry of Justice numbered

11 in 1814, 39 in 1815, 90 in 1816, 245 in 1817, and 348 on January 1, 1818. To put it another way, new pensions numbered 28 in 1814, 54 in 1815, 177 in 1816, and 134 in 1817. Meanwhile, three pensioners died or disappeared from the rolls in 1815, twenty-two in 1816, and thirty-one in 1817.

The budget itself and, thus, the available funds withheld grew substantially. From 1814 to 1815 alone, the number of functionaries and employees subject to the system grew from 148 to 6,532. Salaries grew from 427,300 francs to 11,736,800. Accordingly, the 2 percent withheld went from 8,546 to 234,736. Pensions paid out rose steadily from 15,750.25 in 1814 to 477,075.36 in 1818.[13] All of this was for the Ministry of Justice alone.

Practical details continued to be addressed. An *ordonnance* of February 22, 1821, modified the 1814 *ordonnance* so as to establish the proper proportion between a thirty-year pension and one given before thirty years. For the ten first years, the pension would be one-third of what would be achieved at thirty years, with an increase of a thirtieth for each year above ten.

Reorganization of government ministries and administrations posed problems in maintaining retirement systems, and some *ordonnances* indicate financial difficulties. Thus the *ordonnance* of October 2, 1822, concerns temporary indemnities paid to discharged employees who had obtained rights to a pension. Such payments were made if *caisses de retraite* did not have sufficient funds. In cases where employees were discharged because of reorganization, economizing, or elimination of the work, they received a half-salary indemnity for one year. Thereafter, payment for those who had served enough time to be eligible for a pension would equal what the pension would have been. Those who did not have the required time received the minimum pension corresponding to their salary, and the indemnity lasted as long as their activity in the ministry had lasted. Other articles dealt with dependents and subsequent employment.

Another related matter was that of leaves of absence. An *ordonnance* of November 6, 1822, demanded that presiding judges and prosecutors granting leaves to members of their courts write the ministry within three days. Each leave included a terminal date. Individual dossiers reveal how leaves were sometimes extended and turned into retirements.

Such details concerned pensions asked for and granted. What if retirement was not desired? An *ordonnance* of June 16, 1824, concerned serious and permanent infirmities that might lead the government to contemplate forcing a magistrate's retirement. It called for the creation of a commission composed of the principal judges of the jurisdiction. If it concluded that there was sufficient evidence confirming the infirmity, it referred the case and appropriate documents within three days to the minister of justice, who might then order the court to meet in a general assembly and name one or several commissioners to investigate further. The court would study the case, take depositions from witnesses and physicians, and hear from the magistrate in question. The court might recommend retirement of the magistrate, who would be eligible for a pension and honorary status. If the recommendation of retirement were rejected, it could not be repeated for two years.

The parliamentary debate leading up to that legislation provides a window on the problem of *inamovibilité* and forced retirement for reasons of infirmity. The contradiction between life tenure and the removal of the superannuated would continue to be raised by individuals arguing their own cases, but it came up as a constitutional issue in the spring of 1824. Minister of Justice (Garde des Sceaux) Peyronnet spoke in the Chamber of Peers on April 17, 1824, of the difficulty and sensitivity of dealing with a judge who is unable or unwilling to fulfill his functions. He evoked a "death of the intellectual man" that preceded physical death. *Inamovibilité* has to do with the prince rather than the law or nature, which might have stripped the judge of his "faculty of seeing, hearing, thinking, and speaking."[14] The argument about intellectual or moral death preceding the physical kind owed something to Xavier Bichat and other *idéologues*, but the application of the idea led to discussion of precipitous or arbitrary action by the state and the predicament of the magistrate who is not aware of his own affliction. Asking a demented magistrate to retire might not achieve the desired result. And prejudice, professional rivalry, and hatred might result in unwarranted accusations of disability. On April 22 the Chamber of Peers decided to elect a five-member commission to study the matter. Those elected were le marquis d'Aguesseau, le comte Ferrand, le marquis d'Orvilliers, le comte de Saint-Roman, and le comte de la Bourdonnaye-Blossac.[15] The names themselves resonated with a long magisterial history.

The marquis d'Orvilliers gave the report, softening the language of the legislation, removing a reference to "incurable infirmity" and designating "replaced magistrates" as "magistrates admitted to retirement."[16] The report likened an investigative commission to a "family council." It referred to life tenure as "an acquired right that the King, in his Charter, wished to maintain and confirm, following the example of his august predecessors," and mentioned the 1467 *ordonnance* of Louis XI. A modern sort of legislation was, thus, linked to centuries of royal and magisterial tradition.

Pierre-Denis, Comte de Peyronnet, minister of justice in the Restoration, spoke of the sensitivity required to deal with a judge who was no longer able to fulfill his responsibilities. He evoked the "death of the intellectual man" that preceded physical death.
Yale University Art Gallery

On May 14, the Chamber of Peers discussed the proposed law. The Marquis de Marbois argued against it, claiming that things were done better in the Old Regime. Courts had been well disciplined and knew how to deal discreetly with infirm judges. He was uneasy with the potentially public nature of the proposed mechanism. Blindness and deafness, he thought, were easy to identify, but how would one handle more hidden infirmities? Should wives, children, and servants be called as witnesses? Would doctors and surgeons be required to break confidentiality? What if only a bare majority of the commission opposed forced retirement? The public would find out. And must one refer to the investigation with the same language as a criminal investigation? He preferred "enquête" to "information."[17]

The Comte de Sèze, best known as defender of Louis XVI, recalled Napoleon's assault on *inamovibilité* and warned of the danger of an overreaching minister of justice. He noted that the minister could ignore the commission's recommendation, thus involving the government in a decision better left to the magistracy. He went on to recommend that the pension be pegged at half the salary, distinguishing between an ordinary, voluntary retirement and a forced one resulting from a sudden infirmity: "It is nature alone that is guilty, it is she who renders him victim of the accident of which she is the cause." The moment calls for help, not abandonment.

The Comte de Sèze distinguished between what should be an *indemnité* and a *grâce*, and quoted a Roman legal maxim to the effect that one should not add affliction to the afflicted. Moreover, he wanted to make honorary status automatic, not subject to a ministerial or royal decision. It was not a matter of favor, but of justice. Even the 1807 decree spoke of conserving honor rather than receiving it. De Sèze spoke in magisterial fashion of the honor and hard work of the magistracy, which "renders every day immense services to society and to the government itself," and he quoted Montesquieu on the long labor of magistrates, working "nuit et jour pour le bonheur de l'empire."[18]

Peyronnet responded that it would be inconvenient to have a magistrate sitting while being investigated, but that it would not really be such a serious problem if in the end he were found competent. Suspicions would already exist if he were incapacitated. Infirmity could hardly be kept secret. Thus, the law would end an abuse, not create one. As for the procedure, the roles of minister and judge would maintain separation of powers. On time of service and amount of pension, he appealed to the general rule that only after thirty years did one acquire "an absolute right to retirement." And he thought

Raymond, Comte de Sèze, defender of Louis XVI in his trial in the National Convention, received a reward of nobility in the Restoration and participated in the pension debate in the Chambre des Pairs. He described the plight of the aged or infirm magistrate: "It is nature alone that is guilty, it is she who renders him victim of the accident of which she is the cause."
Bibliothèque nationale de France

that an honorary title was an act of recompense and could not, therefore, be automatic.

Baron Pasquier discussed the poverty of the magistracy and the need for greater pensions. Boissy d'Anglas agreed, saying the magistrate should not have to beg for his bread. It was a matter of personal and magisterial dignity. The Duc de Brissac spoke against an automatic granting of honorary status, offering the specter of a demented judge showing up in his robe and disturbing some public ceremony or court proceeding.

As others joined the debate, issues of rights accrued from paying into the system came up. Baron Pasquier wanted to support half pay for the pensioned. Equity, for him, comes not from getting back what one paid in, but, anticipating twentieth-century welfare state principles, from taking equal chances.

Pushing for greater generosity forced a discussion of the availability of funds. Unlike previous debates, this one generally operated under the assumption that finances were not so terribly limited. Pasquier pointed out that most pensioners would be old. Boissy d'Anglas saw this sort of pension as *dédommagement* rather than *récompense*, the maintenance of the contract that existed between society and the judge. The Marquis de Lally-Tolendal drew an analogy with the military, where the accomplishment of one's duties also resulted in physical and mental wounds, and he too spoke of what society owed the magistrate.

The debate stirred passions, as most of the participants were themselves magistrates, and the issue concerned basic constitutional matters. It also had obvious practical implications. Lally-Tolendal remarked upon the spectacle of a former and current minister of justice disagreeing about whether the decree of 1807 was truly revoked. In the end, Peyronnet said that only the minister can admit someone to retirement, not a court itself. And 99 of 117 votes supported an amended *projet de loi*.

The Chamber of Deputies took up the matter in June. Analyses were similar, but the debate, if anything, was even more passionate. M. Mousnier-Buisson, rapporteur of the commission examining the *projet de loi*, urged its passage. He saw the legislation as an improvement over the 1807 decree and recognized the reality of the problem in the magistracy. *Inamovibilité*, for him, was not threatened. The judge's entitlement is attached to his very service.[19] If judges ruled favorably in each of the two stages of the investigation of a fellow judge, the ministry could do nothing. The magistracy was still policing itself. He did, however, address the financial challenge and warned of the dangers of raiding funds originally destined to pay pensions. He warned as well that the changing population of the magistracy since the Revolution, including people without fortune or other means of existence, posed a strain on the system.

The report remarked in concluding that the commission itself was composed to a large extent of magistrates, most of whom were *inamovibles*, who would not do anything to threaten the most basic principle of French justice. Two days later, the discussion was taken up. The arguments resembled those of the Chamber of Peers, and they examined the legislation from the points of view of the public and the magistracy. Monsieur Colomb discussed the psychological dilemma of the aging magistrate whose attachment to his robe is like that of the old soldier to his armor. Having aged in a profession he loved, he experiences profound sorrow at his abrupt passage to a completely new existence.[20]

M. Duplessis de Grénédan took a more political position. He claimed that Restoration judges were mostly holdovers from the Revolution, that time was gradually removing them, but that the idea was to speed up the process. He saw the legislation as an attack on life tenure, that it would be better to put up with infirm judges. The mere suggestion of removal would lead to humiliation, and even healthy judges would resign. For him, there was no serious problem requiring the legislation. A "secret" procedure for determining the status of a judge could not remain secret for long; the result would be humiliation. He predicted massive resignations from the magistracy.

Garde des Sceaux Peyronnet defended his proposal and claimed a real need. The absence of one judge from a tribunal of three would result in "paralysis" for the justice system. He described one tribunal whose three principal judges were seventy-nine, eighty-seven, and eighty-two years old, while the substitute was seventy-nine. Worse yet, among the three, one was deaf, another blind.[21] He thought the legislation would result in no humiliation for the magistracy, as it simply recognized the humanity of aging and ailing magistrates.

Peyronnet described how the magistracy had changed since the Old Regime. When magistrates owned their offices, at the first sign of serious infirmity, they hastened to transmit them to their children or to sell them. Now, he claimed, there were perfectly good judges without great fortunes. Even if they recognized the need to step aside, those close to them, thinking more of themselves than the system of justice, might encourage them to remain in office.[22] And the separate roles of fellow magistrates and the minister of justice would prevent abuse of the law.[23]

M. Leclerc de Beaulieu disagreed. He cited the dangers of Napoleon's "odious decree" and looked for historical examples from France and elsewhere. His conclusion was that no one had ever come up with such a way of dealing with the infirmities of old age. Even when somewhat infirm, aged magistrates could offer experience and wisdom. The solution would be to let aged magistrates stay and to create more positions for young people to join the magistracy. The talk of infirm judges only reminded him of Greek comedy, and he called for a system in which honorable people would be attracted to a career in the magistracy.[24]

The discussion continued to evoke the self-image of the honorable and self-sacrificing magistrate, the reality of physical and mental aging, and the practical problem of maintaining judicial institutions while older judges contended even with temporary maladies. M. de Gères argued that catarrh, gout, or rheumatism was no reason to push a judge into retirement. The solution, for him, was to increase the numbers of judges while reducing the number of courts.[25]

The last speakers on June 12 continued to evoke both constitutional and financial problems. And they emphasized unwelcomed retirement, but many magistrates already imagined retirement on their own terms. Perhaps another speaker, M. de Vatimesnil, again representing the Ministry of Justice, had those retirees in mind when he focused on the system of withholding from salaries as creating an "aleatory contract." The longer the service, the greater the contribution and the more sacred the right. He saw justice and balance in such an arrangement.[26] The law was passed by a vote of 299 to 29.[27]

The system was set, but some details still demanded attention. An *ordonnance* of August 17, 1824, concerned pensions and aid to be given widows and orphans of magistrates and ministerial bureaucrats. It took into account matters of right and finance. The widow would have a right to a pension if her husband had thirty years of service at his death or if he was already receiving a pension for less than thirty years of service. The widow's pension would be one-third that of her late husband, but it could not fall below one hundred francs.[28]

The year 1824 saw the accession to the throne of Charles X, whose political inclinations were more conservative than those of his brother, Louis XVIII. While historians of the Restoration now emphasize the experiment in constitutional monarchy that would continue after the Revolution of 1830,[29] a strong desire to connect to the Bourbon past is confirmed in the *ordonnance* of November 24, 1824, that proclaimed that service in venal office in the Old Regime magistracy would count toward the thirty-year requirement. In following the order of 15 Floréal, Year XI, it specified that the claimant needed also to have served since January 1, 1792. It respected the thirty years of service, sixty years of age rule, and counted the venal service only to complete the thirty years. The counting of venal service from the Old Regime suggests ideological preferences of the era of Charles X, but the *ordonnance* referred to laws of 1790, 1791, the Year XI, and 1806, providing continuity and complicating the notion that the Restoration was all about forgetting the revolutionary and Napoleonic past.[30] Moreover, the need to have worked since 1792 suggested that pure Old Regime figures would not succeed. There were occasional complaints about this, but soon that cohort would die out.

Complaints about the rules set in 1814–15 or their application were fairly common in the first ten years of the system and again at each change in regime. Debates about fairness and equity reached beyond parliamentary bodies into the world of publication and magistrates' demands. Magistrates easily couched their claims for individual benefits in a language of justice and equity. How could they have done otherwise? It was their stock in trade. But they also needed to adhere to the emerging system.

The ministry circulated printed forms for the bureaucratic presentation of careers and to assist the bureaucrats in their calculations. Legislative, administrative, and judicial services were totaled in printed columns. Printed forms were themselves a sign of the growth of the state. They permitted standardization of the data submitted by aging magistrates, who had each gone to the trouble of amassing proof of a lifetime's work. Gathering that material, from birth and marriage records to letters of appointment, minutes of electoral meetings, letters of recommendation, and publications, meant confronting one's own life. That process, combined with the writing of a demand, constituted a kind of life review.

The process became normalized over time. The Revolution of 1830 saw a number of changes in personnel, but few in policy. Some individuals in the wake of the July Revolution had greater success than in the Restoration, but the remarkable thing is the consistency of decision-making. A rejection in the 1820s was more than likely upheld in the 1830s. Hopeful magistrates continued to ask in an increasingly routinized way. They told their life histories, displayed their needs, and provided the required documentation.

Some change followed the events of 1848. Revolutionary rhetoric again addressed the matter of retirement and revived hopes of pensions for ordinary working people. Yet, again, other matters took precedence. But the idea of retirement, combined with the contradiction between *inamovibilité* and superannuation, led to a major policy shift. Having to judge the physical or intellectual condition of a magistrate was always something that created uneasiness. When a new Napoleonic regime came to power, the next great step in the history of retirement took place. It made a practical administrative change by creating one fund for all the ministries, but it made a significant policy change by opting for a mandatory retirement age.

A report and decree of March 1, 1852, addressed to Louis Napoleon, still prince president of the republic he had destroyed—he took the imperial title nine months later—contended that *inamovibilité* of the magistracy needed to be contained because of continued abuses. It took up the argument that tenure was instituted to protect the people (*le justiciable*) rather than the person of the magistrate. It was not intended to be an impediment to good administration and survived as "a kind of superstitious cult." The report claimed that in human societies there are no "absolute rights" and that the interest of the public should not be "sacrificed to the convenience of the judge." In short, "public order and even the dignity of the magistracy" called for a retirement age.[31]

The report pointed to two earlier pieces of legislation. The first, the law of April 20, 1810, concerned magistrates who had been condemned to forfeiture of their position by proceedings of the Cour de Cassation and the Garde des Sceaux. It was observed that often a disciplined judge was suspended rather than impeached, and that no replacement was named. The new decree would encourage a more definitive procedure. The second law revisited was that of June 16, 1824, which concerned forced retirement for reason of infirmity and has been discussed above. The report claimed that the 1824 law was only a first step, that it was vague and ineffective, that magistrates banded together to slow it down and protect fellow judges who deserved to be forced out.[32] The report argued that "life tenure is not an absolute dogma: it ought to cede to the force of things." It went on to explore the situation of elderly magistrates who, having earned public acclaim, do not always know when to step down. It called for saving them from a painful inner conflict: "Out of respect for their old age, let us not allow them to tarry too long on terrain where they no longer walk except in surviving themselves."[33]

Of course, there were brilliant exceptions, people who retained their faculties deep into advanced age, but the laws are made for the most common experience, and this law would create an obligatory retirement. It recommended a retirement age of seventy years for members of *tribunaux de première instance* and courts of appeal, of seventy-five for members of the Cour de Cassation. The former required greater strength and activity, the latter greater tranquility and sang-froid. The decree stated that the judges in question would have full rights to their pensions without having to document any infirmities, but they would not cease their functions until their successors were named.

That March 1852 decree represented a major step. When combined with the 1853 constitution of a unified fund for civil service pensions, it resulted in a remarkably modern bureaucratic system. But until a mandatory retirement age changed bureaucratic practice, magistrates continued to expose themselves to the ministry's gaze. The demand, increasingly formulaic, still reviewed the life. Such a life review was anything but an open-ended ramble or innocent exercise of memory. Historical experience and the development of bureaucratic procedures called it into being. Legislation that privileged public servants made some lives worthier of reward than others. The retrospective construction of personal lives and public careers depended heavily upon historical circumstances and bureaucratic rules.

4

Restoration, Revolution, and Retirement

Ending Careers, 1814–53

Magistrates who ended careers in the Restoration began them under very different historical circumstances. Although they belonged to a reformist generation, they could not in 1788 have anticipated the radical changes they were about to witness. If they thought about what their careers would look like or how they would end, they might have expected experiences similar to those of previous generations.

In 1786, a young lawyer named Louis-Ferdinand Bonnet, who had gained some fame defending Madame Kornemann in one of the great causes célèbres of the era, gave a speech at the Bibliothèque des Avocats of the Parlement de Paris entitled "Les trois âges de l'avocat." It would be unreasonable to expect a twenty-six-year-old to speak from personal experience of the second and third ages of life, but the oration provides an idea of the lawyer's self-image and the way his career was represented on the eve of the French Revolution. For Bonnet, who placed himself between the first and second ages, the three were concerned with (1) study, (2) oratory, and (3) the calm exercises of the *cabinet*. The third was not quite retirement—indeed, David Bell points out that many lawyers skipped over the second stage—but it did involve a slowing down from the pace of the middle years, and, long before the term entered the French lexicon to designate old age, he described "le troisième âge."[1]

Bonnet's version of the "third age" was a Ciceronian defense of maturity. Only those who had dissipated their "beautiful years" in "the intoxication of pleasures, the languors of laziness, or the insipid amusements of frivolous high society" had reason to fear an age of "privations, solitude and ennui." The responsible magistrate would continue to enjoy public esteem. "The sweetest memories await you there; and if the middle of your life has had greater sparkle, the last part will have even more luster and dignity."[2]

Activity itself engendered a continual love of work and a need to work right up to the end of one's life. Again one wonders whether Bonnet really spoke for his elders, but he certainly spoke for his profession when he presented it as a public duty. He spoke of the "man of genius" as a public patrimony to which his fellow citizens had rights. Neglecting his professional activities would mean committing a kind of crime. Still, one could not expect a lawyer to be an orator all his life. The heat of argument is inappropriate to the old man's physical constitution and the gravity of his character. His debt to the public has changed. He may not be a defender at the bar, but he can still be guide, counsel, and confidant. "His voice is chained, his pen is free; and when young athletes no longer encounter him as a dangerous rival, they ought to find in him a protector and a friend."[3]

The text concerned the life course of the *avocat*. The *magistrat* had different experiences, but, like the *avocat*, he could become adviser, confidant, and writer. And some lawyers obviously became judges.[4] Bonnet wrote as if the old system would long continue, and he suggested that older lawyers might change the language of the law. They would certainly do that, but not exactly as young Bonnet predicted. And the revolutionary and Napoleonic divide created a new world and, within it, another form for the magistrate's third or even fourth age.

History intervened, and lives took odd turns, but the emerging institutional structures of modern France gave careers a "normal" shape and increasingly a reward at the end. Magistrates of Bonnet's age experienced the revolutionary renegotiation of the social contract, and they developed a refined sense of right. Neither the Revolution nor the Restoration was a simple undoing of the previous regime, but a step in the development of a constitutional and bureaucratic order and in the evolution of the modern idea of career. Subsequent revolutions may be seen equally as restorations. They were occasions for limited professional purges, new rounds of complaints, and renewal of demands, but career patterns indicate extraordinary continuity in the magistracy.

The history of the Revolution has often been presented as a history of those who died in it, whether martyrs or victims. It is important, however, to appreciate the history of those who (in the spirit of Talleyrand supposedly responding to the question of what he had done in the Revolution) survived. The French Revolution brought a largely preindustrial France into the modern political world, initiated important social welfare legislation, contributed to the development of ideas of career and retirement in the public sector, and provided rich and dramatic material to be remembered and refashioned as even relatively minor political actors survived and aged.

One might assume it was a revolt by youth against age, as it has sometimes been described as the work of a band of brothers overthrowing fathers (there were sisters and mothers too, but they seem to have been pushed aside).[5] Yet, while the allegorical representation of liberty or the republic was a young woman, the Revolution also used the image of the old man and old woman to give itself a certain permanence, an anchor, and politicians pioneered social legislation, elaborating a right to a good old age and retirement.[6] In part, the concern for old age grew out of rhetoric itself. In part, it grew out of social need. The mass mobilization for war left soldiers' dependents in difficult circumstances. Aging veterans and their widows had already posed a challenge in the Old Regime. The revolutionary and Napoleonic periods only added to the problem, and more and more people began speaking a language of social right.

Some men in public life would benefit eventually from the revolutionary shaping of old age as a stage of life and retirement as a way of managing it. Revolutionary-era bureaucrats gained civil service status and an expectation of full career and retirement. Formal career dossiers and bureaucratic methods of acquiring rights to pensions made their way onto the scene. In the Napoleonic era, postulants designed charts to represent their careers, with references to documentation of particular offices and accomplishments.

Having puzzled over homemade charts, bureaucrats came up with printed forms for organizing the information. One of the models for such a form came from judges' demands in French-occupied Holland.[7] Another came from authorities in Tuscany.[8] Magistrates who had served in areas conquered by the French and were themselves often not of French origin served the French state until they were displaced by international treaties and administrative reorganization. Upon retiring, they informed the ministry in Paris of how their systems had functioned in the Old Regimes of Europe. But even as demands became more formulaic, as rules became clearer and careers themselves were more consistently represented, postulants offered elaborate justifications.

We have already seen how pension demands sent to the Ministry of Justice in the Napoleonic period reveal claims of entitlement and how, in the Bourbon Restoration of 1814 and 1815, the Ministry of Justice came up with a systematic way of handling claims. Royal *ordonnances* of September 23, 1814, and January 9, 1815, set conditions of thirty years of service and sixty years of age, or ten years of service with infirmity caused by the work, to permit magistrates to claim a right. But standardization extended beyond

N° 444

ARRÊTÉ
DE LA JUNTE DE TOSCANE
du 1.er Août 1808.

Supprimé le Mars 1809 1808

CERTIFICAT DE SERVICE DE M. (Antoine) Joseph Louis Marie Barli × Bailli à Figline

servir à la liquidation de la pension ou indemnité à laquelle il peut avoir droit.

NOMS et PRÉNOMS	DATE de Naissance	DATE des commissions brevets ou Ordres	PAR QUI ils ont été signés	NATURE de l'emploi	ANNÉES de service dans chaque emploi	TRAITEMENT FIXE dans chaque emploi. Livres Toscanes. Francs.	SECOURS provisoire annuel accordé par l'arrêté du 29 mars 1808.	OBSERVATIONS
Barli (Antonio) Joseph, Louis, Marie	10 Avril 1748	24 Juillet 1777 9 Juillet 1807	Leopold Louis Marie	En 1770 Officier de Fortune de Marine En 1772 Ducale di Monte Cavallo en suite auditeur Vicaire Giudice Esecutore en fin le .... Vicaire à Figline	38. —	Ton: 1180— Toscl. 1100 2280 1925.20	—	[handwritten notes]

Le présent certifié véritable est conforme aux Brevets de Nomination, Commissions, et Rescrits y mentionnés

Fait à Florence le 27 Juillet 1809

L'ARCHIVISTE GÉNÉRAL
Louis Ludwig

This form provided a summary of the services of Antoine Joseph Louis Marie Barli, a bailiff in Tuscany, in 1809. Faced with a variety of such documents, the Ministry of Justice eventually developed a more standardized version.

AN BB2 10

graphic representations of careers to literary ones. The postulant created his own genre, a narrative of self-presentation that combined years of service with lost health, performance of duties with acts of political courage. A great deal of self-fashioning was called into play. Letters that accumulated in a magistrate's dossier reveal changing strategies. Comparisons are made with colleagues, friends, and rivals. A composite portrait of the aging magistrate emerges: a man typically in his mid-sixties, who claims to embody qualities of stability and competence, writes of his family's history and honor, recounts heroic actions in complicated times, and speaks of health and wealth sacrificed, of honor besmirched, of the public served. He may have contributed to the Revolution, but the safest strategy appears to be the claim of serving France and the magistracy. The rules held out the possibility of counting some Old Regime service as national service; magisterial tradition itself transcended regime.

Demands poured in, but it took time to get some postulants to adhere to the rules. In 1819, a circular was sent to courts throughout France restating official requirements and reminding potential retirees to initiate the process.[9] The circular included a model form for would-be pensioners to fill out and a list of required documents. Legislative, administrative, and judicial services were to be totaled in printed columns. Demands, blending the language of favor and right, would be summarized in reports made by the bureaucracy. Formulas used the average of the last three years' salary and the total years served. Those who failed to receive what they wanted wrote again and again. If they lived until the next revolution (a generational phenomenon in nineteenth-century France), they assumed they would be rewarded with a fairer hearing, but in fact it often made no difference, as the bureaucracy's functioning transcended regimes. One man, Nicolas-Joseph Romer, headed the accounting department of the ministry from the Napoleonic era into the 1830s.[10] He issued reports summarizing careers and determining financial need. Magistrates might earn his sympathy even as he was overseeing the evolution of a relatively objective operation. Needy magistrates cried for help using language of both traditional charity and revolutionary welfare, but virtually all described honor and respect as essential to a good retirement. Unhappy ex-magistrates wrote multiple letters, and some paid to have their complaints printed and circulated in public.

80 CAREER AND RETIREMENT

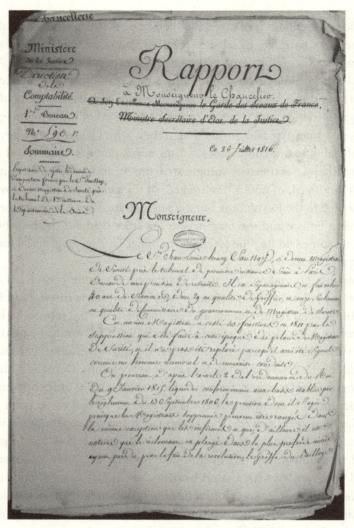

A typical report by Nicolas-Joseph Romer, in this instance on Jean-Louis-Henry Saussay, a magistrate in Paris, writing in the Second Restoration. Saussay had already sought a pension in the empire, the First Restoration, and the Hundred Days. He would try again under the July Monarchy. Romer, who headed the accounting section of the Ministry of Justice from the empire into the first years of the July Monarchy, summarized petitioners' demands and communicated the ministry's decisions. The document, with its crossing-out of the printed salutation and reuse of the page, reflected changes in regime.
AN BB25 30

The pension-demand dossiers of judges—career dossiers per se only came into being in the 1850s—permit a study of retrospective constructions of lives and anticipations of retirement among public officials over the long term. Retiring judges wrote letters and provided documents outlining their public service before, during, and after the Revolution. Many of their dossiers included accompanying letters of recommendation. Thus, who one was or who might intervene complemented what one did, but it was the service itself that was most important. Service in the Old Regime would be incorporated into a long-term career whose interruptions were often remarkably brief considering the turbulence of the period. Representation of that service, of course, depended upon the time of writing. Demands during the Napoleonic era often expressed moderate support for the Revolution. Demands during the Restoration made more of Old Regime service and loyalty to the Bourbon family. Revolutionary excesses were criticized in both periods, but they were viewed as particularly cruel in the Restoration. Nonetheless, a consistent ideal of moderation and of courageous defense of innocent people became the norm.

Pension legislation was perceived as cumulative, and circumstances encouraged the development of new norms drawing upon diverse precedents. The uncertainties of the Napoleonic period left postulants and administrators relatively free to interpret the meaning of "right," but well into the Restoration, individuals described how they thought the decrees applied to them as belonging to classes of public servants. They sometimes used their own lives to criticize the formulas. For example, François Marie Perret presented his career as almost constant judicial service, but demanded that his period of imprisonment during the Terror count as well.[11] The bureaucracy recognized he did not have enough time of service, but the circumstances led the ministry to offer him a temporary stipend. He continued to protest. He would have done well not to quibble with his reward because ministerial investigations in 1816 revealed a more enthusiastic revolutionary. Still, that enthusiasm was expressed in a self-justifying document written during the Terror. Such self-presentation is difficult to assess, but it indicates the need to shape one's memory to the time. When revolution came again, in 1830, he tried again, but regardless of regime, the state was the state, and the rules were the rules. Bureaucracy eventually transcended regime, even as actions and views in one regime became known and judged in another.

The working out of the rules and the correspondence concerning their implementation became a common theme in magistrates' life stories. The regicide Charles François Oudot spent the entire Bourbon Restoration in exile in Belgium. In making his case with the new regime over the period 1830-40, he protested that his mistreatment by the Bourbons should be undone. Not only should he be paid as of 1830—the ministry agreed—but he should be provided back pay for his years in exile, years that had ruined him financially. The ministry interpreted laws of the Napoleonic and Restoration periods as preventing such largesse. Oudot's memoirs analyzed the appropriate laws and recounted case after case of other individuals who had been exiled, stripped of pensions, and then reinstated. His own story consisted of long-term service—thirty-seven years—and what he saw as one great injustice, but its telling involved comparisons with other situations.[12]

Less successful, having served only twenty-five years, seven months, and twenty-seven days—he argued for twenty-nine—was Pierre-François Anfrye, who had risen to be presiding judge of the Civil Tribunal of Versailles before resigning in April 1819 because of "grave infirmities."[13] He mentioned poor eyesight, kidney stones, bladder problems, and gout. That he had resigned before being granted a pension was the sticking point. The themes that recur in his correspondence are service, illness, and lack of resources. He called the law "Machiavellian" and "jesuitical" and claimed a proprietary right, as salaries had been subject to withholding for the creation of a ministerial pension fund. His career history involved an earlier resignation from a judgeship in the wake of Louis XVI's execution on January 21, 1793. Now he found it hard to accept that the government of Louis's brother would mistreat him. He ended his account with reference to an operation for stones.

Writers of demands bent the rules and reminisced about their years on the public stage of history. Gerontologists who have debated the role of reminiscence but agree that it would not live up to the standards of historical research fail to appreciate historians' recent attraction to subjectivity.[14] Historical actors represented their own life histories against the evolving background of public history. Each helped format the other.

Scholars have described how historians and jurists writing in the early nineteenth century made sense of the revolutionary past.[15] Some of that historical and legal thinking made its way into autobiographical writing and the arguments of retiring magistrates. Influences ran both ways, between individual lives and the history of France. Some who were encouraged to retire feigned disbelief and described remarkably good health and a strong desire to continue serving the public. Sometimes it took months or years, sometimes only a paragraph, for resistance to turn to resignation and proud acceptance.

But retirement did not automatically guarantee a pension, and arguments developed over the appropriate amount to be accorded.

At the very least, many postulants asked to be named honorary judges in their former jurisdictions. Thus, they maintained a certain status, expressed both in a formal role in civic functions and in still being listed in the imperial or royal almanac. While some judges wrote generally of a time of repose, others described a classical return to the country and a humanist retirement to the study. But intellectual labors required the material means that post-revolutionary magistrates often claimed not to have. Lists of publications and sometimes samples of legal, historical, and literary work accompanied some demands. Maintenance of a Ciceronian model of retirement would require state support.[16] In the post-revolutionary era magistrates drew on both classical models and newer republican notions of public service.

The model retirement for a magistrate might have been peaceful, but it followed an active life described in terms of adventure and pathos. Aging magistrates employed tales of heroic acts and family woes to sway bureaucrats and officials. The heroism involved standing up to terrorists and fighting brigands and draft resisters. The family woes included illness, bankruptcy, and the premature deaths of sons in military service. Letters blended statements of loyalty to the regime, an accounting of lives used up or sacrificed, and estimates of the cost of leading a suitable life in retirement.

Reading individual dossiers, one is drawn to personal dramas and attentive to the transitions from one regime to another, one kind of loyalty to another. But reading them collectively leads in another direction. It is not that one forgets the major political divides, but that lives don't conveniently fit the political chronologies. They transcend the divides. While we often think of individual lives as shaped by historical events, we ought to recognize how those events fit within the long context of individual lives. Sociologist Andrew Abbot has described this phenomenon in terms of the "historicality of individuals" or a "historical continuity of individuals that provides the sinews linking past and present."[17] For Abbot, historical experience encodes itself on individual actors, and he even provides an example of retirees who "are not just an arbitrary group who happen to be retiring. On the contrary, they bring with them to the moment of the retirement decision quite specific historical baggage."[18]

The treatment that follows is necessarily partial. A thorough history of the magistracy in the period remains to be written. The series of books by Jean-Pierre Royer and other legal historians focuses primarily on the second half of the century.[19] The classic volume by Marcel Rousselet covers only the July Monarchy and is based partly upon a fairly impressionistic reading of retirement dossiers.[20] The *thèse* by Jean-Claude Gégot on the Hérault is based upon a much closer reading of materials, but it doesn't argue any sustained thesis and is not easily used. Thorough as the research is, it is understandable why it has never been published in book form.[21] More recent regional studies tell a story of professionalization, with emphasis on access, promotion, and identity.[22]

The focus here is on the end of the career, but it inevitably concerns the entire period from the end of the Old Regime to the Second Empire. Retirement dossiers contain a collection of materials: an initial letter, often more than one, usually some letters by colleagues and informants, and a form that indicates the circumstances of the demand and summarizes the career. Supporting documents include birth record and proof of each position held, with accounting of years, months, and days served.

Procedures sometimes began with a demand to retire, followed by permission and another demand for the pension. Often a single request covered retirement and pension. Sometimes the procedure began with a letting go of members of a court. In some cases it is clear who had initiated the process, but it is often much more ambiguous.

The Ministry of Justice opened approximately fifty-three hundred retirement dossiers from 1814 to 1852. At first I read all the dossiers in the first half-dozen cartons (around three hundred) and a few others at random, but then, for statistical purposes and to gain a sense of the country as a whole, I selected six departments of France to trace from the 1810s into the early 1850s: Bouches-du Rhône in Provence (including Marseille and Aix-en-Provence), Calvados in Normandy (including Caen), Bas-Rhin in Alsace (including Strasbourg), Rhône in the Lyonnais (including Lyon), Somme in Picardy (including Amiens), and Haute-Vienne in the Limousin (including Limoges). Such geographic diversity encompasses areas whose Old Regime legal structures and revolutionary tendencies differed significantly. Thus, we can include the more patriarchal (Roman law) south and the somewhat more egalitarian (customary) northern areas, as well as the more Jacobin Haute-Vienne and the more "federalist" Caen, Lyon, and Marseille. The following courts are included:

Appeals courts
Aix-en-Provence, Amiens, Caen, Limoges, Lyon

Tribunals of first instance
Bouches-du-Rhône: Aix-en-Provence, Marseille, Tarascon
Calvados: Bayeux, Caen, Falaise, Lisieux, Pont-l'Evêque, Vire
Bas-Rhin: Saverne, Schélestadt, Strasbourg, Wissembourg
Rhône: Lyon, Villefranche
Somme: Abbeville, Amiens, Doullens, Montdidier, Péronne
Haute-Vienne: Bellac, Limoges, Rochechouart, St-Yrieix

The six departments of France in the sample.
Map by Amy Anderson Troyansky.

Some individuals made moves into other departments. The sample is determined by the magistrates' final posts. Some jurisdictional changes occurred over time. There was, for example, a tribunal in Barr (Bas-Rhin) at the beginning of the century and not one at Saverne. I have also traced justices of the peace, whose jurisdictions might encompass rural communes or urban neighborhoods.

The sample includes 480 dossiers, ranging from 60 in the Rhône to 106 in the Somme. The following chart breaks them down into groups: magistrates, widows, and children (receiving and not receiving pensions or aid):

Dossiers by Department

Department	Magistrates with Pension	Magistrates without Pension	Widows with Pension	Widows without Pension	Children with Aid	Children without Aid	Total
Bouches-du-Rhône	48	20	13	12		2	95
Calvados	40	23	21	6	1		91
Bas-Rhin	27	9	19	9			64
Rhône	33	12	14	1			60
Somme	60	20	17	9			106
Haute-Vienne	31	14	14	3		2	64
Total	239	98	98	40	1	4	480

The following series of graphs indicates the years in which careers were ended and the proportions of retirees receiving pensions. In five of six departments, the period of the Restoration is a critical one. The retirements in the Bouches-du-Rhône and Calvados are particularly numerous in 1816; there is something of a cluster in the early years of the Restoration in the Rhône, Somme, and Haute-Vienne, but little to speak of in the Bas-Rhin. Overall, the number of new retirees evens out across the next three decades, but there is another peak at the end of the period, the result of a few people being pushed out in 1848 and of mandatory retirement beginning in 1852, a year that saw a large number of pensions accorded in the Bouches-du-Rhône.

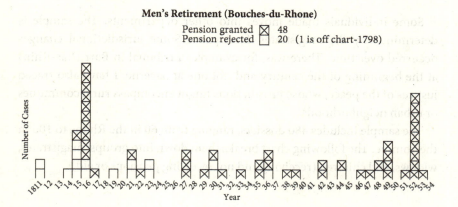

Men's Retirement (Bouches-du-Rhone)
Pension granted ⊠ 48
Pension rejected ☐ 20 (1 is off chart-1798)

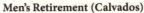

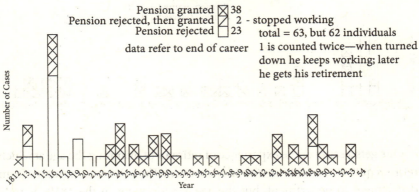

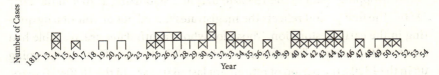

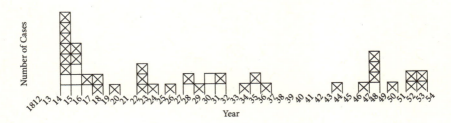

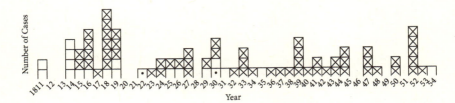

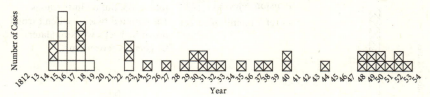

One gets a sense of the experience of retirement by noting the age at which retirees quit work (with or without pensions). There is some variation from department to department, but the age at retirement in the 1810s is relatively early (though not by late twentieth- and early twenty-first-century standards): 65.6. It then goes up to 69.8 in the 1820s and 71.8 in the 1830s before dropping again in the 1840s to 67.2 and stabilizing at 70.4 in the early 1850s. The first period reflects the magistrates forced out or voluntarily quitting in the early Restoration. Those for whom death dates are available had another 10.1 years to live outside of office. With the age of retirement going up in the 1820s, the period of retirement lasts 6.0 years, in the 1830s 5.0 years. In general, retirement occurs in the late sixties or early seventies, with death intervening in the mid- to late seventies. The following charts provide figures from the six departments:

Ages of Retirees by Decade (where known)

Department	1810s Number of Cases	1810s Average Age	1820s Number of Cases	1820s Average Age	1830s Number of Cases	1830s Average Age	1840s Number of Cases	1840s Average Age	1850s Number of Cases	1850s Average Age
Bouches-du-Rhône	19	64.8	10	65.2	12	74.6	11	65.4	11	75.1
Calvados	22	64.6	13	73.2	6	73.3	13	68.2	3	57.7
Bas-Rhin	3	70.3	9	71.0	9	76.9	10	65.9	2	72.0
Rhône	15	64.3	8	67.5	8	67.5	6	62.7	5	69.7
Somme	26	67.8	13	69.0	18	69.2	14	68.8	8	67.5
Haute-Vienne	12	64.4	6	73.3	9	70.8	7	70.9	6	71.8
Total	97	65.6	59	69.8	62	71.8	61	67.2	35	70.4

Ages at Death by Decade (where known)

Department	1810s Number of Cases	1810s Average Age	1820s Number of Cases	1820s Average Age	1830s Number of Cases	1830s Average Age	1840s Number of Cases	1840s Average Age	1850s Number of Cases	1850s Average Age
Bouches-du-Rhône	2	59.5	13	76.6	6	71.0	8	81.4	3	83.0
Calvados			11	76.6	10	78.0	3	85.3	3	69.3
Bas-Rhin	1	80	5	76.0	5	80.3	8	79.3		
Rhône			10	76.6	9	78.4	5	80.0	1	88.0
Somme	2	66.0	9	74.8	15	81.3	18	76.2	1	75.0
Haute-Vienne			7	75.8	10	79.7	2	80.5	2	78.5
Total	5	66.2	55	76.1	55	78.7	44	79.0	10	77.7

Years of Retirement by Decade (where known)

Department	1810s Number of Cases	1810s Average Years	1820s Number of Cases	1820s Average Years	1830s Number of Cases	1830s Average Years	1840s Number of Cases	1840s Average Years	1850s Number of Cases	1850s Average Years
Bouches-du-Rhône	12	6.7	6	8.7	8	4.9	2	1.0	3	4.0
Calvados	7	9.4	9	3.4	6	4.2	4	4.3		
Bas-Rhin	2	3.5	5	4.6	7	5.1	6	3.1		
Rhône	11	15.0	8	7.6	5	2.3			1	2.5
Somme	17	10.7	8	7.1	11	7.0	8	1.8	3	19.0
Haute-Vienne	6	9.0	4	4.3	7	4.6	2	2.0	1	5.0
Total	55	10.1	40	6.0	44	5.0	22	2.5	8	9.6

Relying upon averages is somewhat misleading. There were some who retired only in anticipation of death and others who would have ten or twenty years in retirement, perhaps allowing them time to pursue projects in the last stage of life.

Figures derived from widows' dossiers confirm the advanced age of the magistrates in the sample. Those who die in activity, leaving widows, die around 68.6 years of age. Those who had a period of retirement retired at 71.9, dying at 75.6. All deaths average 71.8.

Ages at Retirement and Death of Men Whose Widows Seek Pensions

Department	Retirement Number of Cases	Retirement Average Age	Death of Retirees Number of Cases	Death of Retirees Average Age	Death in Office Number of Cases	Death in Office Average Age	All Deaths Number of Cases	All Deaths Average Age
Bouches-du-Rhône	7	70.1	7	73.4	10	65.3	17	68.6
Calvados	11	74.5	11	76.5	12	71.5	23	74.1
Bas-Rhin	4	70.5	4	73.3	10	68.3	14	69.7
Rhône	7	69.1	7	75.3	6	66.5	13	71.2
Somme	8	73.0	8	77.8	4	74.5	12	76.7
Haute-Vienne	4	71.3	4	76.0	9	67.3	13	70.0
Total	41	71.9	41	75.6	51	68.6	92	71.8

For the entire run of dossiers in the department of Calvados, a total of ninety-one, twenty-seven concern demands for widows' pensions, and one concerns an orphaned daughter asking for aid. Fourteen of the men died in office. Ten available ages at death range from 62 to 78 and average 73.2 years of age. For fifty-seven individuals who retire, the average age is 68.0. A few retired very early for reasons of health. Ignoring the five who retired before age 55, the average rises to 70.1.

There was some movement from the beginning of the period to the end. Consider the chart that traces the years when magistrates ended their active careers and distinguishes between those who receive pensions and those who do not. The years when individuals ended their careers were fairly evenly spread except for a peak in 1816, and the chances of receiving a pension went up dramatically by 1823. Earlier on, large numbers of prospective retirees were turned down. Over the course of the period, twenty-five were initially rejected. Three would eventually receive pensions. Eight were simply not eligible. Of them four were *greffiers*, ruled out by the *ordonnance*. One supplied insufficient documentation. Three were no longer at their posts in September 1814 and, thus, did not fall within the regulations. Sixteen of the applicants did not have the required years of work. If they tried to argue that they had infirmities caused by the work, they were not believed because they had been pushed aside before asking to retire. Eleven were pushed out for political reasons. But of them, only one had worked enough years to satisfy the law, and he would eventually get a pension in 1818 after being turned down in 1816. So the bureaucracy could certainly claim, if somewhat disingenuously, that its decisions about pensions had very little to do with politics. The ministry failed to reappoint some magistrates in 1816. If they did not have the required years—it was only twenty-six years since 1790—their rejection was not ostensibly political.

In the other departments reasons for refusal of pensions were comparable. In Haute-Vienne, thirty-one magistrates received pensions, and fourteen were refused. Three were ineligible, one having been *révoqué*, one having only been a *greffier*, a third having waited too long after retirement to apply. The remaining eleven did not have the years, and seven of them may have had their careers shortened for political reasons. In the Rhône, thirty-three were granted and twelve refused. Of the twelve, ten did not have enough years of service, one died before the process was completed, and one resigned. Four of the ten may have been let go for political reasons, one was reappointed, and two were considered not up to the job (weak or having no talent). In the Somme, sixty received pensions, while twenty were turned down. Of the twenty, thirteen did not have the years, and only two of those were clearly in political trouble. Four were ineligible (*greffier, huissier*), two died, and one provided insufficient documentation. Here and there were mentions of *moeurs*, incompetence, mental instability, or writing obscene verses. In Bas-Rhin, twenty-seven were granted pensions, and nine were refused. Four of the nine had insufficient time in service, three died while the process was occurring, and two were ineligible (*greffier* and one who becomes a *maire*). In Bouches-du-Rhône, forty-eight were granted pensions, and twenty were turned down. Of the twenty, fourteen did not have enough years of service, and five of them had political problems. Two lost jobs for incompetence, one returned to work and died in office, another died while the process was still on, and two had ended their careers too early.

A big year for careers to end was 1816. There were eleven definitive rejections and one temporary one. Of the eleven, ten were replaced for political reasons. Revolutionary ideas and actions could be held against applicants, but loyalty to the Bonapartist regime was the greater offense. Ten of the eleven pushed out for political reasons suffered that fate in 1816. Only one seems to have been pushed out in 1848, or so the applicant claimed.

Because of the large number of people pushed out at the start of the Restoration, the age in the 1810s was relatively low: 64.6. Although not shockingly low, the age went up as the system became more stable. Thus, it went up to 73.2 in the 1820s and 73.3 in the 1830s, but then dropped to 68.2 in the 1840s and 57.7 in the 1850s. My suspicion is that retirement became more attractive by the 1840s, perhaps due to economic or political crisis. The drop in the 1850s was possibly a result of a shakeup following the 1848 revolution. Time in retirement grew. Of fifty-seven individuals, we have twenty-six dates of death. Age at death in the 1820s averaged 76.6, in the 1830s 78.0, in the 1840s and 1850s combined, 79.2. For those pushed out in the early Restoration, time in retirement was long: 9.4 years. It dropped to 3.4 in the 1820s and rose slowly to 4.2 in the 1830s and 4.3 in the 1840s. Of course, if we had access to those without death dates, the average might go way up. And the averages mask great variation. Of the twenty-six, nine experienced 0–2 years of retirement, nine experienced 3–5, five experienced 6–10, two 11–15, and one 19.

One gains a clearer sense of careers and retirements from graphing them. The following charts illustrate the lives of magistrates for whom we have all the basic data: birth (B), years of work counted toward a pension (solid line, with years not counted in parentheses), year of retirement (R), and year of death (D). I have also included a few magistrates who died in office and whose widows demanded pensions. Individuals are arranged in age order. Obviously, there were other magistrates who died in service, knew they were ineligible, or whose careers extended beyond the limits of the study. But we can use this sample to visualize the shapes of careers, their critical points, and their durations.

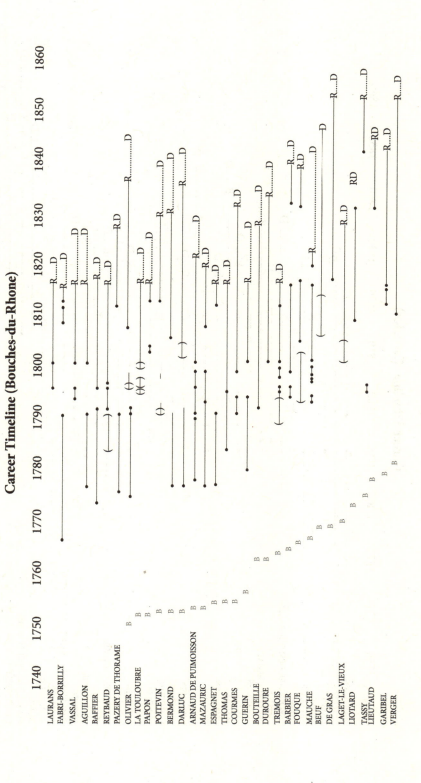

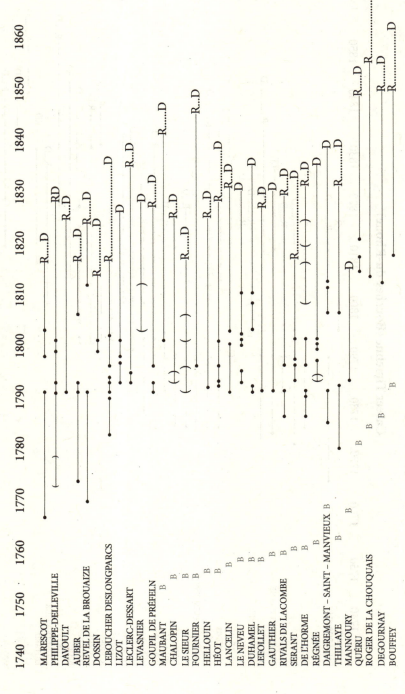

Career Timeline (Bas-Rhin)

	1740	1750	1760	1770	1780	1790	1800	1810	1820	1830	1840	1850
TASSIN												
ZAEPFFEL		B										
KERN		B										
SILBERRARD		B										
FANGET		B										
FRIANT D'ALINCOURT	B			•———————•				R..D				
KOHL		B							D			
CORHUMEL		B				• •			RD			
FELS			B		•———•				R..D			
LAUGIER			B						R..D			
GÉRARD			B			( )————————————•				R.D	R....D	
LUTHER				B						R..D	R....D	
DEVILLE						•———+——•				R..D		
NANCÉ										R.D		
SADOUL					B		• •( )•			R.....D	R....D	
RAFFARRA				B				( )•			R...D	
GONET				B							RD	
DE KENTSINGER			B								R....D	
ZEYS				B				( )				
WOOG					B				D			
HAMELIN										•———D		
DORON						B				( )—( )—•		R..D

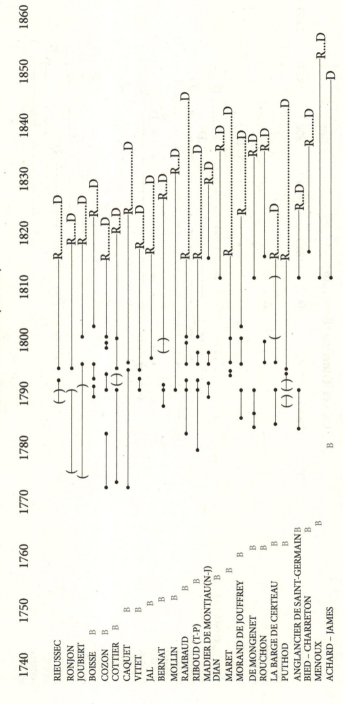

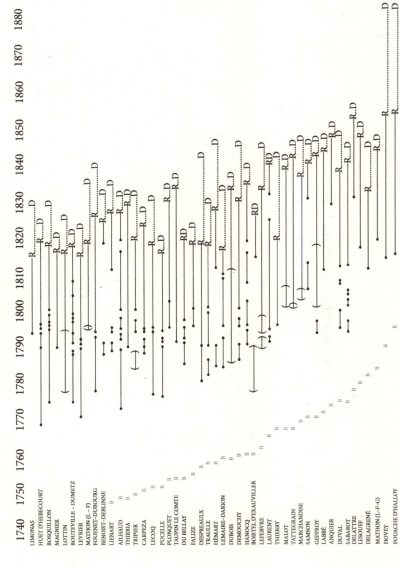

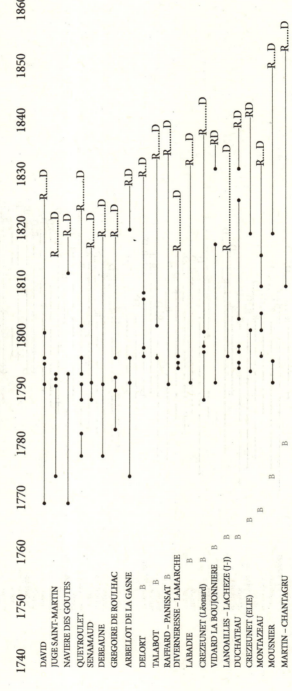

Some breaks are predictable. The years 1789–90 saw the end of the Old Regime system of justice and a scramble for new posts. Some career interruptions were brief, but others lasted into the Napoleonic era and even into the Restoration. The period of the Jacobin republic saw further changes, as many magistrates took on legislative functions or went into hiding or exile, and the end of the Terror saw the return of some who had dropped out of sight. The new Napoleonic judicial system made 1800 a period of reemployment for some and the very beginning of other careers. As we saw earlier, the Restoration yielded many retirements, some forced, some simply coinciding with the cohorts born in the 1740s and 1750s having worked both in the Old and New Regimes reaching old age. Another wave of retirements in the 1820s and 1830s involved people whose careers in public life often began in the Revolution; those in the 1840s were more often postrevolutionary creatures and, as mentioned above, may have been reacting to current conditions.

The turbulence of the period and breaks in public service lead one to conclude that indeed this is a period of dramatic change. However, the careers that continued demonstrate a remarkable continuity. The titles were new, the court system and legal structures changed, but people with legal expertise, family traditions of service, and the desire to keep working made for a kind of professional stability. A focus on institutional structures might obscure that important fact.

Examination of different departments permits the elaboration of divergent patterns and life experiences. Without reading too much into the differences, we might, nonetheless, surmise that disparate cultural tendencies and political experiences yielded a variety of patterns. Age patterns varied, and political conflicts resulted in transformations of the magistracy.

The sample from the Bouches-du-Rhône indicates a great many Old Regime magistrates, born before 1760, eventually reentering the system and retiring under the Restoration, when the kinds of authorities they had, in effect, grown up with were back in power, or as late as the July Monarchy, at which point they really seemed to be holdovers from a distant past. To put it another way, the judiciary in that department may have struck people as a gerontocracy. A study of ages of all those active at any given time would be needed to clinch that argument, but the sample of retirees is enough to suggest as much. At the same time the lengths of interruptions in careers are a sign of the kind of conflict that raged in the region throughout the 1790s.

Ten- to twenty-year gaps beginning in 1790–91 stand out in the careers of Fabri-Borrilly, Aguillon, Pazery de Thorame, Olivier, Poitevin, Bermond, Darluc, and Espagnet (eight of thirty-three).

In Calvados, where resistance to revolutionary Paris had been a notable feature, we find very few products of the Old Regime surviving past the Revolution, but many people who came into the system under the Revolution survived in public life through the Restoration. And compared with the Bouches-du-Rhône, ten-year revolutionary gaps are fewer: Auber, Revel de la Brouaize, Duhamel, Daigremont-Saint-Manvieux, and Thillaye (five of thirty-three). Once in place they stayed; few retired in the early Restoration. This suggests that there was not as dramatic a reaction in that period or perhaps that there was a strong sense of institutional and professional continuity.

It is difficult to speak of a pattern in Bas-Rhin at all. The data appear quite scattered. What does emerge is a new stability under Napoleon, with experienced or new magistrates joining the system in 1800 or 1810. Another odd feature in the department is that some much older men became magistrates late in life, including at least one distinguished Protestant church leader. Thus, people of retirement age were joining the magistracy for the first time after having pursued other careers. Retirement, in fact, seems an exceptional phenomenon. Whether this is a function of the Protestantism of the region or the need to speak German is unknown.

In the Rhône we find a great many brief interruptions and retirements in the early Restoration followed by long periods of retirement. While those long retirements may indicate a cultural difference from what obtained in Alsace, they may also indicate the strong political differences that characterized the area of Lyon. Yet the relatively brief periods of inactivity during the Revolution indicate an overcoming of famous political differences in a region that tried to resist Parisian hegemony.

The Somme included lots of retirements and impressive continuity. Old Regime magistrates experienced brief interruptions (only four lengthy revolutionary gaps out of eighteen who had begun in the Old Regime and the total of forty-seven magistrates in the department's sample) and adapted fairly successfully to the new system.

In the Haute-Vienne we find Old Regime people retiring in the early Restoration. Again we may be dealing with demographic facts but also political psychology, as pre-revolutionary people retired under a regime with which they were comfortable. The revolutionary creatures in what had been a very Jacobin area tended to remain in place through the Restoration or, in a couple of cases, returned in the July Monarchy, but two began long retirements at the Restoration.

Léonard Diverneresse-Lamarche had been a clockmaker before being elected *juge de paix* in the northern district of Limoges in 1793. By the Restoration, his eyesight was compromised, the *procureur général* claimed he really did not have the knowledge appropriate for the post, and memories of his revolutionary opinions had not been forgotten. Whichever of those factors was primary, his pension was granted.[23]

More complicated is the case of Jean-Joseph Lanoailles-Lachèze, the younger of two brothers who had been priests in the Old Regime and become justices of the peace in the Revolution. Their father had also been a magistrate. Pleading illness, vision problems, harassment by anonymous enemies, and the need to support three children, he retired with the expectation of a pension. Bourdeau, the *député*, called him "one of the best justices of the peace in the Département" and suspected that his disgrace stemmed from his previous clerical status. Critics among his superiors, Roulhac, *procureur général*, and Larivière, *premier président*, claimed he had no financial need, especially as his wealthy nonagenarian father would soon die, and that he spent his funds on hunting, maintaining six dogs, and leading a licentious life. The ministry took its time reaching a decision, ruled against him in 1818, then for him in 1819. When the Bourbons were again overthrown, he sought to be reappointed but without success. Meanwhile, his older brother, Léonard, *juge de paix du canton de Chateauneuf, arrondissement de Limoges*, from 1798 to 1816, also a former priest, received nothing.[24]

Two notable cases are those of François David, *conseiller à Limoges*, whom we encountered in the Introduction, and Jacques-Joseph Juge Saint-Martin, *commissaire du roi à Limoges*. The first represents an almost uninterrupted career of almost fifty-six years followed by a six-year retirement. The second, while turned down for a pension because of insufficient years of service or financial need, represents the development of a life of vital retirement, including considerable agricultural and intellectual activity.

David was a distinguished magistrate who managed to remain in some official capacity almost constantly. His *État* listed the following services:

SERVICES OF FRANÇOIS DAVID

Subsitut du Procureur du Roi près la Cour
de l'Election de Limoges
October 1, 1768–September 30, 1790   22 years, 0 months, 0 days

Juge au Tribunal de District de Limoges
December 9, 1790–November 26, 1794   3 years, 11 months, 18 days

Juge au Tribunal civil du département de la
Haute Vienne
November 12, 1795–June 19, 1800   4 years, 7 months, 8 days

Juge au Tribunal de première instance
de Limoges
June 20, 1800–August 19, 1801   1 year, 2 months, 0 days

Conseiller à la Cour Royale séant à Limoges
August 20, 1801–November 4, 1825   24 years, 2 months, 15 days

Total   55 years, 11 months, 11 days

His demand described a career that was even longer and fuller. He began with his reception as *avocat au parlement de Bordeaux* at barely twenty years of age in 1762 and mentioned some municipal posts that were not to be counted. For him, legal work transcended regime, and, when he began asking for a pension back in 1821, he cast his eyes both behind and ahead: "My entire life has been devoted to the bar, to the magistracy; this honorable career has equally become that of my children. My son, procureur du Roi, au tribunal civil de Limoges, already counts twenty-five years of service, while my grandson is on the verge of completing his studies at the law faculty of Paris." He spoke of the zeal and assiduousness with which he had worked and of the growing weight of years that was becoming too much. He asked to be admitted to retirement with the title of *Conseiller honoraire* and as consolation in his old age and recompense for his long service to be replaced by his son. Despite his having the support of the department's deputies, the ministry, while expressing respect, rejected the exchange, recognizing that the people of the Corrèze wanted representation in the court. Yet, by 1825, David got his wish. And when he died in 1831 at the age of eighty-nine, he was accompanied by a grandson and grandnephew who had both launched careers in the magistracy.[25]

Juge Saint-Martin also evoked his position in a lineage of magistrates. Following in the footsteps of his father and grandfather, he was provided in 1773 with the office of *conseiller du roi en la sénéchaussée et siège présidial de Limoges*. He then became *commissaire du roi près le tribunal criminel du département de la Haute-Vienne* from December 1791 to September 1792.[26] At that point, having seen his position suppressed but also having purchased *biens nationaux*, he carved out a space of active, rural retirement and humanist leisure.[27] He wrote in philosophy, agriculture, arboriculture, and social history. He idealized the rural retreat of the local notable, what a recent historian of the region's châteaux and châtelains describes as "otium cum dignitate." For him, a retreat to the agricultural world permitted escape from the decadence of the city and the dangers of revolutionary-era politics. Philippe Grandcoing uses him as a model for a new form of bourgeois retirement to the country, identifying eight former magistrates or lawyers residing in their châteaux in 1836.[28]

The nature of retirement for these magistrates had something to do with the time of cessation of active life, but it also had much to do with the nature of interruptions in the career. Among those ending up in the early Restoration, many had experienced the Revolution as a parenthesis. For them, Old Regime service was most important. Augustin-Honoré-Louis d'Espagnet was born in Aix-en-Provence in 1754. He served as *conseiller au Parlement de Provence* for fourteen years, seven months, and twenty-eight days from February 3, 1776, to October 1, 1790, experienced an interruption of twenty years, just longer than his active career, which continued July 1, 1811 to March 28, 1816 at the Cour Royale d'Aix. His letter spoke of emigration and the loss of his fortune by the sale of his *biens*. He died a widower two years later at his country home in Lambesc, where he was discovered by the forty-eight-year-old mayor of Rogne and a forty-one-year-old gardener.[29]

His contemporary and fellow Aixois, François-Pierre-Joseph Pazery de Thorame, the son of a *conseiller au parlement*, also served in that court from 1775 to 1790. He joined D'Espagnet in the Napoleonic-era and Restoration Cour royale on the same day, July 1, 1811, but lasted in office longer, retiring in May 1827, only to die in December. One of the witnesses was an aging *conseiller*, the other an Adolphe d'Espagnet, *propriétaire*. His emphasis is on age and infirmities; he employs a very common phraseology: "My age and my infirmities no longer permitting me to fulfill the [position's] functions, without endangering my health, with the zeal that I ought always have brought during my long career..."[30]

The letter smoothly elides the interruption. Likewise, Honoré-Sauveur Fabri-Borrilly, another Aixois, skips quickly over experience of emigration, but he does want the emigration counted toward a career, which would then add up to fifty years.[31] But he provides no details of life as an émigré. So too for Pierre-Gabriel Aguillon, *conseiller à Aix-en-Provence*, who returned in 1800.[32]

Typically, those who left in 1790 complain about losses upon their return but provide few if any details about life in emigration. They contrast markedly with those who moved around Europe pursuing careers in the French empire. Those itinerant magistrates recount expenses of housing and of educating children, missed professional opportunities back home, and the difficulty of speaking a foreign language. But those who worked into the early years of the Revolution had a great deal to talk about, often in very dramatic fashion.

Thus, Charles-Antoine Guérin, *président à Aix-en-Provence*, presents himself as a devoted monarchist inexplicably forced into retirement in 1816 at the age of sixty. Twelve years later, he would die in his hometown of Vence. For him, the Revolution was an attack upon himself and his family. His father and brother had been judges in Vence, and his brother died in Toulon when, it was claimed, he tried on July 28, 1792 to appease a crowd.[33] He was incarcerated for royalism in Nice in October 1793 on the orders of the younger Robespierre and Ricord, *représentants en mission*. He had also been a victim of the antiroyalist Fructidor coup four years later. Moreover, he claimed he had behaved well upon the restoration of the monarchy. He denied having been a partisan of *l'usurpateur* and had complimented the king and the duchesse d'Angoulême on June 3, 1814. He had encouraged his son's pursuit of Napoleon in Sisteron with the national guard of Aix. That one of his sons was killed in the Spanish campaign and another was wounded did not make him a Bonapartist; he did not want to see his other sons taken similarly. So it was difficult for him and, on his account, his neighbors to understand why he was let go. He understood that it had had something to do with his connection to Maréchal Massena—a *calomnie*, he complained—but he pleaded that Massena had protected him and his fortune during the Terror and that he himself should not be associated with Massena's administration as governor of the eighth division. The story was filled with twists and turns, but it was presented so as to add up to a consistent life, one part of a three-generation story of service in the magistracy.[34]

Still another *président à Aix*, François Baffier, served 1773–91 and 1795–1817, and claimed consistent service to the king. He was born in Aix, worked in Corsica, then made his way back to Aix. He spoke of forty years of service (actually thirty-nine years, four months, and nineteen days).[35] One gets the sense that these retrospective shapers of careers pretended there was no interruption, especially those ending careers in the Restoration. They tried to match the legitimacy of their careers with that of the Bourbons. Some made the comparison explicitly. For others, very brief interruptions seem not to have upset essentially continuous careers. Jean-Baptiste Arnaud de Puimoisson, for example, began his career as a small-town *maire* and *juge de paix* before moving to Aix, retiring as *procureur général* in 1821 at the age of sixty-eight, and dying in his country house back home in Puimoisson eight years later.[36]

Joseph Lombard, *substitut à Aix*, wrote of twists and turns in his career and the particular problems of magistrates in border areas. He served in Nice before it was part of France, but he claimed having been naturalized French. He kept an eye on his contemporaries, particularly one named Trémois, who had been born in Monaco. He spoke of distributive justice, and he gave a good sense of transcending particular regimes.[37] Thus, he wrote that he had served under all governments from 1794 to 1816 with appropriate "fidelity, moderation, and impartiality," and without the least interruption. When he wrote again in the July Monarchy, he had been a judge in Draguignan, and he presented himself as a man of 1789. He suspected his "impartiality" was not appreciated in 1815, and he allowed himself to be a little less impartial in airing suspicions of political opponents. He saw the triumph of his own principles in a new regime with a "Citizen-King at the head of the State." His appeal, however, was unsuccessful.

Even if they could have imagined awaiting revolution in 1830, many died in the 1820s. Consider a few examples of magistrates from Calvados ending their careers in the Restoration. Gilles-Jacques-Charles Chalopin, *juge de paix* in Tilly-sur-Seulles, was mayor of his town from December 1792 to April 1794 and *juge de paix* from then until January 1824. The ministry's report described him as not very knowledgeable but careful and a good conciliator.

By profession he was a clockmaker. While he was viewed as honest, he was not considered a royalist. But in his letter of December 3, 1823, he alluded to his having been born the same year as the king, and thus not able to begin another career. He claimed that France was now experiencing "the most complete joy." He retired in 1824 at the age of sixty-nine and died two years later.[38]

An early Restoration letter came from the man in the middle of three generations of magistrates. Jean-Baptiste-Augustin Daigremont, *juge à Caen*, who later died in office, leaving a widow seeking help, described his father, Jean-Louis, as possibly the oldest magistrate in France, a man of more than eighty who had worked from age twenty-one to seventy-seven. The father's greatest regret was said to be that he could not work into the Restoration. He wanted the *croix d'honneur* from the hand of the king, whom he compared to "le grand Henry."[39]

A *juge de Caen* who had served continuously from 1790 to 1816 fell short of the thirty years required but also ran afoul of Restoration authorities for his politics. Dutrone was replaced in March 1816 and presented himself as worthy of reward. His was a story of persecution during the Revolution and of financial need. He had begun life with greater wealth but was orphaned at twelve, served in the military, studied the law, and spent a month in prison during the Terror. He emphasized his help for a monarchist who had spent nine months in prison—the man's wife had displayed a white flag and cried, "*Vive le Roy*." He claimed to welcome the return of Louis XVIII, "the best of Kings." But the ministry knew him as a "fanatical Bonapartist, bad and dangerous according to all reports; *fédéré* and recruiter of this impious horde; in a word an incorrigible man and declared enemy of the Government."[40]

When a *président à la cour de Caen*, Le Follet, fell just short with twenty-seven consecutive years of work from 1790 to 1817, his letter chiefly concerned the problem posed by the Bonapartist interlude, particularly the Hundred Days, when he had accepted the *articles additionnels* and sat in the Chambre des Représentants. He tried to get back in the good graces of the monarchy, explaining his behavior and that of his colleagues. He wrote of the pride and independence of the lawyers of Caen, claiming it was wrong to assume that those in position under Napoleon were all Bonapartists. He raised a similar question looming over those implicated in the Revolution. What of those in place since 1789? For him, the worst government was better than anarchy, and he appealed to a monarchy that calmed factionalism and guaranteed Frenchmen the enjoyment of their rights. The king should have "nothing to fear from supposed partisans of Bonaparte." Le Follet may have hung on, if he was the same Lefollet (Hervé-François) who retired in 1826 as *président honoraire à la cour royale de Caen*.[41]

After long careers, some magistrates explained away missteps. Philippe-Martin-Antoine Morel, *procureur du roi à Falaise*, tried to excuse his having served in the Chambre des Représentants by arguing that he had no "bad intentions" and that he had never signed the *articles additionnels*. He went on to describe his behavior during the Revolution, when he helped victims and bought no *biens nationaux*. But the most recent crisis was evidently the one that mattered, and he was declared ineligible for a pension.[42] Similarly, Pierre-François Rousselin, *président à Caen* and a member of a distinguished family of magistrates, claimed he was essentially forced into activity during the Revolution. A representative on mission in Calvados named him to an administrative post, and he dared not decline out of fear of being declared a suspect.[43]

One former *substitut près le tribunal civil de Falaise*, Louis-François-Salomon Lecouturier, understood that politics was his undoing in 1816 and did not bother asking for help until the July Monarchy, under which he had greater expectations. But, as in so many cases, he discovered that a rejection under the Bourbons would be upheld under Louis-Philippe.[44] The treatment of a *juge* from the same town of Falaise, Pierre-Michel Serant, indicated that suffering from asthma and gout might make a difference, and he collected a pension from 1826 until his death at seventy-one in 1832.[45] More certain was having completed thirty years of service. Thus, Jean-Baptiste Hellouin, *juge de paix d'Aunay*, whose service began in 1791, even overcame political opposition. He was eased out primarily because of the political and antireligious opinions of his son, with whom he resided. The prefect thought he was a capable man but that he was irreligious and politically suspect. M. Romer concluded that even if there were good reason for his replacement, he still had a right to a pension at sixty-nine and having served thirty-three years. The Conseil d'Administration of the ministry, which handled difficult cases, agreed.[46]

Even in the late Restoration, there were survivors from the ancien régime, many of whose careers were interrupted in the early Revolution and resumed in the Directory. Thus, Jean-Pierre Rivals de Lacombe, *conseiller à la cour royale de Caen*, had begun as *lieutenant particulier assesseur criminel en la sénéchaussée et siège présidial de Montauban* in 1785, found himself without a post in 1790, and returned to the judiciary in 1795. He moved from the Somme to Agen and finally Caen, where he retired in 1828. In asking for that retirement, he proclaimed his royalism, referred to his long service and devotion to the sons of St Louis, good Henry, and Louis le Grand. Rivals de Lacombe died in January 1831, at the age of seventy-one.[47]

Even greater continuity emerges from the dossier of Jean-François Philippe-Delleville, whose breaks lasted a month or two. He began as *procureur du roi au tribunal des maîtrises des eaux et forêts à Bayeux* from 1772 to 1778, became *lieutenant particulier de l'amirauté de Bayeux, Port et Asnelles* from 1778 to 1790, *président du tribunal de district de Bayeux* from November 6, 1790, to August 25, 1792, member of the Convention and Conseil des 500 from September 21, 1792, to May 19, 1798, *premier vérificateur à la commission de comptabilité intermédiaire* from July 19, 1798, to March 21, 1800, and finally *conseiller à la cour royale de Caen* from May 21, 1800, to April 15, 1828. Four months later he was dead at the age of eighty-eight years, six months. His movements from post to post were more numerous than those of others, but they added up to almost constant activity for the public good. Only his early service in the *tribunal des maîtrises des eaux et forêts* failed to count, so the formula permitted forty-nine years, three months, and nine days.[48]

In the July Monarchy, creatures of Napoleon could point to thirty years of service, but retirees of the 1830s still included people who had been serving since the Old Regime. Take the example of Barthélemy-Fleury De L'Horme, Lyonnais who became *premier président de la cour royale de Caen*. His official service only added up to nineteen years and ten months. But he provided details that helped fill in the gaps—imprisonment during the Terror and a legitimate stay in the colonies after the Year VIII—and permitted him to claim a full career as a *fonctionnaire* since 1786. He described leaving the "prisons de la Terreur" for Paris, where he and two colleagues spent five months seeking bread for Lyon from the Comités de Salut public, de Sureté générale et des subsistances. The committees provided fifteen million assignats used to buy grain in Marseille. He was perhaps reminded of his actions in the 1790s when, from October 1830 to January 1831, he visited Paris to talk with the ministry. His letter suggested a keen awareness of what had happened to colleagues. When he was *procureur général à Lyon* during the ministry of le Marquis de Marbois, all other *fonctionnaires*, whatever their conduct, received pensions and honorary titles. More recently, he remarked that M. Le Ménuet, who replaced him, had had a six-thousand-franc pension. If Le Ménuet now received a salary, he himself should receive the pension, and the budget would be the same. But his expenses were greater. Le Ménuet came from Normandy, but the Baron de L'Horme found it financially daunting to return to his native Lyon.[49]

At its start, the July Monarchy signified an opportunity for revolutionary creatures to reassert their political principles, but as time passed, it became possible to emphasize only the part of the career beginning under Napoleon. Pierre-Adrien Maubant, for example, had mentioned revolutionary service and accusations of federalism in a Restoration-era demand of 1826. But when, in 1839, he recounted his almost forty years in the one post of *conseiller à la cour royale de Caen*, he had no need to describe service before 1800, except when providing a total. He wrote in a shaky hand that having "arrived at the age of 87 years, and soon having 50 years of functions in the Magistracy, I feel the need to rest and to abandon definitively every sort of judicial work." He had come a long way, the son of an innkeeper. And when he died at ninety-two in February 1845, perhaps he had felt most comfortable with people of his earlier rank, as the two witnesses to his death were both carpenters.[50]

Large numbers of post-revolutionary figures reached retirement in the 1840s and early 1850s. Still in Calvados, we have Adrien-Pierre Rousselin, *conseiller à la cour royale de Caen, fils d'un marchand tanneur*, who had occupied two posts, one after the other, from 1812 to 1846. When he retired he was sixty-nine, having worked thirty-four years.[51] Pierre-Marcel Rousselin, son of the earlier-mentioned Pierre-François, had begun occupying four successive posts on the same day as Adrien-Pierre in 1812 and stepped down in October 1849. It was a simple matter of having served over thirty-seven years.[52]

In such a way, families of magistrates constituted dynasties despite the supposed turn toward professionalism and individualism. Old Regime legacies naturally sought to maintain family traditions, but even revolutionary creatures balanced merit and lineage. Thus, what had begun in revolt continued in an institutionalized manner. As we have seen, recent scholarship has alluded to a related problem in treating the various meanings of Jacobinism, from a revolutionary sensibility to professional loyalty to the centralized state.[53]

But it took some time for revolutionary passions to subside. Among the old revolutionaries, we might examine several from the Bouches-du-Rhône. Pierre Barbier was *juge de paix à Châteaurenard*. His service included stints in 1793–95 and 1798–1815, but both ended because of his political opinions. The July Monarchy brought him back to active life from 1831 to 1839, when health reasons led him to resign. He wrote of how he had emerged from the revolutionary era politically pure and impoverished. But Barbier went on to describe the difficulties of serving a very divided jurisdiction and how his work had ruined his health. By the 1830s he found himself identifying with the Orleanist regime.[54]

Some magistrates were so implicated in revolutionary activities that they had little chance of success in the 1820s. Jean-André Callamard, *juge au tribunal civil de Marseille*, tried to convince both Restoration kings of his honorable service. In 1825, he called himself "doyen d'âge et de rang" of his tribunal and appealed to Charles X: "But, Sire, today your royal Cry of forgetting and unity is truly the order of the day." But his service had only been for twenty-one years, eight months, eighteen days, and the ministry reported that he openly proclaimed his having been a Jacobin and that he was a married former priest.[55]

Callamard's fellow *juge au tribunal civil de Marseille*, Louis Long, also continued to be known as a Jacobin.[56] His earliest service had come in the Year II. He failed to receive a pension in 1818 and tried again in 1830, writing his prefect on September 8, claiming that his only crime was that of having obeyed his conscience in swearing to the government of the time the oath of fidelity prescribed by the laws. He pointed out that the charter of 1814 called for the principle of *inamovibilité* and that that disastrous epoch was unjustly given the beautiful name of Restoration. He appealed to the new regime by making a comparison between its respect for truth and legal liberties and the Restoration's despotism and lies, and he claimed the hour of justice had sounded with the July Days of 1830 and the coming of a "government repairer of all injustices," correcting the crimes of the Bourbon regime, which had returned "under the influence of foreign bayonets." Proclaiming his attachment to the "national cause," he repeatedly evoked his service, his need at age eighty, and his political opinions.[57]

Still another *juge au tribunal civil de Marseille* from the revolutionary period, Antoine-Paul-Joseph Courmes, had more than thirty-five years of service, 1790–93, 1798–1831, so his demand should have posed no problem. However, there was a dispute over whether he had simply resigned his position or followed proper procedure. The confusion led to his writing at great length and seeking the help of the *procureur général* Borely, who supported him strongly and resisted insinuations of wrongdoing coming from the *bâtonnier* of the order of *avocats* of Marseille. Courmes expressed reticence about speaking of himself so made full use of Borely's letters, but he did claim that thirty years of service constituted a right to his retirement. He appealed to the Charter of 1830 as disallowing executive meddling and asserted his good faith.[58]

Courmes's argument, like those of others, sought to use political principle wherever useful but fell back on a kind of commonsense careerism. Describing careers was a way of speaking about public life in the nineteenth century, a way of transcending the ideological and personal battles of the revolutionary, Napoleonic, and Restoration eras. Pensions could always be associated with loyalty to a particular regime, but they increasingly became expectations in a more stable world.

When Revolution came again in 1848, the problem of workers' retirement reappeared, and in the early 1850s mandatory retirement came to the judicial system. But already in the 1830s, demands were much more formulaic than they had been for those who had begun careers either under the Old Regime, the Revolution of 1789–99, or Napoleon. For those who experienced the early bureaucracy, reconstructing careers and recounting memories were parts of the process.

We think of bureaucracy as impersonal, but a developing bureaucracy demanded the writing of autobiographical texts. At least in the first generations, we have writing to bureaucrats that provides wonderful source material. The state, with its bureaucratic apparatus, encouraged a consciousness of career and of aging. Industrialization, the modern labor market, and the welfare state will have their roles in the construction of the aging self. But an early experience came in the development of public sector employment and the concomitant elaboration by individuals of their life histories, the shaping of political and personal memories into something to be cashed out.

The juxtaposition of personal experience with history and right permitted aging magistrates to impose a certain continuity of career across a period of turbulence and sudden change. They cited laws and affirmed norms and understood how to address the regime of the moment. We have just examined the shapes of careers, but the very language they used was an important ingredient of their demands.

PART II
THE LANGUAGE OF RETIREMENT

5

Entitlement and Complaint

Creating a Rhetoric of Retirement

A cultural history of retirement must reach beyond legislation and the tracing of careers to an exploration of themes and rhetoric in pension demands themselves. Such an approach is important as it reveals the emerging logic of entitlement. Postulants evoked a range of concerns. Demands for pensions and honors employed themes of politics, career, wealth and poverty, health and sickness, honor, and family life. Ideas of entitlement and the voicing of complaint grew easily out of the succession of regimes from Bourbon monarchy to the fall of Napoleon. Echoes of Old Regime honor and revolutionary displacement, of loyalty to republic, empire, or monarchy, provided ingredients for representing individual lives. Themes of judicial tradition and public service fused with the language of everyday life and aging. Rhetorical strategies emerged for representing lives in subsequent decades that solidified magistrates' self-understanding and rights. Later those strategies became available to broader swaths of the French population.

Organizational change had serious consequences for personnel. During the Napoleonic era, forced interruptions of career, as in the aftermath of the Sénatus-Consulte of October 12, 1807, occasioned an important round of dismissals, retirements, and correspondence. Decrees of March 24, 1808, sought to implement the new order, identifying sixty-six judges who should cease their functions, six retirees, eighty resignees, and thirteen who had not yet responded to a demand that they resign.[1] The issues had to do with aging, illness, disability, and politics. Regardless of political circumstances, the 110 dossiers that preceded the 1814–15 *ordonnances* anticipated the language of the early Restoration (and the Restoration-era dossiers include many letters written under Napoleonic rule), so the creation of a rhetoric of retirement becomes all the more visible when we examine pension demands from both eras.[2]

The mixture of private and public spheres meant life course and politics could take turns occupying foreground or background. That blend of private and public is most recognizable in the use of familial language. Discussion of family concerns varied from description of economic losses in the Revolution to traditional family service to the state and loyalty to the House of Bourbon. Demands linked notions of lineage, including traditional service in the past and hopes of replacement by a son, nephew, or son-in-law, with appeals to humanity and sympathy.[3] Family travails included illness, poverty, death, guilt by association, the need to educate children, and the desire to avoid shameful dependence upon others. Charts that might in the past have justified the noble status of a family were now displayed to demonstrate labors expended for the public or the nation or the king. The nature of the pension had been transformed from a reward at any time to a reward at the end of a working career, but continuity of lineage was still sometimes evoked. Revolutionary trials and tribulations were dramatically narrated in order to gain sympathy.

Some voices complained of impoverishment brought on by the Revolution, with particular reference to legislation and property seizures, the consequences of emigration, debt, and imprisonment.[4] Others complained of the loss of a post: "The loss of the position of Receiver of the Great Chapter of the Cathedral of Strasbourg, which for more than a hundred years was like a fief in my family, that I was occupying at the time of the revolution, was only the beginning of my woes."[5]

Of course, revolution occasioned death, but also a host of infirmities resulting from imprisonment, deprivation, fear, and stress.[6] Stories of military casualties and occupation by foreign armies were common,[7] sometimes ending in suicide of a returning soldier.[8]

Particularly in serving a continental empire, displacement was a common theme. One individual complained that in Year XI he was required to move within forty-eight hours to the Tribunal civil de la Justice des Deux Ponts (Zweibrücken) despite not understanding German.[9] Another lamented a move to a rural location he saw as unsuitable for an aging magistrate.[10] Postings abroad could be expensive. Jean-Jacques Gros spoke of spending nine thousand francs on six round trips between Paris and his posting in Hamburg (later recalled as four trips costing ten thousand francs, but also confusing 9 Thermidor and 9 Messidor).[11] Responding to denunciation was a common theme. Louis-René Crespin, prosecutor in l'Île de France (Mauritius), wrote, "If I had really asked [of the English] to serve in the new order of things, would I have dared to present myself in France to my family, my fellow citizens, my government?"[12]

Reorganizations of the judiciary system and changes in boundaries and institutions as a result of warfare caused magistrates to feel the impact of world-historical events. Silvestre Alvigini of Genoa wrote in extraordinarily gushy language of his gratitude for being retired in June 1811 even though he was one of thirty-three magistrates suffering the same fate when appeals courts were closed in Montpellier, Limoges, Genoa, and Aix.[13] Michel-Ange Antonini wrote similarly from Rome in April 1813 upon the suppression of the criminal court, expecting that all employees terminated in the former Roman states would be granted pensions.[14] Pierre Baudoin, a former Flemish administrator and archivist in the Chambre des Comptes of Brabant, expected the French regime to honor his sixty years of service by paying a pension.[15] Anton Luigi Barly, *juge de paix de Regello*, wrote in May 1809 from Florence, confessing trouble with his eyes and ignorance of French while proclaiming his "sincere attachment" to Napoleon and the hope that, in conformity with old Tuscan practice, his income would continue in his needy old age.[16] A former judge in Parma, François Bertioli, did not need to appeal to regional tradition, but identified two colleagues, Carmignani and Baistrocchi, who, in July 1811, were already receiving pensions, but by September he would be dead.[17] The daughter of a former presiding judge in Mayence (Mainz) described how her father had lost much of his wealth as a result of the emigration of two of his sons, only to lose even more when the property he himself acquired in Mayence lost nearly all value.[18]

Since so many dossiers concerned people who had been employed in imperial territories, opportunities arose for comparisons between systems. Count Corsini, in supporting the widow Fabroni, explained that in the Tuscan system a fund for widows' pensions was based upon legislation of 1800, 1804, and 1805.[19] Salsciccioni, *juge de paix à Livourne* (Livorno) had served fifty-two years and reached the age of eighty. The *premier président de la cour d'appel de Florence*, Montiglio, wrote that his *greffier* had had to do his work, but his main point was that justices of the peace in the Grand Duchy of Tuscany were *fonctionnaires*, a status that Old Regime equivalents in the French interior had not had.[20] A ministry official in 1811 remarked on the need to treat magistrates from annexed territories and recommended grouping their demands together.[21] Among dossiers of French magistrates, that of Charles Joseph Derivaux, *ancien conseiller en la cour de Nancy*, who had begun his career in 1783 in the Principauté de Salm, convinced the ministry that his services for the Prince de Salm-Salm ought to be considered as if he had worked for France itself, as the territory had been joined to France in 1793 and more definitively in 1814.[22]

Many dossiers from the empire concerned people who had served greater France. Thus, Altanic St. Ougal, former *président de la cour d'appel de l'Isle de France*, returned to France after a long absence at nearly seventy-five years of age, and, writing from Vannes, told a tale of particular woe. His wife had lost her wealth in the Revolution. He complained that he was not treated as well as his colleagues who had remained in metropolitan France. To cap it all off, he described the plight of his six sons. The two eldest were killed in the army of the Rhine, the next died in a shipwreck, the next was shot at Vannes, a fifth suffered from epilepsy, and the sixth was employed in the *droits réunis*.[23]

Life histories involved considerable drama. Jacques Besson, a priest (former Bénédictin) turned administrator, recounted adventures in Ste. Lucie, Guadeloupe, St-Domingue, the United States, and southern Italy. He wrote Napoleon of his own "bravery" and "devotion." He includes a 1799 article from the *Monitore Napoletano* that recounted his heroism at resisting pirates who threatened his boat with pistols and sabers.[24] The same carton includes pleas from others who had served in Saint-Domingue and encountered dangers in the Haitian Revolution.[25]

One magistrate bragged that his services should not just be counted but weighed.[26] Another explained how he had managed to save many émigrés and refractory priests by slowing the mechanisms of justice.[27] Still another thought that the patriotism expressed by having nine surviving children deserved reward.[28]

Complaints were accompanied by claims of right. Nicolas-Joseph Guyot, *membre du bureau de consulation et de révision* in the Ministry of Justice used the term "droits acquis" five times in his letter of May 18, 1815.[29]

What of the credibility of postulants' accounts? The ministry faced the same problem that confronts the historian. At least one contemporary thought the ministry too credulous when presented with rumors of wrongdoing among candidates for appointment.[30] That may not have been so serious a problem at the end of the career. Documentary evidence was required for time of service, and confidential reports were requested of colleagues or local administrators. So conflicting views were aired, and much of the basic material is trustworthy. But some claims, especially concerning matters of motivation, demand greater skepticism. Change of regime occasioned changes of mind about whether to retire or hold on. The crisis of March 1814 led one judge to resign, but the arrival of a replacement occasioned a change of mind, and the timely death of that replacement allowed the original to stay on for a few more years.[31]

Until the bureaucratic process became firmly established, postulants reviewed their lives by emphasizing the themes that they thought would elicit a favorable outcome and that helped them make sense of their world. They were beginning to work toward a perspective at the end of a career that made sense of the whole. Yet, certain information was expected: age, service, infirmity, and often need. Consequently, demands typically included that information and often were structured by that evidence.

Even before the Restoration system was put in place, Napoleonic-era demands often began with such references. Many blamed their service for having whitened their hair.[32] Some were referred to by others as doyen or Nestor of the court.[33]

Age was relatively self-explanatory. Nicolas Acher had the support of a Dr. Cara, former physician in charge of the general hospice of Lyon, who declared him "subject to respiratory infections, which were more debilitating last winter because of the more extreme cold." But Acher, in a letter of June 3, 1810, thought his having reached his eighty-third year was itself his "principal infirmity."[34] In writing about the above-mentioned Barly (or Antoine Joseph Louis Marie Barli), Carelli, *procureur général impérial en la cour d'appel de Florence*, described a man whose effective age was greater than his sixty-two years.[35]

Infirmity was usually spelled out in considerable detail. Poujade suffered from paralysis and had gone to the waters of Balaruc-les-Bains (L'Hérault).[36] His colleagues had kept quiet about his health in hopes that he might recover, but he failed to respond and was incapable of speaking. Guerin du Loiret wrote of declining eyesight within the previous month and very painful paralysis of the lower extremities.[37] Fournier, a *juge* in Bergerac, suffered from apoplexy and failure of memory.[38] He went to nearby Sarlat to recover. His doctor reported that he could not enunciate and had been weakened intellectually. Bevalet, *juge au tribunal de première instance à Pontarlier* (Doubs), was paralyzed on the right side of his body, so his wife wrote for him.[39] So did the wife of Josse Philippe Vanandenrode, appeals court judge in Brussels, who discussed her husband's partial paralysis and his having become "Melancholico-maniaque," the term used by his physicians.[40] But he persisted in making his way to court on crutches. The *procureur-général impérial*, Beyts, referred to the judge's condition, less charitably perhaps, as one of "imbécilité."

Some resisted such characterizations. Phélippes de Coatgoureden de Tronjolly claimed he was "neither mad nor infirm," but it did no good.[41] Others accepted their infirmities. Louis Bousquet, *juge en la cour de justice criminelle du département du Tarn*, suffering from bad eyesight and swollen legs, wrote from Albi on June 28, 1810, of his obligation to step down. He desired a "pension proportionate to my infirmities, my needs, and my advanced age."[42] Sarrey, *juge de paix du canton de Fleurance* (Gers) wrote on July 24, 1810 of his constant work since the start of the Revolution, but the work itself had so damaged him physically that he could no longer write more than a few lines, and those very slowly and with indescribable pain.[43] Vespasien Biandra, *vice-président du tribunal civil de Turin*, wrote in January 1811 of his heroism fighting brigands and assassins and his approval by all governments in Piedmont, but his long service, he claimed, was responsible for an attack of vertigo five years earlier and loss of an unexpectedly large quantity of blood during an unfortunate bleeding operation. He had recently begun spitting blood and suffered from an enervated stomach and a dangerous cough. Things only got worse, and he feared developing consumption. His doctor, Alexis Gillis, claimed that his ailments were the result of "a too sedentary life."[44]

The ministry also received demands from employees who were not magistrates. They made comparable declarations and demands. Jean Baptiste Demorest was *Executeur des jugements criminels de Grenoble*, but he had been suffering from epilepsy for six years. He wrote of his wife's poor health and a desire to be replaced by his nephew, who had been his adjunct and had to support four children and a mother-in-law. In closing, he offered wishes that might be considered unusual coming from an executioner: "[He] will not stop addressing wishes to Heaven, for the prosperity and conservation of your days."[45]

In a letter of September 28, 1811, the *procureur impérial du tribunal de première instance* in Castres, Carayon, went into excruciating detail in describing the result of the blindness of Jean Antoine Auger, *juge de paix*. He could no longer read the law or other documents, and he could not determine whether a seal on a door had been tampered with. The population deserved better.[46]

Physical infirmity made resignation necessary in the 1812 case of Antoine Giscard, *conseiller à la cour impériale séant à Montpellier*. He spoke of a "grave malady" that had disabled him for six months. His doctors were more precise, saying that he was suffering from "a disease of the anus known as proctalgia, which makes him endure severe pain in this part, in the general area and notably in the right thigh and leg." They claimed some temporary success in treatment but recurrence when he returned to work. They blamed the latest flare-up on his having to travel twenty-five *myriamètres* (250 km) on horseback over mountainous terrain in bad weather to install a new tribunal, but they thought the intensity of the ailment derived from the stress and conditions of his occupation.[47]

Whether a magistrate was incapable of continuing was often a matter of debate. Bladviel, *juge au tribunal de première instance à Figeac* (Lot), having been informed upon by a colleague, reacted with incredulity when he received an April 13, 1809, letter from the *grand juge* saying that the *Décret impérial* of October 2, 1807, obliged him to request his retirement because of infirmity. Bladviel responded on April 21 that he had only taken a small fall. But that was not the opinion of the *président du tribunal civil*, Gach, who wrote on June 2, 1809, of Bladviel's difficulty walking, hearing, and speaking, and that his way of compensating was to adopt the opinions of colleagues he happened to like.[48] Bladviel gave in on June 28, 1809, asking that the ministry take into account his seven children, one of whom had died in the army in Italy.

Medical certification also became part of the process. While some postulants claimed that age itself should be proof of deterioration, a medical discourse about the particular hazards of the magistracy and of the aging of the magistrate evolved. Falling off a horse or cart while on judicial business had immediate consequences, but the more sedentary labors of judges also could be life-threatening. Doctors and surgeons described the strokes and heart attacks, gout and asthma, blindness, deafness, paralysis, the difficulty urinating that caused pain, or the incontinence that kept a judge at home. But they went beyond describing illness or disability, and argued that the job itself caused the disability. Long hours of work in unhealthy environments, the emotional strain of the court, and the need to learn new law codes took their toll. Medical arguments passed from doctor and surgeon to judge, colleagues, and bureaucrats. Occasionally contradictory testimony made its way into the dossier, and sometimes a medical practitioner seemed to write just what the judge ordered, as in cases where he desired either to be succeeded by a son or to continue working—the certificate indicates that retirement, though desirable, was not yet medically necessary. Whatever the evidentiary status of the medical certificate, and whatever the peculiarity of the magistrature, the physical and "psychological" descriptions of the aging of magistrates combined representations of a particular group of individuals and of physiological processes that applied to everyone. Their summing up anticipated that of broader populations in the later nineteenth and twentieth centuries.

Complaints of physical infirmity humanize accounts of aging magistrates and contribute to a portrait of the aging body. Parliamentary debates over 1824 legislation encouraging forced retirement for infirm judges explored the vocabulary of "permanent" or "incurable" disease, and Minister of Justice Peyronnet described magistrates unwilling or unable to recognize their disabilities.[49] But many first-person accounts themselves displayed both acute and chronic ailments without shame. Throughout the first half of the nineteenth century, medical documentation formed only one part of the dossier, but it was the one supported by scientific expertise.

Approaching his seventy-third birthday, Jean André Barges, *juge au tribunal de première instance de Bourgoin* (Isère), reported in October 1809 how a long illness had led him to ask in April for an indefinite leave of absence to try to recover his health. He recalled some temporary improvement and the impact of good weather that encouraged his traditional zeal and caused him to ignore the advice of his doctor, return to work at the end of May, and withdraw his request for a leave. Over the course of the summer and early fall, his health gradually deteriorated, so now he renewed his request for a leave or, short of that, a retirement. The ministry requested his *acte de naissance*, and he responded in December, when he claimed that his condition was critical, that he could barely move without having difficulty breathing and that he suffered from chest and stomach pain. A postscript mentioned complete deafness on the right side, weakened hearing on the other, and problems of eyesight.[50]

Focusing on medical histories allowed magistrates to take politics and morality out of the picture, but colleagues did not always cooperate. When sixty-six-year-old Jean De Sèze missed his thirty years by a few months in 1830, he claimed a ten-year illness, but his colleagues doubted its severity and announced that he had made it known that he did not want to serve the new regime.[51] Infirmity was an issue in the case of Etienne Laurent Paschal Laforé, *président du tribunal de première instance séant à San Remo*, but it was not the only one. Description of cataracts and age was accompanied by accusations of corruption. A report to the *grand juge* in February 1810 indicated that his salary was insufficient to support his expenses and that his domestic servant had control over him and extorted large sums of money from those who appeared in court.[52]

Jean Casimir de Sèze's admissible service, as laid out in a typical bureaucratic form, did not quite reach the thirty years required to receive a pension; the form indicates that nine months and four days did not count. Jean, brother of Raymond de Sèze, defender of Louis XVI, consequently sought another kind of help by claiming a ten-year illness. His colleagues doubted its severity and reported that he had let it be known that he preferred not to serve under the July Monarchy. Whatever he thought his career meant, in the ministry it was represented in a form like anyone else's.
AN BB25 272.

Physical and mental ailments themselves were sometimes matters for debate. Claux, *ci-devant magistrat de sureté pour l'arrondissement d'Aurillac* (Cantal), was surprised by his unsolicited retirement in May 1811. He admitted an obvious infirmity, as he had only recovered partially from paralysis on the left side, but did not think of it as a disability. Only sixty-three, he still walked to the courthouse and his country residence. He wrote perfectly well with the right hand and boasted that he was perfectly clearheaded.[53] He was certainly more capable than Jacob Cohendet, *garçon de bureau* for the Ministry of Justice, whose brother and doctor confirmed a state of complete dementia and paralysis for more than a year before his death in 1810.[54] Jean Jacques Coremans, *ci-devant conseiller* in the imperial court in Brussels, recounted a career of seamless moves from government to government but could not escape the degeneration of the body, especially the urinary tract and prostate.[55]

Seekers of pensions had other things on their minds as well. Need came in the context of political and meteorological events, economic losses, family traditions, and such intangibles as honor and dignity. Many of the letters presented retirees as *pères de famille*. Some used the phrase *famille nombreuse* (or *nombreuse famille*), which would later justify special assistance in the modern welfare state. Many mentioned grandchildren.[56]

Demands for pensions read like what gerontologists have termed life reviews (*récits de vie*), albeit motivated life reviews. We find a blend of autobiography, family history, national history, honor, disgrace, dealing with catastrophe. Retiring magistrates engaged in impressive self-dramatization. Legislators, administrators, and employees built upon Enlightenment, revolutionary, Napoleonic, and "Restoration" ideas. Whatever the revolutionary impact on the family, the succession of events, turnarounds, personal tragedies, gains, losses, and pain pushed people to make sense of their lives, as public figures, private individuals, and members of families.[57]

Political differences existed, purges occurred, forced retirements as well as voluntary ones, but an experience of Revolution, whose benefits also brought catastrophe, led these people to seek security for themselves and their families. By seizing upon memories of past loyalties and betrayals, family histories, revolutionary rhetoric about social debt and equity, by also humanizing the royal family as a family,[58] *fonctionnaires* were working out the cultural origins of what eventually would be called a welfare state. It would be wrong to think that the rhetoric of career and retirement can be mapped onto simple political differences. Styles ranged from melodramatic complaint to bureaucratic accounting. As we have seen, they included emergency calls for help, pathetic tales and complaints, and formulaic claims of professional dignity.

Some dossiers demonstrate a gradual process of withdrawing from the workplace. Individuals were given less taxing work while their colleagues covered for them. Thus, Gouan, *juge au tribunal de première instance de Lodève* (Hérault), wrote in 1809 of his having become director of the jury rather than sitting and hearing cases.[59] De la Buisse's widow recalled taking dictation from her infirm husband while he was still officially active.[60] Claude Aubry, *juge au tribunal de première instance* in Château-Thierry, suffered from a weakened leg that kept him from public court proceedings but still managed to work in his chambers.[61]

Age and infirmity might also lead to negotiation over intergenerational succession. The already-mentioned octogenarian Nicolas Acher, appeals court judge in Lyon, wanted a quick retirement and replacement by his son.[62] Charles Joseph Auvynet, seventy-two-year-old *président du tribunal de première instance séant à Napoléon* (La Roche-sur-Yon, Vendée), claimed infirmities in February 1814, but with three hundred thousand francs of wealth asked for no pension. He only wanted to be named *président honoraire* and to be replaced by his son.[63]

It took some time to eliminate that sort of succession. In a compromise between a personal pension and a ministerial one, Joseph Marie Fabre wrote on February 1, 1816, that his successor had promised to pay him a pension until the official one came through.[64] But the state was already retiring people to avoid having close kin serve in the same jurisdiction. Thus, Jean Marie Bal, who had been *président du tribunal de première instance* in Moutiers, recognized his obligation to step down in October 1812 when a relative became *procureur-impérial du tribunal*. He spoke dutifully of ceding his position to one of his own students.[65]

Some individuals debated the system. François Louis Cetty, *président du tribunal de première instance de Colmar*, listed the relevant laws of August 22, 1790; 15 Germinal, Year XI; September 13, 1806; and October 2, 1807, in his letter of May 4, 1809.[66] Others found out the hard way that *démissionnaires* were not eligible for pensions. Thus, the *procureur impérial près le tribunal de première instance à La Rochelle*, La Villemarais, found himself writing again and again in 1809.[67]

Individuals expressed uncertainty about how the system would function. Concerning the case of Jean Baptiste François Guyet, *juge à la cour d'appel de*

Paris, the *premier président*, Antoine Jean Mathieu Séguier, asked on August 4, 1808, whether the pension would be a prescribed amount or proportioned to time in service and need, whether it would come from general funds or deducted from the successor's salary. He did not want a return to a system of venality but suggested that the system would benefit from having judges drawn largely from a cultured elite of means. Only a few talented poor would then require a pension.[68]

That would not be the system of the future, but individuals did make comparisons with colleagues. Denizot, *ancien juge de Paris et de Nogent-le-Rotrou*, wrote Minister of Justice Régnier, Duc de Massa, from Paris, March 15, 1811. He complained about losing the position with which he had hoped to end his days. He wrote again on June 4, 1811, insisting on the legitimacy of his demand and comparing himself to M. Lormeau, a colleague in Nogent-le-Rotrou, who was wealthier, less hardworking, and enjoying a pension.[69] He went on to surmise that his unnamed enemies had written unfavorable notes concerning his service; if presented with the evidence, he would be able to identify them. He recounted how he had always acted in disinterested fashion, consoled the afflicted, and freed the oppressed. Thank-you notes he had kept would reveal his virtuous behavior.

Some discussed the proper mechanism of payment.[70] They based arguments upon notions of justice. Thus, Thenaisie, *juge de paix du canton de Beaupreau* (Maine et Loire), who began seeking support in 1800, wrote Napoleon on May 6, 1808, that he had been a victim of the Revolution for fourteen years, that he had unjustly lost a post as *Directeur du droit d'enregistrement et des Domaines* in Angers back in July 1793, and that two reasons had been given for his rejection. First, it was alleged that if he were granted a pension, ten thousand other victims of the Revolution should also be rewarded. The second was that he only had twenty-five and a half years of service. Responding to the first, he claimed that his office continued to exist and pay pensions. To the second, he said that he had fewer than thirty years only because of injustice.[71]

Demands blended notions of justice with tales of victimization. Joseph Honoré François Régis Gispert Dulçat complained on May 10, 1809, of being persecuted and did not really want to step aside,[72] but he had begun complaining a year before. In that demand of September 29, 1808, he told his life history beginning with a description of his plight: "Seated on the edge of my tomb, at the end of a long career entirely devoted to the public good, circumstances force me to have recourse to your authority, Monseigneur, to obtain an honorable repose, either in the tribunals or in retirement. I believe I have a few rights to this favor."[73] Note the language of right to favor. He quickly went back to the service of father and grandfather, both singled out for praise by *le chancelier d'Aguesseau* and providing a model for his own career as a magistrate. But he also discussed his work as a historian of Roussillon and noted that his observations on the treaty of 1258 drew praise from Old Regime figures Vergennes, *ministre des affaires étrangères*, and Lamoignon de Malesherbes, *garde des sceaux*, as well as Merlin, *président de l'assemblée constituante*, thus emphasizing continuity into the Revolution. He continued to serve as a magistrate in and around Perpignan from 1790 until the Terror (*le terrorisme*, as he put it), which he described as a tempest that forced him from the tribunal. But he benefited from the protection of Maréchal Augereau, and greeted with relief the rise of Napoleon and his return to office in the Year VIII. The result was that, without asking, he had become doyen of the magistracy of the department. His story ended with victimization in a cabal.

Gispert Dulçat was willing to accept retirement, but his strong preference was for continued service. By contrast, Cetty expressed gratitude and asked when to step down.[74] Garcin Clary spoke of persecution and his own heroism in fighting brigands and saving *caisses nationales*. His children were in America and Africa.[75]

Common revolutionary narratives celebrated, or at least accepted, 1789, resisting excesses in the Terror while faithfully answering the call of the population, and welcoming the coming to power of Napoleon. Victimization was one of the themes of Jal's story of the Revolution, but he survived "in an obscure retirement."[76] He described having been forced to accept a post and wanted recompense for his labors and help in his old age. He was hardly alone in speaking of having to accept a task. It was not appropriate to admit to political ambition. People wrote of how "they elected me" or "I was appointed."

Victimization came in various forms. D'Espagnet was a victim of emigration.[77] Tassin was a victim of revolution,[78] Bonière of counterrevolution.[79] He lost two fingers in trying unsuccessfully to protect his father from being killed by Chouans. Tarlet spoke of two victimizations, first when a regime of laws gave way to that of the Terror, then when he was falsely accused of being a *fédéré*.[80] His account of the Terror provided clues as to how one tried to avoid detection. He claimed to have kept his head down in the *administration des ponts et chaussées*. Some forms of public service were evidently more visible than others.

Demands commonly spoke of calumny. Jean Gaspar Bodart, *ex-président du tribunal de première instance* (Ourte), wrote Napoleon on January 15, 1812, saying the minister of justice himself would vouch for him.[81] And an April 20, 1811, letter of Branquart, former *juge de la cour d'appel de Douai*, spoke of "slanderous noises" and "a reputation made by more than forty years of work." He believed that obtaining his retirement would wash away "a suspicion that would poison the rest of my life." He asked how a magistrate whose wife was employed at seven and a half sous a day in making bed linen for the military could be open to corruption.[82]

Suspicions of enemies' machinations were common. Charles Foncez, appeals court judge in Brussels, wrote the Duc de Massa at least twice in May 1811. He began one of those letters with a story of victimization: "Victim of calumny, I am the only one among nonreelected magistrates to be denied a retirement pension, without having been heard, without knowing the crime I'm imputed with, and without being able to justify myself." Actually, he did have an idea of what the accusation might have been. He alluded to a particularly controversial case, "the fatal trial of Plissart," but suspected that he had been accused of "an illicit relationship with my governess." He went on to explain that having been abandoned by his wife in the Year II and having the responsibility of caring for a son wounded at Maestricht and two girls (fourteen and five), and having been imprisoned in the Citadel of Valenciennes on orders of Representative of the People J.-B. Lacoste, he left the children with one Françoise Foubert, who was already taking care of six children. Upon his own liberation he took charge of the six orphans and lived with Foubert in the most virtuous of households.[83] The granting of a pension would be a way of re-establishing his honor.

Demands typically offered as justification for pensions age, infirmity, and financial need. Others were more original. Jean Cazabonne, *ex-juge* in Agen, seventy years old and hard of hearing, wrote in 1813 of hopes for retirement and his primary concern, that his eighteen-year-old son not be embarrassed by a father's mistreatment after forty-two years of service. He thought the result might be "some unhappy brawl."[84]

Pierre Jean François Chrestien, *ancien magistrat à la cour des aides de Paris*, wrote Napoleon on March 2, 1811, of his distinguished service going well back into the Old Regime, including reconstituting the archives of the Cour des Aides after a fire in 1776, and he appealed to the emperor by evoking the birth of the Roi de Rome.[85] When the widow of De la Buisse wrote for help in 1809, she referred to the new moment of peace as a propitious one for seeking government attention, and included his own memoir from around 1805.[86] In it, he referred to Napoleon's healing the wounds of France and presented himself as having sacrificed his being. He emphasized patriotic service and the liberal and electrifying ideas of 1789. He recounted having presided over a political club early in the Revolution but protested what he claimed was the subsequent degeneration of those *sociétés*. He then went into a long narrative of risking his life during the Terror. His was a Revolution easily reconciled to the rule of Napoleon.

Descombles, *magistrat de Nantes*, recounted a career that began in Old Regime institutions, including the Parlement de Bretagne, and took dramatic turns in the Revolution. His acceptance of a post of justice of the peace was a response to his fellow citizens' solicitation, but the Terror in the person of Carrier ended one phase of his career, and his wife's loss of wealth in St-Domingue two years later led him to reenter public service. He went on to express disappointment that his new post was two hundred leagues from his home in Nantes. For eight years he worked in Besançon, far from his family.[87]

Salvy Barthelemy, former *juge au tribunal civil de Gaillac* (Tarn), in a letter to the *grand juge* dated May 17, 1811, cheered Napoleon: "It remains for me to repeat, every day: *vive l'empereur*: long live his dynasty in desiring the continuation of your days and of your protection, in ordinary life, where I am returning."[88] Jean Ambroise Barrois, former *juge au tribunal de Dreux*, searched for the proper terms in writing the *grand juge*, the Duc de Massa. First he begged. "He throws himself in the arms of your excellence ... to present to his majesty the chart of his good and long services, as well as that of his multiple needs, ever more urgent." Then he identified his object: "The title of Honorary Judge and a pension appropriate to that title." And then he hunted for the right words: recompense, grace, hope, justice, protection.[89] Pacou, *ex-magistrat de sureté à Corbeil* (Seine et Oise), wrote in 1811 some lines of poetry to place beneath the emperor's portrait.[90]

Jeannette Catherine Goebbels, widow of Guillaume Willems, *juge suppléant au tribunal de première instance à Liège*, wrote "Her Imperial Highness Madame Mother of his Majesty the Emperor and King, named Mother of the poor and protector of the unfortunate by her August son the Emperor." It may have helped. Just over a month later, the emperor's mother's secretary wrote a supporting letter.[91] Another widow wrote of the need to have a personal intercessor. Marguerite Lansemant, widow of Jean-Pierre Pecheur, *président de la cour d'appel de Metz*, wrote in August 1809 both to the *grand juge* and the emperor. She tried again in March 1810, noting that she had heard from Monsieur Colcher, *législateur*, that there were no funds destined for widows of *présidents*, but that a petition presented by "a person of high repute" might work. In this case *l'architrésorier* would make the approach. She assumed that the marriage of the emperor was a propitious moment: "They say in Metz that all petitions presented to his Majesty the day of his marriage will be received."[92]

Royal weddings, like births, were traditionally auspicious times for the granting of favors, but the Napoleonic period also saw varied attempts at claim-staking. A *procureur* in Châlons-sur-Saône, Alba, wrote that he had fallen victim to an intrigue in Dijon, and proceeded to "unveil all the horror of my position." In one paragraph he described how, at the age of fifty-four, he was reduced to having no bread, with family to support and debts to pay. Then he described his status as third generation in the magistracy, from a family that had obtained its letters of nobility in 1673. The next paragraph described his quitting private practice for government service in the Year VI, the resulting poverty, and the charitableness of the emperor. He compared his own situation to those of other displaced *fonctionnaires*: "MM. Chamborre Juge au Tribunal de la Seine, le président de ce même tribunal, et Dechevannes Juge à celui d'Autun."[93]

Life histories involved work both inside and outside the magistracy. Jacques Gaudin, *juge au tribunal de La Rochelle*, was a man of letters as well as a judge. A former Oratorian, he had translated Plutarch, written on ancient and modern politics and history, and published a well-known treatise on the celibacy of the priesthood. Supporting letters in 1808 emphasized his age (seventy-three) and infirmities (difficulty urinating and deafness), and listed his judicial service, and one of his own demands summarized his life as "constantly occupied with useful works."[94] In a letter of April 29, the *procureur général impérial près la cour d'appel de Poitiers*, Béra, emphasized Gaudin's need to educate a particularly talented son, a thirteen-year-old math prodigy.[95] Leroyer la Tournerie, *juge au tribunal de première instance de l'arrondissement de Domfront* (Orne), recounted his early education, career in the magistracy, raising of his children, studies of Norman law, and publishing in the Year II a *Manuel des jeunes républicains, ou élemens d'instruction à l'usage des jeunes élèves des écoles primaires*, a sign of his revolutionary patriotism.[96]

The Restorations and intervening Hundred Days saw a series of scrambles that tested loyalties and complicated life histories. Jean Baptiste Belloc, former magistrate in Millau (Aveyron), demonstrated uncertainty but typical rhetoric in writing the *chancelier* on July 16, 1814. He spoke of losing his employment as a result of the "happy events that have all at once rendered to France her legitimate sovereign and the peace that has put an end to the diverse disastrous governments that have succeeded each other since the fatal epoch that covered our sad fatherland in shame and mourning." He went on to describe his own situation against the background of high politics and to claim loyalty to the Bourbons while describing continued public service. He wrote of traversing "the storms of the revolution with all the wisdom and moderation that are suitable for a true Frenchman." His service to the republic came at the behest of "the healthiest portion of our electorate."[97]

Negotiating political transitions became critical in some cases. Michel Fasse, former *conseiller à la cour royale de Bordeaux*, was retired in July 1816, but he told a story of loyalty to the monarchy despite continuous work across the succession of royal, republican, and Napoleonic regimes. He writes of having traversed the Revolution without participating in its excesses and manages to adopt the royalist term for Napoleon: "l'Usurpateur."[98]

A few magistrates got caught in the contradictions inherent in some of the legislation. The *ordonnance* of September 23, 1814, was supposed to have been clarified by the *ordonnance* of January 9, 1815, but in a complicated case, François Guerrier, who had begun his career as *conseiller au parlement de Metz* on June 18, 1781, and experienced a gap between 1794 and 1800, complained that his career was again interrupted by the Treaty of Paris (May 30, 1814), which eliminated his jurisdiction. By his calculation, he was owed a pension of one-half of his salary for more than thirty years of service. That his post no longer existed in September 1814 was not his fault. But the ministry read the 1815 *ordonnance* as requiring reference to the *décret* of September 13, 1806, and a pension of one-sixth his salary. He wrote at length and prepared "Observations sur l'ordonnance royale du 9 janvier 1815." While his analysis did not have the desired end, an internal memo of May 9, 1818, indicated it did make some impression on bureaucrats seeking guidance.[99]

It was one thing to walk through the minefield of revolutionary history. It was another when the bureaucracy's own failing complicated one's predicament. Baron Jean Marie Noël Fabre, former *procureur général près la cour royale de Montpellier*, was born December 28, 1750, retired February 9, 1816, and died February 28, 1819. In a letter of August 21, 1815, he claimed he had been confused with other Fabres, two of whom had signed the act of federation. They were not members of his family. An 1814 *Vie politique des Députés à la Convention* also confused him with another Fabre, an error that was then disavowed by the editor. Fabre admitted to having signed the *acte additionnel* because of pressing circumstances and having made decisions in order to maintain public tranquility.[100]

He followed up his demand with a request to be replaced by his son-in-law, Marc Antoine François de Gaujal, Baron de Tholet. Gaujal himself wrote the ministry, as did Fabre's son, Fabre Barral, who on August 20, 1815, addressed the problem of regime change and his father's behavior: "My father himself had had striking evidence of discontent by his superior authority for not having pursued persons who had shown themselves overtly hostile to Bonaparte." But Fabre's own demands under different regimes revealed him to be more of a weathervane.[101] On December 3, 1814, he not only claimed not to be either of the Fabres of the Convention Nationale but pledged his fidelity and devotion to the House of Bourbon; on April 14, 1815, he changed his tune. He admitted that he had signed, with the other members of the Montpellier courts, the Adresse au Roi, but he blamed it on circumstances, argued that the language of the address was not his style, and declared his faith and devotion to the emperor. Upon the second restoration, he again blamed circumstances when he wrote on August 7, 1815, that his signing the Acte Additionel was more "the effect of error or fear than any bad intention." He repeated his case with two more letters within the week.

Those who discussed revolutionary politics sometimes lined up on either side of a revolutionary-era debate, but often they placed themselves above the fray. Well-known political commitments were almost unavoidable. But the passage of time influenced the form of representation. Some identified with political principles, whether of the Old Regime or 1789. Others carved out a position of moderation for which they had been punished in one regime or another, or wrote more matter-of-factly about material losses. Thus, poverty, whether discussed in terms of monetary amounts or conditions of dependence, was explained in political as well as economic terms. Appeals to authority included mention of promises by ministerial administrators or statements of allegiance to the current (paternal) head of state. Expenses of educating children, of treating a family member's illness, of having had to move from jurisdiction to jurisdiction were recounted in considerable detail. Occasional demands from former priests made the point that they had no family support; many explained the sacrifices that came necessarily with government service.

A position of political moderation was key to the demand of Silvain Pepin, an Old Regime magistrate who served as *Député à la Convention Nationale* and the *Conseil des 500* before completing his career as *juge en la cour d'appel de Bourges*. He described his education, his legal work in the provinces and Paris, his enjoying the esteem of his fellow citizens, his collegial relationship on the Comité de Législation with Cambacérès, Merlin, Roger Ducos, and others, his large family, and his debts that contributed to a general decline in his standing. He reported that he had had ample opportunity to take advantage of his public position and enrich himself but had always refused. His first desire was for a new post, his second for a pension. Pepin enclosed his own printed "Opinion de Silvain Pepin, Député à la Convention Nationale, par le Département de l'Indre, sur le procès de Louis Capet; imprimée par ordre de la Convention Nationale," in which he explained that he had been absent for the vote on whether to judge Louis but favored an appeal to the people in the name of national sovereignty. He went on to explain the delicacy of his situation. For one thing, some of his official papers were burned in his house in Châteauroux by individuals influenced by "l'effervescence révolutionnaire" and confusing them with "monumens d'aristocratie ou de féodalité." But he also claimed a reticence to speak openly about health problems: a growing weakness in seeing and hearing and episodes of vertigo over the previous four or five years. Because the onset of the vertigo was preceded by severe headache, he was able to hide his ailment from others, including domestic servants. But the frequency had gotten worse in the course of a year, a turn that he attributed to the loss of a daughter.[102]

As we have already seen, the succession of regimes was lived intimately. Having retired on November 13, 1814, François-Siméon Bezard, *conseiller à la cour royale d'Amiens*, returned to service in the Hundred Days. The Second Restoration was his undoing, and his pension was suppressed in 1816. When he wrote again in 1830, he claimed that the pension was based upon withholding and, thus, his property. The ministry disagreed, saying that withholding only began on January 1, 1815, but it did re-establish the pension, referring to a law of September 11, 1830.[103]

Bezard was hardly alone in seeing possibilities of justice in the July Revolution. When the Bourbons were overthrown, a host of their enemies (or just people denied satisfaction previously) wrote again. Jean-Nicolas Méaulle's sons wrote in 1830, lamenting the fact that their father, a member of the Convention, exiled in 1816, did not live to see recent events.[104]

Yet many former revolutionaries did not have to await the 1830s to be rewarded. Indeed, those who failed to get pensions but allied themselves to the Bourbon cause were scandalized by the successes of non-émigrés and even revolutionaries (nonregicides) in the Restoration.[105] Slowly but surely a bureaucratic mechanism was being created.[106] But the personal accounts kept coming in. Pleas for help sought to grease the wheels of bureaucracy; sometimes they worked, but bureaucratic mechanisms were becoming more fixed.

One former *Procureur criminel* in the Meuse, Dominique-Christophe Bazoche, who was serving in the Chambre des Députés in 1816 referred to that body's own legislation and the justice minister's words of concern for aged prosecutors in demanding his pension. The passage spoke of loyalty, dignity, the king's justice, and right. He feared that if he were not properly rewarded, not only would his family suffer material consequences, but his reputation at home would be damaged.[107]

Some of the judges married two or three times. They were old by any measure, and they still had young children.[108] The cost of educating them was a common argument for aid. Their military service was also enlisted as an argument. Three sons or grandsons died or disappeared in Russia.[109] The priest who did not marry during the Revolution and consequently had no family support presented his continued celibacy as a virtue.[110] Another who married needed to support his family.[111] By contrast, local informants who revealed that another former priest had married a nun, abandoned her, and then set up house with another woman had some impact on the bureaucrats.[112]

Fraternity may have been a revolutionary ideal, but some magistrates distanced themselves from their own revolutionary brothers. For one Scellier, it should be no crime to have "as a brother a member of the too famous Revolutionary Tribunal of Paris."[113] One's own actions were accompanied by excuses. *Conventionnel* Poullain de Grandprey claims to have tried to save Louis XVI.[114] And referring to the critical day that brought down Robespierre, Thuriot remarked that while he may have been a member of the Committee of Public Safety, he presided over the Convention on 9 Thermidor and served the royal family well.[115]

It is a challenge to judge the sincerity of claims written in the heat of the moment. But we should remember that the "moment" refers to the reaction to a ministerial judgment and the triggering of memories of revolutionary *journées*. While passions may have run high in the early Restoration, the events of the Revolution were much less recent. Even those writing in the Year XI looked back a decade to the Terror, and those dealing with the early Restoration ministry were looking back twenty-five years to 1789. They had

had plenty of time to shape and reshape their memories, and revolutionary events were only one part of longer-term reflections on career and life course.

Life might have been melodramatic, but melodrama was also deployed in an instrumental way to obtain something of value, and pathos was clearly a device for making a more convincing argument. But dossiers sometimes included odd combinations of materials that added up to a pathetic case. Antoine Simon Lambert des Ardennes, *ex-juge de la cour d'appel à Metz*, was victim of the purge that followed a Sénatus-Consulte of 1808, and wrote multiple times through 1813. He described accusations of dishonesty and continuous conflict with his colleagues, which included disagreement over his applauding a line in a play concerning vindication in legal proceedings. In one letter he described waiting in vain to petition Napoleon in person when the emperor failed to stop at the temporary *arc de triomphe* set up at the entrance to town. A *littéraire* who cited Rousseau, Voltaire, and La Rochefoucauld, he even produced two versions of his own epitaph, one written soon after being thrown from a horse, the other following his recovery.[116]

In an original attempt at providing supporting documentation, Claude Lauxerrois, *procureur impérial près le tribunal de première instance séant à Tonnerre*, demonstrated a history of infirmity and important personal connections by including dinner invitations which he had had to decline for reasons of health.[117] Thus, he simultaneously leveraged ill health and a social network, something more than prosaic accounting or a formulaic claim of professional dignity.

The support of professional colleagues was more routine than that of patrons. In a letter of support dated November 15, 1815, Brochet de Verigny, the *préfet du Gers*, commented on the naiveté in the way Jean Joseph Abadie, *juge de paix de l'arrondissement d'Auch*, sings his own praises, but he assured the minister of justice of the accuracy of Abadie's testimony.[118] Brochet de Verigny may not have read all that many demands, as the language was not really unusual. Abadie began with his age (eighty-five) and deafness in seeking "the pension to which the eminent services he rendered society during his long career guaranteed him his rights." He described thirty-five years of Old Regime service as notary and prosecutor, ending with the Revolution, a "very limited fortune," and "a reputation so great and so extensive that he had earned the confidence of all the former Sénéchaussée." Then came revolutionary service that was only ended by people envious of his probity and virtue. In the election of justices of the peace, he received all votes save one, and then displayed "his impartiality, Enlightenment, patience, and severe probity." In appealing to the new government, Abadie referred not only to the restored dynasty but to the "Restauration de la France."

A postulant who had a heroic tale to tell might put the story in others' voices. Thus, in September 1811, Berthier, *ancien juge* in Tournon (Ardèche), told of coming to the aid of imprisoned Lyonnais, but he included their own memoir in which they described his interventions in Tournon and Privas. He mentioned his own ill health, but the crux of his demand concerned his providing innocent victims with clothing, sheets, and money, and spending entire nights consoling them.[119]

Event history has rarely been the province of historians of aging and the aged, but the history of events provides us with an opportunity to examine the workings of memory and the way in which historical circumstances forced awareness of one's own career and how it might end. Alan Spitzer has shown how political memory was deployed by politicians of the Bourbon Restoration. Memory and forgetting played important roles in political careers spanning various regimes, but they were also key to the aging self. Already in the late eighteenth and early nineteenth centuries, some individuals were constructing aging identities by looking back across a turbulent era and trying to make sense of it all.

Quite a few had played a role in notable events. Petit, former criminal court judge in Paris, wrote in 1811 of eighteen years of services including in Paris's fifth arrondissement in Thermidor, Year II, and during the reaction overseeing lengthy trials in Nantes. He went on to speak of trials of the *Septembriseurs*, trials having to do with the *journées de Vendémiaire*, the trial of Babeuf and his accomplices, the trial of the *machine infernale*, and the conspiracy of the Opéra.[120]

Some of the narratives referred not to the long-remembered events of the Revolution, but to less well known incidents. A former criminal court judge in Chartres, Etienne Simon Paillart, wrote in 1811 of Old Regime service followed by "revolutionary storms and a grave illness." But he was most specific about his preparation of the case of the criminal bandits known as the Brigands d'Orgères (Years VI and VII), his related travels throughout the Départements of Seine, Seine et Oise, and Loiret, his discovery of forty to fifty containers of stolen goods, and "the arrest of more than 80 brigands."[121]

Arguments often referred to justice, paternal kindness, right, equity, welfare, humanity, and need. A customs judge from Rennes argued that "distributive justice and equity agree to treat equally those who in the last three years had equal functions, ranks, and salaries." There was the former justice of the peace in Beaumont, arrondissement de Castelsarrasin in Tarn et Garonne, who does not want to retire. He only suffered, at age sixty-one, from a slight attack of gout, and asked: "Is there anyone in the universe who does not know that our august monarch Louis the desired who is afflicted with the same infirmities, doesn't cease to perform good services to his subjects. . . ?" Thus, a new version of the king's two bodies.

We have been examining the nature of postulants' arguments. Also important are the models of retirement they seemed to have in mind. One was the classic retirement to the country, to one's property. There is the humanist retirement to one's study, as in that of a former court archivist in Lille. His ancestors had performed that task for two centuries, and he wanted to continue to perform historical and literary labors. He claimed to have returned from exile in 1802, volunteering to take care of the local hospice archives. He enclosed some of his research and asked for support in his studies. But he received nothing, as he had not worked for the ministry since the beginning of the Revolution. Such a judgment was considered scandalous by some, who found it difficult to believe that a restored monarchy was favoring creatures of the Revolution over servants of the Old Regime. Another volunteered during his retirement to accept the functions of president of the tribunal of commerce of Brive. A former priest, who had become a judge during the Revolution, now wanted to return to the clergy, but while collecting a pension for his secular work. Others announced their poetic works, often including samples. A former censor, for example, offered reflections on freedom of the press. Another was reported to be writing obscene poetry.

We learn of a supposed colony of retired Frenchmen receiving pensions from a government agent in Monaco. We have tales of family woes, descriptions of the aging caused by difficult labors, including the sedentary labors of judges. While medical certificates were required to prove that disabilities had been caused by the work, some postulants claimed that their general deterioration, nothing in particular, ought to be proof enough. We learn of justices of the peace who have fallen from their horses or carts, no longer able to ride to the scene of a dispute or crime.

One judge asked if he should destroy his robe. He would rather not. The brother of the abbé Sieyès, Joseph-Barthelemy, after thirty-nine years of service, had too much difficulty reading in the dark of winter, even during daylight hours. There is the rich dossier of Claude-Honoré Antiboul, former magistrate from Toulon, whose life story reads like a novel. At least he wrote it that way. He told how he had saved the navy from a plot of prisoners of war and how he had fought against brigandage in his arrondissement. He has passed his retirement working a little, settling labor disputes among fishermen, and writing poetry. When he failed to gain a retirement pension, he opened a public subscription and advertised in the press.

Virtually all the well-known modern gerontological models made their appearance. Although the institutionalization of retirement was based largely upon notions of decline and disengagement, individual life-histories spoke of creativity and activity. And much of the first-person writing expressed a large dose of narcissism.

Some expressed a fundamental ambivalence. For example, Meller, *ci-devant président de la cour de justice criminelle du département de la Roer* (Aix-la-Chapelle), wrote the Duc de Massa from Paris on May 28, 1811, thanking him for his pension and expressing contradictory desires. On the one hand, he looked forward to the comforts of private life; on the other, he still desired to be useful to the public.[122]

Sometimes there was fear of the impact of retirement. Crevel, *procureur impérial à Neufchâtel*, wrote Fouquet, *procureur général impérial près la cour d'appel de Rouen*, on August 25, 1808, about one Martin, *juge au tribunal de première instance séant à Neufchâtel* (Seine Inférieure), that he could barely speak or care for himself but that talk of complete retirement might put him in his grave.[123] Fouquet followed up a week later that he was the senior judge in the area, that he had been a hard worker with a reputation for integrity and incorruptibility, but that a state of paralysis has existed for more than six months. Martin's own lawyer, Concedieu, explained the paralysis as the result of a fight in the woods on a hot day while he was serving as a forestry inspector. Still, Fouquet worried about how to broach the subject. In general, he thought, people in public life have a hard time adjusting to inactivity, and Martin was particularly susceptible to shock at receiving news of his retirement.

Expressing anger about being pensioned, Marquier, a *juge* in Perpignan, wrote in June 1811 of his fears of being "deprived of the means of providing for the subsistence of my family" and of being shamed. He explained his pensioning as a result of resentments stemming from "a dispute relating to two French individuals who had committed a theft in Spain [and were] wanted by the Spanish government under international law."[124] Fear of shame was also the principal theme in a letter of the *premier président de la cour impériale de Metz*, Voysin de Gartempe, on October 4, 1812, concerning Marchoux, *ci-devant président du tribunal de première instance séant à Vouziers* (Ardennes). Voysin de Gartempe wrote that Marchoux suffered from "infirmities that had occasioned a sudden mental derangement as a result of which he engaged in a few acts of delirium unfortunately too glaring" and that he desired recognition of his service "and to escape from suspicion of misconduct that stains *fonctionnaires* whom one sees return home at the age when they would seem to be able to continue functions that experience renders easier to fill."[125]

Maintaining dignity, an issue that exercised lawmakers working out public pension policy, was clearly important to individuals negotiating their own retirements, and that dignity evidently required fending off both tarnished reputation and bodily decline.

To sum up, the Napoleonic and early Restoration dossiers yield insights into the last years of professional life and memories of earlier political and personal crises. The range of themes is impressive. As the system became more regularized and bureaucratic, procedures became more fixed, the details of work were recounted down to the day, and the life histories adhered to more typical patterns. Dramatic stories of revolution and empire would begin to fade, but the language of magistrates' demands would borrow in subsequent decades from that turbulent period.

6
Changing Content and Expectations

Implementation of pension legislation combined with years of political and career experience led to the adoption of a language of right, and cries for help gave way to expectations of and demands for normal bureaucratic functioning. A close reading of a large sample of demands and simple quantitative analysis of themes confirm that shift but also reveal more precise changes in content and expectations. The documents also permit a comparison between male and female demands, but here we examine retiring magistrates' own choice of themes. In essence, men claimed entitlement with relatively early and increasing assurance, that assurance formed the basis for complaint, and the discourse of the magistrate became part of a broader self-understanding of the government *fonctionnaire*.

Patterns become visible as we cross three broad periods. The first, when the system came into being, can be examined through the first nine cartons in the series, BB25/30–BB25/38, from the years 1814–15; they include 283 usable files (out of a total of 390), of which 244 concern men and 39 women. Taking nine themes and dividing them by gender, we arrive at the following:

	Themes in Demands, 1814–1815			
	Men		Women	
Theme	Number	Percentage	Number	Percentage
Age	137	56	8	21
Career	237	97	36	92
Right	85	35	18	46
Honor	59	24	7	18
Politics	172	70	19	49
Favor	105	43	28	72
Need	155	64	38	97
Infirmity	101	41	8	21
Family	128	52	32	82

Entitlement and Complaint. David G. Troyansky, Oxford University Press. © Oxford University Press 2023.
DOI: 10.1093/oso/9780197638750.003.0007

Career was most important in men's letters, need in women's, although husbands' careers were also crucial for their widows' chances. Support for family was important for both, but especially for women. Politics played a greater role for men but a significant one for women as well. For both in this period, life stories were closely tied to public events. Revolutionary experience combined public and private impacts. They would be separated later, especially after 1830.

To see what happens over time, we can look at comparable numbers for the next decades. To do so, we will use the sample of six *départements*. Thus, for the period 1816–29, the themes can be charted as follows:

	Themes in Demands, 1816–1829			
	Men		Women	
Theme	Number	Percentage	Number	Percentage
Age	82	71	6	23
Career	115	100	25	96
Right	34	30	9	35
Honor	50	43	8	31
Politics	55	48	12	46
Favor	7	6	2	8
Need	42	37	18	69
Infirmity	63	55	5	19
Family	42	37	15	58

Looking at the next period, 1830–49, for the same six *départements*, dossiers running from BB25/122 to BB25/219 reveal the following:

	Themes in Demands, 1830–1849			
	Men		Women	
Theme	Number	Percentage	Number	Percentage
Age	62	63	15	25
Career	97	99	45	76
Right	73	74	46	78
Honor	25	26	4	7
Politics	12	12	1	2
Favor	5	5	4	7
Need	25	26	20	34
Infirmity	67	68	8	14
Family	19	19	11	19

References to politics and family leveled off in the approach to 1820 and then fell noticeably. Among women, right was rare before 1825, and politics rare after 1826.

The simplest observation is that for both men and women favor decreased in importance and right increased. Favor was at 43 percent and 72 percent for men and women at the start but fell to single digits subsequently. For women, favor disappeared after 1838, for men after 1836. At first politics went into gradual decline, then fell precipitously. For men the decline went from 70 percent at the start to 48 percent in the 1820s to a mere 12 percent in the 1830s and 1840s; it fell off after 1839, with a very slight increase in 1848. For women, politics was evoked in 49 percent at the start and 46 percent in the 1820s, but then it becomes almost nil (2 percent).

Need and family also declined in frequency of mention, a reflection of bureaucratization, a process by which time served was the key. However, infirmity increased for men, again something prompted by the system in many cases but also something men were used to revealing (41 percent to 55 percent to 68 percent).

Putting the data for men in one chart, we arrive at the following:

Percentages of Men Evoking Particular Themes in Three Periods

	1814–1815	1816–1829	1830–1849
Age	56	71	63
Career	97	100	99
Right	35	30	74
Honor	24	43	26
Politics	70	48	12
Favor	43	6	5
Need	64	37	26
Infirmity	41	55	68
Family	52	37	19

Age was always at least an implicit part of the dossier, but these percentages, always a majority, referred to explicit references to age. Career was a constant, often full of great detail. Family, need, and politics became less common, favor virtually disappeared, and right and infirmity emerged as important. Along the way, honor enjoyed a resurgence during the Restoration but then settled back to a quarter of the dossiers.

The shift from favor to right, as has already been suggested, was one of the big stories of the period, and it appears simple enough. But in particular demands the language could be blurred, and it was even possible to claim a right to someone's favor. Moreover, right itself might have referred either to someone else's will or to a more abstract principle. The former included the fairly mild "droit à la bienveillance,"[1] or "quelques droits aux bontés de sa majesté,"[2] or "droit à la justice de votre Grandeur";[3] among the latter there emerged the standard and more assertive *droit acquis* or even "un droit acquis et bien acquis,"[4] but also "droit précis" or "droits incontestables."[5] Right down the middle, or speaking old and new languages simultaneously, some spoke of a right to favor. The report on Barthélemy Fouque, *ex-juge de paix* in Tarascon, referred to both "droits à cette faveur" and "droit à la retraite."[6] In the dossier of Felix Cordier, favor was evoked but then replaced with justice: "cette faveur, ou mieux, cette justice."[7] As we move across the period, we see more and more assertions of abstract right or simple justice, but individual demands also multiplied the justifications.

Thus, a magistrate's right consisted of the sum of multiple factors; he might have evoked dramatic events and a "very violent fit of rage," but overall, "His age, his infirmities and his long services ... give him a solid right to the retirement pension that he solicits and that the law seems to accord him."[8] And in one magistrate's dossier, which mentioned the magistrate's daughter's mental illness, his uncertainty about whether he wanted to retire, and his problems of memory and eyesight, the *procureur général* wrote: "His right to a retirement pension has been in some sense implicitly recognized."[9] But recognition of that right was more than implicit when it was *acquis*, although Romer, in speaking of *droits acquis*, clarified that it had to be approved by the king with royal *ordonnance*. He could still have asked a person to continue in office if the ministry or local officials favored it.[10] Even under the July Monarchy, we find that devotion to the Bourbons will generally not be held against someone who has his *droit acquis*.[11]

A magistrate who presented himself as a victim of the Revolution wrote the king in 1816, blending praise of the king, self-presentation as a supplicant, and assertion of rights, but he expressed some ambiguity between seeming and incontestable rights: "by an effect of this beneficent justice that [His Majesty] has signaled each day since the happy and memorable epoch of his return to the throne of his fathers, to accord the supplicant the retirement pension to which his known services and sorrows seem to have acquired for him, in some sense, an incontestable right."[12] Right was still open to debate in the early 1830s only because of confusion over whether a judge had resigned his position and, if so, whether he acted for political reasons. Enemies had accused him of trafficking in his position, but the ministry determined that Antoine-Paul-Joseph Courmes, *juge au tribunal civil de Marseille*, had resigned for health reasons after thirty-six years of service. It was cleared up just before he died at seventy-eight.[13]

Politics was often evoked in the early years of the system. Sometimes it had to do with political principles and with the authors as political actors, especially when postulants expressed loyalty to the regime. For example, Revel de la Brouaize expressed in 1823 "a constant attachment to the true principles of the monarchy."[14] Similarly, Bruyas described himself as "retired to the bosom of his family" and his conduct as offering always "the guarantee of his love of order and the loyalty of his sentiments for his King and for his fatherland."[15] In 1828, Rivals de la Combe activated a long royalist memory, speaking of "my long services, and my inviolable devotion to the sons of St Louis, of good Henry, and of Louis the Great."[16]

A demand that presented the Bourbon Restoration as a revolution came from Mme Bruges, widow Zaiguelius. Her husband died in Russia or Poland in 1799; they had spent time as émigrés. She was imprisoned. Now she referred to the "salutary Revolution that we have just experienced."[17] Pierre Joseph Louis Magdeleine Debézieux, *ci-devant procureur du gouvernement près le tribunal ordinaire des douanes de Nice*, also spoke of restoration as revolution.[18]

By the time of the Restoration, and especially the July Monarchy, memories of the Revolution were already fairly distant. And political principles may have evolved. Lombard proclaimed loyalty and compared his plight with others' and named names. By 1830 he was rejoicing at the latest revolution and describing his patriotism as owing everything to 1789: "Today as my principles have triumphed and as I see a Citizen-King at the head of the State, I have confidence that justice will finally be rendered me."[19] Aligning 1830 with 1789 was also the strategy of Friant d'Alincourt, *juge au tribunal de Strasbourg*, who wrote the Garde des Sceaux, on December 1, 1830, "Old Patriot of 89, I have seen with the keenest satisfaction the principles of that epoch triumph and place at the head of the constitutional government Philip I as king of the French!"[20] Similarly, Lancelin, who had begun seeking his pension before the July Revolution, took the occasion in September 1830 to appeal to the new regime: "I am convinced that, under a beneficent Government whose principal basis is justice, my demand will soon be welcomed."[21]

The critical moments in people's memories varied. Villemoney, who spoke of the *malheurs de la Révolution*, was even more outspoken in his opposition to the empire. He claimed to have chosen resignation in 1807 rather than continue working for Napoleon, whom he described as a "monster."[22]

The key moment for Carpeza appeared to be 1791. There was a dispute about whether he had abused his wife—they divorced—and hastened her death and whether he had extorted money from his mother-in-law. He was accused of immorality and drunkenness. But even as his behavior during the Hundred Days opened him up to criticism, he was seen less as a Bonapartist than a liberal or *Constitutionnel de 1791*.[23]

How one behaved in the Revolution contributed to one's reputation and career, but other steps were also important. Mourrier was committed to revolution in 1793 but also, by some accounts, a *fédéré pendant les 100 jours*.[24] How do we understand the "true" politics of someone living through multiple regimes?

Continuities and discontinuities emerged from reconstructions of careers. The discontinuities were often presented as the result of being subject to others. Consider how one magistrate recounted political events and intrigue in processing memories. Sauty was considered in the Restoration an "enemy of the government," but he expressed resentment toward several regimes. He had lost wealth from *rentes féodales* suppressed in 1793 and a post in 1800, but was again removed from office in 1815. He referred to "secret authors of my displacement" and to his faithfulness to the laws of his country. He mentioned being removed from office by Bonaparte in 1800 and replaced by a schoolteacher. "Tired of being the sport of intrigues and passions," he moved from the Department of the Corrèze to the neighboring Department of the Haute-Vienne and established himself as a lawyer at the Appeals Court of Limoges. In 1811 he was named judge in the Civil Court of Limoges, an appointment he resented, as it meant giving up what had become a lucrative legal practice. Being removed again in 1815 hardly made him any happier. He had many moments and regimes of which to complain.[25]

One approach by postulants was to recount political decisions but then to explain them as either having had to do with the moment, and, thus, not necessarily characteristic of the entire career, or as typical of what everyone else was doing in a time of great pressure. As one put it: Yes, I was in the *chambre des représentants*, and I swore the oath to the government and accepted the *acte additionnel*, but so did everyone else.[26] In other words, it was about circumstances and norms. D'Anglancier de Saint Germain, in explaining gaps in his service from the perspective of 1824, referred explicitly to "the force of circumstances" and "the proscription that pursued former magistrates."[27] Similarly, Morel, accused of being a Bonapartist, claimed to have helped victims of the Revolution: Yes, I was in the *chambre des représentants*, but I had no "bad intentions."[28]

Sometimes a self-proclaimed victim of the Revolution just claimed to want "repose and tranquility."[29] And sometimes, as with Trémois, we hear that the individual opposed Bonaparte in the Hundred Days and that public opinion would support him.[30]

Sometimes it had to do with making comparisons with others. Comparisons with others may have had much more to do with rights and experiences than with anything having to do with politics.[31] Pierre-Suzanne-Marie Delamardelle, former attorney general in the Royal Court of Amiens, and the son of a magistrate (Guillaume-Pierre-François) in Saint-Domingue who had written on judicial reform, compared himself to others replaced in 1815. They had been granted retirement. He wanted it too. Born in Port-au-Prince, he was known to be familiar with the colonial world and, after retirement, was sent on mission to Martinique.[32]

Leroy-la-Cocherie compared himself with colleagues getting more support for less service and argued about the legislative basis of the amount of his pension.[33] Ailhaud, in 1827, argued that his "rights are equal to those of...," and he named lots of others. Describing a retirement in 1816, a return to service in 1818, and another retirement in 1827, he included a three-page printed biography, which served to illustrate his claim that he could not bear the cold of Picardy. Having begun in Provence, Ile de France, St Domingue (where he was a *commissaire* with the more famous Polverel and Sonthonax), and Aix-en-Provence, he found himself in Paris and then Amiens. In making comparisons with others he signaled an assault on his reputation.[34]

Life stories often included tales of victimization. Manel claimed to have been persecuted for his royalism.[35] Maret blamed his "hatred for anarchy and attachment to the old order."[36] Claude-Marie-François Puthod, *chevalier de l'Empire* since 1809, described himself as a reluctant revolutionary and compared himself with others who had gotten pensions.[37] He claimed to be looking well beyond his own individual case and even the narrower question of retirement pensions in a printed examination of how to indemnify French colonial refugees from Saint-Domingue.[38] This text, published in 1825, described the difficulty of arriving at an amount for each property that had been lost. After recommending the creation of a special commission, he concluded by blessing Charles X as "father" and "consoler." Such blessing was short-lived. After 1830 he condemned the Restoration and revealed himself to be a real weathervane. After several years of the Orleanist regime, he submitted an 1835 pamphlet critical of republicanism and warning about the dangers of freedom of the press. He had published a *Discours sur l'amour de la justice* in 1813, and the magistracy remained a source of continuity even as he negotiated changing political circumstances. No doubt he would have welcomed the Second Empire had he not died in 1844.

He was not the only Puthod to adjust to prevailing winds. François-Marie Puthod de Maison Rouge, well known for having produced pioneering cultural work as a member of a revolutionary-era commission on monuments, in the Restoration praised Louis XVIII as a new Louis IX.[39] That was a remarkable attempt at creating continuity over a very long period of time, an understandable strategy in legitimizing a restored monarchy. Some aging magistrates could opt for a similar strategy, but the successive regime changes created opportunities for missteps. Dutrone, in Caen, based his claim not only upon health (gout), poverty, and the need to support his family but on Old Regime service and his having been persecuted during the Revolution.[40] Nonetheless, he was let go without pension as the ministry saw him as a dangerous enemy with insufficient years of service. He had tried to emphasize his Old Regime loyalty and revolutionary-era arrest, but a more recently earned reputation trumped outdated loyalty.

The acceptance of a post could often be seen as a modest act of service or acceptance of an honor, but it could also be the result of an emergency situation. Thus, P.-F. Rousselin, having been declared a suspect, judged it prudent, if not necessary, to accept an appointment.[41] While the Restoration regime was wary of both revolutionary and Napoleonic creatures, often seeing continuity between those regimes, individual lives did not necessarily conform. Boisard presented himself as a victim of the Revolution, having lost a fortune, but he still found himself in difficult straits for having supported the Napoleonic *acte additionnel*.[42]

Monarchists complained when they found revolutionary creatures doing better than they. Baudard, *ancien conseiller du Roi*, was particularly prone to complaint.[43] He and others referred to the challenge of learning new laws. Other political principles were evoked in the aftermath of 1830, when some complained of victimization by the Restoration, and just after the Revolution of 1848, when republican beliefs were presented as reasons for earlier mistreatment.[44] Remembrance and deployment of political details, perhaps in part a simple function of the presence of documentation (even occasions for copying old documents), in part a function of critical events having been burned into memory, were used to normalize experiences and to construct an idea of public functioning.[45]

The idea of the *fonctionnaire* permitted the removal of lives from the political arena. But such a neat separation was not always so easily accomplished, as political power intersected with the magistracy. Nonetheless, as the bureaucratic system developed, magistrates emphasized service to the state and transcending politics. They were, in effect (and increasingly self-consciously), high- and intermediate-level *fonctionnaires*.

Life stories of *fonctionnaires* also appeared to be about cashing out particular forms of service, and in the first decades, there were attempts at negotiation. Jean-Jacques Gros wanted years of Terror and exile to count double.[46] His dramatic account was one of several on cashing out political experience. Barge de Certeau claimed persecution in the early Revolution in the Dauphiné and a return to office in 1795 but continuous attachment to the Bourbons and, therefore, wanted to count time he was a fugitive.[47] Similarly, Rieussec, saddened at being retired against his will, thought back to his arrest in the Year II, his time spent hiding in the country, and his constant adherence to the king; time of persecution, he argued, should count as time of service.[48] Such strategies were analogous to those of exiles seeking recovery of old properties.

Noel-Joseph Madier de Montjau, a conservative deputy to the Estates-General and *conseiller à la cour royale de Lyon* as of 1815, writing in 1829, recalled that he was going to go into exile in 1791, but that Louis XVI told him to stay in Paris. He listed critical *journées* and periods of the Revolution: April 4, June 20, August 10, Terror, 18 Fructidor. And he asked that deportation count like military service. He was refused, and his son, Joseph-Paul (himself father of Alfred, a revolutionary in 1848), eventually wrote the new Garde des Sceaux Courvoisier, thinking he would be more accommodating than his predecessor, Portalis.[49] Also relying upon the military model of doubling or tripling service in time of war, Devérité, whom we encountered previously, drew the parallel between the military and the revolutionary-era judiciary.[50]

While family was an important theme for both men and women, among men it was often about traditions of family service. Discussion of multiple generations of service combined memory of private ownership of positions with ideas of public duty.[51] Honor was also linked to the rhetoric of family and lineage, but family concerns also involved present and future needs to educate and support dependents.

Infirmity was moderately important at the start but became increasingly important across the period. For those who did not have the absolute right based upon sixty years of age and thirty years of service, it was essential, and medical certificates connected the infirmity to the service itself. These might have been as easily comprehensible as Fanget's gout, near-paralysis, and ulcers[52] or Lemaire-Darion's falling from a horse and fever.[53] Falling from horseback was part of eighty-year-old Liénart's story in 1827, along with incontinence and weak fingers of the right hand that prevented him from writing.[54] But arguments were made about less visible health conditions, such as the role of anxiety in revolutionary times. Thus, De Boisse, *Député de la noblesse à l'assemblée constituante*, claimed in 1823 that "the seven-year interruption had to do with a serious disease that was the result of fear and worry occasioned by revolutionary threats directed at him for having been a member of the departmental commission that preceded the siege of Lyon."[55]

Politics might still have been in people's memories, but a shift had occurred from political themes to themes of right and infirmity. A political phenomenon was becoming a more natural one. Just as pension legislation had spoken of the natural course of aging, so did individual claims. When Pazery de Thorame in 1827 "solicits a repose that nature commands of me,"[56] he seemed to echo the very language of parliamentary debates.

Finally, we should look at the management of these populations. In a sense we are dealing with human resources to be managed. At times we see it in the awareness individuals had of others, whether active or retired. At other times we see it in attempts to have particular responsibilities that were easier to carry out.

Jalabert, only fifty-two years of age but prematurely aged (*blanchi*), wanted an "honest retirement in an appeals court."[57] His demand illustrated a desire to transcend individual regime. He claimed others depicted him as having more affection for one than another. He resisted publicly taking sides. "They judged ill of me; they knew nothing of what happened in my heart." A victim of others' ambition, he lost everything in the *orage révolutionnaire*, but the more recent *orages de 1815* had made him a virtual leper. He should have been recognized as having honored the magistrature no matter the form of government. And he still wanted to serve, albeit in an easier post: "to live rather than to vegetate." To his mind, that was possible in a court of appeal.

The *chambre d'accusation* fit the bill for Jallu, who suffered from gastritis and rheumatism. He wrote on September 20, 1829, that a three-month leave to take the waters of Aix-la-Chapelle failed to improve his condition—he was even worse—but he preferred to die in office than give it up.[58] The *chambre d'accusation* was mentioned by Antoine Morand de Jouffrey, son of the well-known architect and victim of the Terror, as a less taxing assignment, but we learn from his 1822 case that it was impossible to place every old magistrate there.[59]

At still other times, we see the bureaucracy itself attempting to manage personnel. Thus, in considering Diverneresse-Lamarche, who had given up his trade as a clockmaker to become a justice of the peace, the attorney general said it would be bad for public morale to see him devoid of help.[60] And the attorney general overseeing Volbret mentioned "too intimate relations with ministerial officers" and the inadequacy of available funds.[61]

Some give us a window onto the preparation of the demand. Fouenet-Dubourg wrote in 1826–27 not only about having been incarcerated in the Terror but about having recently received help from two *employés* of Romer in preparing "l'état de ses services." They had given him assurance of two months that should have counted.[62] And there was some flexibility at times. Michel Dian, *conseiller à la cour royale de Lyon*, did not have enough years of service and seemed to have sufficient wealth, but the administration granted a pension in order to encourage retirements.[63] The administration said of Edouard Casimir De Burle, *juge au tribunal de première instance de Tarascon*, that by 1849 he had been in office too long; he suffered from apoplexy and paralysis.[64]

All concerned were developing images of retirement. Trie wanted to retire to la Grande Chartreuse. Perhaps he imagined conditions that would have permitted him to write. He had already produced a guide to Roman and French law. But Romer was critical of his legal knowledge and gave him bad marks, in effect confirming reasons for his having lost his post of *Substitut du Procureur imperial, tribunal civil de Marseille*, in 1811. Meanwhile, he was retired chez Bergasse.[65]

Papon was another who received low marks. He had been replaced because of supposed ignorance of the law. Yet he thought his plight resulted from political calumny. A former *doctrinaire* and brother of a historian of Provence, he turned to history in order to complete his brother's unfinished, hostile book on the Revolution.[66] He complained about having been posted to Monaco: "miserable rock, burned by the sun, where my eyesight weakened every day."[67] Pierre Antoine Maurin, *ancien juge au tribunal de première instance séant à Marseille*, wanted an "easy and honorable retirement."[68]

In some cases, the retirement might have been overdetermined, a result of both politics and disability. Senépart, a *juge de paix* in the Somme, was accused of bad principles, but others said favorable things. Even though he was not strictly eligible, calculations were made and his politics were excused.[69]

Thomas's retirement had multiple motives. He was considered an "awful man and doomed to public scorn. He voted for the *acte additionnel*. To dismiss as soon as possible." Portalis was more sympathetic, but also saw the need for his replacement: "aged and very gouty. His health allows him almost never to sit. . . . He is esteemed, but we think he ought to be admitted to retirement."[70]

We saw earlier that some magistrates expressed shock at being replaced. The correspondence with the ministry might take place on political grounds, but often it referred to health, need, and honor. Vassal reacted badly to being replaced by a younger person in 1817. He claimed not to be infirm and declared serious financial need. He had had to sell his library.[71] Grégoire de Roulhac, who had been mayor of Limoges in the early part of the Revolution but stepped out of political life before the most radical stage, was less careful during the Hundred Days. Still, such missteps were forgiven in correspondence in 1818.[72] The dossier of Joubert, father of the general who had died at Novi, evoked the cost of burying the son, but the key issue for the ministry was the father's health. He claimed not to have serious infirmities. The ministry thought otherwise.[73]

Even when the ministry had doubts about an individual's morality, the law might assure a pension. Hellouin, described as having no religious principles and having raised a son who had authored an antireligious brochure, "Catéchisme du Bocage," was replaced in 1824. He still got his pension.[74] In 1825 a magistrate accused of unethical behavior was still rewarded with a pension. Benoist-Deblinne's reputation for having rescued an officer of the Swiss Guard at the Tuileries on August 10 and sympathy for his having had his family château burned trumped accusations of wrongdoing.[75]

In the case of Laget-le-vieux in 1827, there were serious accusations about supposed wrongdoing, but there were reasons for the ministry to sympathize. During the Hundred Days he had supposedly been persecuted by revolutionary agents, and he had eleven children. Complaints were well known, but he was permitted to resign for reasons of age and infirmity.[76]

A year later, Poitevin remarked about the problem of applying a theoretically sound system to people whose careers happened to correspond to a turbulent period. In principle he supported the idea of a right earned at sixty years of age and thirty years of service, but his career and those of many colleagues had been interrupted. In future, there would not be a problem, but for now he proposed legislation that would permit eligibility at age seventy, with fifteen years of service.[77]

Seventy was a critical age, according to Demouchy, who wrote in 1829, "At this stage of life, moral and physical forces tend toward more or less rapid decrease." His letter described "more than 34 years of judicial and administrative services" as well as the loss of his wife, "who had managed their properties outside Compiègne."[78] But upon being told that there were insufficient funds, he expressed a willingness to press on.

It bears repeating that after 1830 appeals to right and claims of infirmity (for men) were on the rise while politics played a lesser role. We find individual cases of political missteps and punishment (and some magistrates voluntarily leaving office because they refuse to support a new regime), but the overall evolution is toward a more professionalized and bureaucratized system. Thus, Mollin's devotion to the Bourbons was not held against him, and his *droit acquis* was confirmed. Increasingly, people saw themselves as part of a functioning professional body.

It could also take time for officials to distance themselves from political battles and replace an ideological lens with a more purely administrative one. Thus, someone who was victimized in 1830 could have his claims received more favorably later on. For example, François Jean Alexandre Prosper Cabasse, *ancien procureur général près la cour royale de Limoges*, a man who had served thirteen years in Aix-en-Provence (and written about the history of the Parlement de Provence), almost three years as *procureur general près la cour royale de Guadeloupe*, and four months on a commission of the Naval Ministry organizing the colonial judiciary, found himself victimized in 1830. Health problems—doctors referred to gastrohepatitis, bronchitis, and spitting blood—required him to return to France from Guadeloupe, where he claimed to have worked to improve the situation of *gens de couleur*, and then to retire to Naples. The Revolution of 1830 occasioned the end of his career; he complained that the minister of justice in the second half of that year, Dupont de l'Eure, future president of the provisional government of 1848, was the "instrument" of his enemies. When by 1833 his health showed little sign of improvement, he called not for a new appointment but a pension. He wrote again in 1839. The ministry, having considered his infirmities and the parallel case of Morand de Jouffrey, granted him the pension in 1840.[79]

Fitting the profile of the victim of the Bourbon Restoration welcomed back in the July Monarchy was Pierre Jacques Vidard la Boujonnière, *juge de paix du canton du Dorat*. Fired in 1816, he was brought back in September 1830. But he found himself unable to continue and asked for a pension from the "Benevolence of our good king Louis-Philippe." He also tried to get his brother-in-law named as his successor, but that effort failed, and he only enjoyed the pension for the last four months of his life in 1835.[80]

Political adventure during the revolutionary "orage" or "tourmente" could flatten out as an unexceptional part of a long career. Adrien Maubant, *ancien conseiller à la cour royale de Caen*, exercised posts in the revolutionary era, but as one associated with the federalist revolt he was imprisoned under the Convention. Looking back at the entire career, the federalist episode could largely disappear after forty years in the same post from 1800 to 1840. It was mentioned in his documentation in 1826 but essentially overlooked in 1840.[81]

Pierre Barbier, *juge de paix du canton de Châteaurenard* (Bouches du Rhône), described himself as having "emerged pure out of the political turmoil." He found himself briefly out of favor in 1795, seen by his superiors as too attached to the "principles of the French Revolution" and then again "dismissed as a result of political events" in 1815. Born in December 1764, he returned to service in the July Monarchy, serving from 1831 to 1839. One of his demands described both the geographic and physical challenges of the post; it was hard to make his extensive professional rounds because of problems with his legs, urinary tract, sight, and hearing. The emphasis on infirmity was to some extent necessitated by his total years (twenty-seven) not quite reaching thirty, and he made the point that his return to service came when he was already quite aged. His original demand in February 1839 invoked the justice and equity of the king. He saw himself as having emerged pure from the political storm and claimed that his entire life demonstrated his devotion to country and attachment to "the august dynasty whose origin is entirely national, protectress of industry and French civilization." Clearly he had an idea of how to address the Orleanist regime. Or perhaps his notary knew in what terms to couch the demand. The notary Rouget wrote the *procureur général* Borély in October 1840 to speak of Barbier as "the Nestor of the patriots of St Rémy" and then in December to remind him of a conversation they had had in Aix.[82]

By the 1840s, a great many magistrates had had no professional or political experience of the Revolution. Born in 1792, Léopold Erasme Oberlin, *ancien juge de paix du canton de Soultz-sous-Forêts*, wrote at fifty-one in 1843 of his physical and mental ailments, including memory problems. Most of his fortune belonged to his daughter.[83] For Eloy Josse Ledieu, *ancien juge de paix du canton de Villers-Bocage* (Somme), whose service began in 1821 and ran to 1844, the emphasis was on proper standards of living. He was not impoverished, but the *premier avocat général près la cour royale d'Amiens*, Caussin de Perceval, reported that he was too poor to live honorably.[84]

Continuity was implicit in the dossier of Pierre Jean Baptiste David, *ancien conseiller à Limoges* and son of the previously mentioned François David. He had served in 1791–94, for some unstated period beginning in 1795, and then in 1801–15 and 1818–44. His own claim was very brief, as the procureur général Dumont-Saint-Priest wrote at greater length. At forty-seven years, five months, and sixteen days of service, he demonstrated continuity; if we include his lineage back to the Old Regime and his being succeeded by his own son, we see a good deal of continuity in a region long characterized by support for the French Revolution. Bureaucratization has won out.[85]

Those whose pension demands clustered around 1848 generally had no service in the 1790s. François Jacques Nicolas Doron, *ancien juge de paix du canton de Truchtersheim* (Bas Rhin), was said by Casimir De Sèze, *premier avocat général près la cour royale de Colmar*, to be suffering from mental illness. A letter of 1847, when Doron was all of fifty-seven, predicted that he would not last six months. In fact he died four months later.[86] For Antoine Emile Lepeytre, *ancien procureur général près la cour royale de Caen*, who had entered the magistracy in the wake of 1830 and felt the need to retire at age fifty-one, the problem was physical and environmental. He had already suffered from chronic irritation of the larynx in a previous post in his native south and now had difficulty adapting to the colder climate of Normandy. He wrote emotionally about what might become of him.[87]

When Joseph Pétiniaud, *ancien juge de paix à Pierre-Buffière* (Haute-Vienne), spoke of his being victimized by a Comité révolutionnaire in Limoges in 1848, he spent more time speaking of advanced age (almost seventy when replaced) and ill health (gastroenteritis and hemorrhoids).[88] While Pierre Courrent, *ancien procureur général près la cour d'appel d'Aix*, occupied his final post from March 1848 to January 1849, the year of revolution was seen less in terms of politics than sheer overwork. He could speak of around-the-clock labor during the "extraordinary crisis of ten months" and his failing eyesight.[89]

The year 1848 represented an important shift in the magistracy and its relationship to politics, as in so much else, but in the history of retirement it revealed the process of bureaucratization had taken hold. Over the course of the first half of the nineteenth century, the history of French politics had played its role, but it had become normalized in the late lives of an important group of professional servants of the state. No matter what their particular politics—and defining them might be problematic—they were all speaking the language of right, often comparing themselves to colleagues, and admitting to the ways in which they were human beings, subject to the aging process even as they might present themselves as heroes, victims, or innocent bystanders. Their careers had made them *fonctionnaires* with entitlements that transcended politics. Their distress was a reaction less to political rejection than to physical decline.

Scholarship on the nineteenth-century magistracy emphasizes periodic purges and the social evolution of personnel away from local notables toward middle-class professionals. Some local studies rule out expectation of retirement at the end of a predictable career. But even though retirement was not mandated at a particular age until midcentury, significant numbers of individuals made retirement a part of their lives. Even today, in a wide range of occupations, if we look closely we find people in a wide range of occupations who emphasize having been forced out and others who behave as if everything flowed from their own choice. Retirement was expected and chosen by some. For those upon whom it was forced, it entailed some retrospective refashioning and imagining what life's last years would bring.

The end of a career might have been brought on by removal in periods of transition. Less dramatically, some found themselves not being renamed to a position. But whether the cessation of activity was forced or voluntary, it led to a more routinized process of seeking and receiving a pension. And even more dramatic cases would be followed by such a process. The distinction between leaving at one's own initiative and being pushed could become blurred as the status of *honoraire* became more common. And such blurring might benefit all concerned. Individual histories and memories were subsumed under the rubric of retirement.

7
Gender, Widowhood, and the Limits of Entitlement

In the history of pensions and retirement, women have often occupied the margins either as dependents or as widowed seekers of recognition and support. Nonetheless, their demands, though less numerous, merit attention and comparison with male writing. Sampling men's and women's demands reveals important differences in the gendered nature of complaint and offers a sense of how things changed over time. Reading widows' demands also allows us to tease out how a particular group of women experienced middle and late life.

Degrees of entitlement were outlined in the original *ordonnances*, and widows' rights were worked out over time, but from the earliest correspondence matters of right were evoked either implicitly or explicitly. Women were less inclined than men to complain, whether because they were less confident in their rights as they themselves had not performed judicial service or because they were less equipped rhetorically. They sometimes echoed their husbands' political positions, but politics was often filtered through descriptions of practical and familial challenges. Widows whose own families participated in the magistracy could speak of honor and service. More commonly widows communicated need and identified what they took to be an appropriate standard of living. A few referred to their own occupations; many more spoke of their family histories and private experiences of public history.

The break in the life course that magistrates themselves discussed was retirement itself. Wives of course felt the consequences of that moment in their husbands' careers, but when they became widowed they were confronted with a differently gendered notion of the life course and often what might be considered middle age. Some contemplated impending isolation.

On September 15, 1815, fifty-two-year-old Marie Claire Julie Tattegrain, widowed for twenty days and looking ahead in Paris to a lonely old age, wrote the Garde des Sceaux:

> I was wife and mother, and here I am abandoned, without help and without support; my husband has just succumbed to an illness as long as it was painful; my older son fled his country when it was ravaged, and he is now living abroad. A last conscription has devoured my unfortunate younger son; he was employed, Sir, with his father, in the offices of your Ministry, and there his estimable qualities and talents were noticed by his superiors. It is from the fruit of my husband and son's labor that I received my subsistence and I was able to ease the pain of my ill health. Today in my frightful isolation, I have nothing more, absolutely nothing, to live on; and my misery would be complete, Sir, if I were not sustained by the hope that you will deign to come to my aid, by granting me a pension.[1]

She and other widows who presented themselves to the Ministry of Justice sought to take advantage of a provision in the pension ordinances of September 23, 1814, and January 9, 1815, that, like pension legislation throughout the revolutionary period, granted widows and orphans a share.[2] As we have seen, judges and other employees of the ministry had to demonstrate that they were sixty years of age and had worked for thirty years or had become disabled or infirm after ten years of service. Widows' fates depended upon their husbands' careers, to some extent on their material circumstances, and, on some occasions, their ability to elicit sympathetic responses from bureaucrats, officials, and others close to power. In such cases they might have activated professional and kinship networks.[3] The *ordonnance* of August 17, 1824, affirmed the widow's right to a pension if her husband had worked his thirty years or had already begun receiving a pension. She would receive one-third the amount of his pension, but at minimum one hundred francs. Widows learned over the period 1814–53 how to use the law and to represent their own predicaments in addressing the Ministry of Justice.

The years before the *ordonnance* of 1824 saw considerable uncertainty among widows about entitlement. Augustine Malfillatre, widow of Hippolite Dobignié, *Directeur des Domaines et de l'Enregistrement* in Anvers, wrote the king after having earlier been turned down by the Napoleonic

Administration de l'Enregistrement. Her husband, who died in 1813, only had twenty-eight years of qualified service, so she asked that two other years as *inspecteur* in Mons during the Directory be reinstated. But obviously he had not worked in Justice and was, thus, doubly ineligible. She presented her husband as a political victim, a man whose moderate principles were too much for "a republican government." She combined principle with name-dropping, asserting that the family's allegiance to church and king and "the losses and persecutions that she suffered during the Revolution are known by Monseigneur the Archbishop of Reims, who wishes to honor her with his esteem."[4] Amélie Marie Joseph Goguillon, widow of Claude Louis Sainson Michel, *ancien procureur général à la cour d'appel de Douai*, at least had the right ministry when she wrote in 1814, assuming she would be well received as the widow of a revolutionary-era prisoner, but she made clear that she did not really know whether she had a right.[5] With more self-assurance, Marie Jeanne Le Dem, widow Faucheur, called on March 11, 1815, for a pension promised by the September 23, 1814 *ordonnance*.[6] Magdeleine Cécile Delphine Justy, widow Fossé, wrote upon her husband's death in 1812 that the family had been left in complete indigence. Their older son served in the military, a younger son was in demi-pension at the lycée de Bordeaux, one daughter was at the maison impériale d'Ecouen, and another resided with her mother. One of her sons wrote for her from 1817 to 1819, asserting, "Our rights are real." When refused, he said his mother did not want to overwhelm the state but that she really needed help. He tried again in 1824, reporting that she had been taking care of her sister and mother, age eighty-six. When she wrote again in 1828, she referred to a desired life of honorable *médiocrité*. Administrator Romer was sympathetic, but Fossé had not been in office in 1814, and so the rules made her ineligible.[7]

Especially in those early years, officials contemplated potential acts of kindness. In June 1816 Marie Pauline Poulliande, widow de Laistre, appealed to the king, evoking his "august family." She wrote as a mother and spoke of her own career without specifying what it was and focused on her husband's death back in 1806, leaving their twin eight-year-old sons without a father. He had been at odds with the Napoleonic administration, and while she failed to gain the support of the Restoration regime, an internal memo remarked: "Perhaps we should at least address a polite response."[8] When Ursulle Jacquette Roullière, widow Boulmer, mother of four and grandmother of seven, asserted "my rights to your benevolence," Romer tried to help but was overruled.[9]

Things were clearer in the last years of the Restoration, but even in the 1840s widows might try to skirt the rules. For example, Héloïse Rose Honorine Gonet, née Schaub, born in 1804 and married in 1836, was widowed in 1844. In 1845 she documented a marriage of seven years, nine months, and one day and received a pension of 210 francs. But she remarried, September 1, 1846, and therefore became ineligible. This did not stop her from begging to have the pension continued. Her new husband was a businessman who had been widowed five months earlier. She claimed he had no fortune and was raising five children from his previous marriage; yet she must have imagined some benefit, as she revealed she had contracted the second marriage in the "unique interest of my poor children."[10]

The ordinances themselves determined some of the basic contents, but the variety of demands suggests room for individual self-fashioning. They blend genres of autobiography, family history, and national history, but compared to the writing of male postulants, women's narratives tend toward the matter-of-fact presentation of loss and need. They especially emphasize the challenges faced in family life.

An initial comparison between male and female demands that refer explicitly to family can be made from the first 252 career dossiers from all over France.[11] One hundred seventy-five (69 percent) include letters of men and women evoking private or family concerns, which vary from discussion of family losses in the Revolution to traditional family service to the state and loyalty to the house of Bourbon. Family travails include illness, poverty, death, guilt by association, the need to educate children, and the desire to avoid shameful dependence upon others. The royal ordinances and the developing bureaucracy required evidence of age, service, infirmity, and need. Seekers of pensions clearly had other things on their minds as well. Need came in the context of political events, economic losses, family traditions, and such intangibles as honor and dignity.

Until the bureaucracy became firmly established, postulants reviewed their lives by emphasizing the themes they thought would elicit a favorable outcome and helped them make sense of their world and of their entire careers. Forty of the 175 demands came from women (thirty-nine widows and one daughter). The following chart displays the themes taken up:

164   THE LANGUAGE OF RETIREMENT

	Themes Evoking Family			
Raised in 175	Men (135)		Women (40)	
Demands	Number	Percentage	Number	Percentage
Revolutionary losses or role	47	35	7	18
Poverty of the family	37	27	12	30
King's family and paternal solicitude	29	21	13	33
Tradition of family service	33	24	7	18
Dependence	28	21	10	25
Illness in family	28	21	10	25
Education of children	18	13	13	33
Honor of the family	22	16	3	8
Sacrificing family to state service	12	9	6	15
Moving expenses	16	12	0	0
Celibacy of priesthood (previous state)	6	4	0	0
Minister's family or paternalism	4	3	1	3

The gendered distinction between public and private life is evident. In addressing the ministry, the men spoke more of politics, honor, and even expenses incurred in moving from post to post. A third of the women sought the paternal support of the king and talked about the education of children. These differences are hardly absolute; it is more a question of emphasis.

Men and women spoke of family, but men made more of the continuity of a family's service to state, nation, or community.

Many of those themes are visible in the 1824 demand of Mme Françoise Pétrouille Bonhomme de Lapouyade, widow Senamand de Beaufort. She wrote on August 15, 1824, to the *garde des sceaux* that just before his death, her husband had demanded his retirement; a year and a half later, she hoped to share in the recompense owed him. A blind mother of four, she appealed to the minister's magnanimity: "You are the protector of the widow and the orphan, your administration is thoroughly paternal; and because of that I dare hope that after having verified the accuracy of my story, you will deign to grant me a pension or at the very least place advantageously my eldest son Pierre-Baptiste Félix Senamand-Beaufort, who has been a lawyer for eight years and whom his father destined to succeed him."[12] Thus, we learn of a desire for professional succession, financial need, disability, and a paternalist idea of the government. At first she was turned down because the husband had retired before the *ordonnance* of August 17, 1824, but the ministry overturned the decision in 1828, so she benefited for four years before dying in 1832.

Reaching beyond the rhetoric of family, our sample drawn from six *départements* of France, from 1814 to midcentury, permits a look at the evolution of broad themes evoked by women. The extended sample includes seventy-seven women, overwhelmingly widows, with just a few wives and daughters.

Percentages of Women Evoking Particular Themes in Three Periods			
	1814–1815	1816–1829	1830–1849
Age	29	23	25
Career	92	96	76
Right	46	35	78
Honor	18	31	7
Politics	49	46	2
Favor	72	8	7
Need	97	69	34
Infirmity	21	19	14
Family	82	58	19

It may seem odd that the theme of family declined in importance after 1830, but it makes sense when we recognize that the more organized and systematic the process, the less recourse to particular tales of woe became necessary. Favor too was less often mentioned, as was politics. The one theme that increased in frequency was right, another marker of recognition of a maturing process. But we should also dig deeper into individual demands.

Wives occasionally wrote for their sick or disabled husbands.[13] Widows and daughters usually wrote within weeks of the man's death, but the timing varied from ten days to several years. Three of the widows' dossiers no longer contain their letters. Forty-three of the widows who initiated demands provided evidence of age, which averaged fifty-seven years, ranging from forty to seventy-seven. Letter-writing continued if the first demand was not met or if circumstances changed. Age at death, known in twenty-three cases, averaged seventy years of age, ranging from fifty-five to eighty-three. Age consciousness varied, as sometimes a statement contradicted the evidence of birth and death records, but age, especially for women, may have been less a number than it was a quality. And the fact of widowhood was far more important than the attainment of any particular age.

Women's letter-writing undoubtedly stimulated greater self-consciousness, whether in middle or old age.[14] Writing for publication or even corresponding with a government entity was a male enterprise, but the need to put one's life into words stimulated new forms of self-presentation in women. Less practiced than the men, they nevertheless were asked to put pen to paper. Some of them dictated letters, and sometimes a nephew wrote in his aunt's voice.[15] A widow and her son might both testify that he could not afford to help her. Even when the letter indicates the solitary voice of the aging woman, there may have been an intermediary. But she was fashioning an identity in making the demand, and even while describing a life of dependence, compromise, and service, until the bureaucracy began to function more automatically she constructed an image of herself.

Widows and orphans provided a familial context for understanding their predicaments. Often they told a history of loss. Marie Joseph Seigneuret, daughter of a former magistrate, told of the consequences of her family's emigration as Catholics fleeing the Revolution for Spain in 1792.[16] Similarly, Mme d'André, widow Defranc, spoke of losing everything in the Revolution, of taking refuge in Paris, of devotion to the king, and of imprisonment in the Temple, La Force, and the Conciergerie in the period of 18 Fructidor. Her husband had been *conseiller au Parlement d'Aix* and in the *cour royale d'Aix*, the sixth magistrate in his family.[17]

Also emphasizing revolutionary victimhood, Anne-Marie-Thérèse Demeuré, widow Oberlin, spoke of loss and mentioned that her own lineage also included magistrates. Her husband had died in 1819, and now, as she wrote in 1820, infirm and responsible for an unmarried daughter and septuagenarian sister, she wanted more than the one hundred francs in aid she had been receiving. She wrote the Duchesse d'Angoulême, January 30, 1824, of her own family's contribution to the Old Regime magistracy in Lower Alsace and losses in the Revolution. Her husband's family suffered the "same calamities." She drew a parallel between her family and her husband's, and appealed to the royal family.[18]

Revolutionary-era loss and family tradition were themes of Catherine Barbe Simon, widow Herrmann, in 1826. Her husband's father had lost a pension from the Grand Chapitre de Strasbourg as a result of the Revolution. It was a post her husband had had hopes of inheriting. She also provided details of the family's remaining property and her own need for charity or a place in a hospice if she did not receive a pension.[19]

Mme Leblanc de Chatauvillard (Adelaide Victoire Denise), widow Chaillon de Joinville, despite a lack of eligibility, wrote of the "goodness and justice of the King" and provided data on lost property and investments and the consequences of emigration.[20] Mme Bruges, widow Zaiguelius, wrote of having emigrated and been imprisoned for twenty-two months. She said her husband had died in 1799 in Russia or Poland and asked for aid following the Restoration, which she considered a "salutary Revolution that we have just experienced." She presented herself as someone who ought to be rewarded in the Bourbon regime, but, in the name of humanity, she also spoke the language of "droits acquis."[21] Marie Madeleine Rey, widow Gonet, wrote in November 1814 of losses in assignats and her small income from some houses in Nîmes and knew to refer to legislation of September 23, but her husband had died at fifty with only thirteen years of service, and perhaps most decisively the death had occurred back in March.[22]

Revolutionary-era losses were presented with greater drama by Mme Legier de Beauvais, widow Saulnier, writing from the rue des Rosiers and recalling her husband's Old Regime service in the Parlement de Paris. Having mentioned family members killed in revolutionary violence and herself being heir to a woman strangled in the Ile Saint-Louis on October 24, 1794, and being forced by brigands to renounce that succession, she claimed she had been feeding a friend who had saved members of the royal family. Dambray thought she had no right but nonetheless recommended her to the king.[23]

A few women presented their husbands' careers as the men had done, evoking dramatic events. Consider Mme Jeanne Brenot, widow Vitet, writing in 1825. She described the "glory and danger of the siege of Lyon," imprisonment, and the absorption of the family's wealth by her husband's debts. Age and need for repose had led her husband to retire, but he still desired to engage in humanitarian service, offering legal aid to those in need and serving on the municipal council. She considered continuing his pension for her as "a grand act of justice," appealing as well to the "goodness of the King."[24]

Some dramatic revolutionary-era stories were less about politics than about the sheer difficulty of life. Marie Jeanne Henriette Humbourg, widow Besson, spoke of revolutionary-era property and financial loss in France and Saint-Domingue that had affected her husband before their marriage. His career had taken him from Digne to Saint-Domingue, Minden, Strasbourg, and finally Aix-en-Provence. He returned from Saint-Domingue in 1794, and the next year they married in Strasbourg. He accumulated debts, and there were costs of last illness, burial, and inventory when he died in 1825 at age seventy-eight. His earlier history and their peregrinations together became part of her story, including attachment to the Bourbons and being forced by need to accept a Napoleonic appointment.[25]

Some heroism was not necessarily political. Clarisse Lecuyer, widow Monier, described in 1826 her thirty-nine-year-old husband's working himself to death. As she wrote (and Romer copied): "He has perished, victim of excessive work and a pleading of five hours, at the closing of last year's sessions.... This effort produced a chest irritation that no remedy has been able to heal and to which he succumbed after six months of suffering."[26]

As time passed, loss and heroism were presented in a post-revolutionary context. Frédérique Marie Madeleine de Reck, widow of Joseph Quentin Leroy, *juge de paix du canton d'Albert* (Somme), told a pathetic tale of a large family (fourteen children, of whom eight survived) uprooted, farm buildings and crops burned in 1827. She estimated losses of thirty thousand francs and reimbursement of six thousand by the *caisse départementale*. Her husband had received thirty-seven wounds in military service under Napoleon; a bullet remained in his chest, and then two accidents in 1842, including one fifteen days before his death, delivered the final blow. The youngest two daughters were ill, and the widow, born in Nuremberg, had trouble retrieving her *acte de naissance*. We have a sense of how far we have come from the Revolution when we note that her twenty-six-year-old son, witness to her death in 1844, was employed by the Paris railroad.[27]

In some cases, former colleagues of a magistrate tried to help his widow. Marie Anne Laure Talandier, née Meyrignac, was widowed in 1844. Her late husband had been *president de chambre à la cour royale de Limoges*, and his brother attempted to obtain documents for her. The *procureur général*, Dumont-Saint-Priest, wrote for her, referring to need and a sick child. He also evoked concerns not only of the magistracy but more generally of "the elite of the population of Limoges."[28]

A stroke affecting the right side supposedly brought on by forced intellectual labor led to the 1835 retirement of Jean Henri Bellidentis-Rouchon, *ancien conseiller près la cour royale de Lyon*. His son wrote for him because of his paralyzed right hand. A year later he was dead, and Verne de Bachelard, a *député du Rhône*, tried to intervene for the widow, Mme de Labastide, widow Rouchon.[29]

The widow of Auxile Joseph Olivier, *conseiller à la cour royale d'Aix, chevalier de la légion d'honneur*, Elisabeth Toinette Emilie Olivier, née Barbier, who reviewed her husband's career, including his taking on responsibilities reinstalling members of the tribunal after the Revolution of 1830, claimed to speak for her husband's colleagues in 1845: "This magistrate whom it is not appropriate for the widow Olivier to praise, but whom his superiors and colleagues esteemed as one of the most enlightened and most worthy, died *after thirty-three years, six months, and seventeen days* of judicial service."[30] But no pension could be continued when she remarried after a couple of years of widowhood.

The women displayed little of the elaborate culture of complaint in which the men indulged. Men's dossiers bulge with letters seeking sympathy, constructing tragic or melodramatic life histories, justifying past decisions, and exposing their physical ailments to the gaze of both medical practitioners and government bureaucrats. The ministry demanded proof of illness, and both men and women complied, but the women were much less expansive. They had some notion of what they deserved in their station of life, and after an initial period of uncertainty their letters stated the facts and appealed to the appropriate ordinances, but their demands contained much less melodrama, and they rarely made the kinds of comparisons with other women that men routinely made with other men. An exception was Françoise Eléonore Lesouef, née Sangnier, who claimed that another widow, Gautier, had received half, not a third, of her husband's pension.[31]

Women were learning to make their claims. Catherine-Françoise Barbette Delignereux, widow Grisart, made her case matter-of-factly. Her husband had been an *employé* who died right after retiring. Her language was not elegant, but it did speak of his *honnêteté*, a quality that harkened back to the Old Regime. She wrote from Paris on January 26, 1815, appealing to the *chancelier*'s justice and humanity and reporting on her poverty, her fifteen-year-old daughter, and the fact that her late husband had known he would not live to reap the benefit of his pension.[32]

Eugenie Ursmarine Prisse, widow Pillot, mentioned the debts her husband had left.[33] Thérèse Bouteille, née Fouque, widowed at sixty-four in 1834, appealed simply to "justice and welfare." She died in 1842, age seventy-two.[34] Rarer was the old-fashioned language of favor employed as late as 1838 by Mme Pallu de Sourdé, widow in her early seventies of the late *Président du tribunal de Rochechouart*, Dupuy: "I dare expect this grace from your justice and your goodness."[35] Equally unusual was the more philosophical and revolutionary rhetoric of 1832 from the sixty-seven-year-old Marie Anne Louise Françoise Piquet, widow of Antoine-Paul-Joseph Courmes: "You have proclaimed 'the power of the law as the basis of stability of human societies.' Out of this conviction, I lay my humble prayer on the steps of your popular throne." Perhaps she wrote those words, but at one point the letter pointed toward a male writer (*Pénétré . . .*).[36] Perfunctory letters stating a right and those that were little more than lists of accompanying documents were becoming common in the late 1830s and 1840s.[37]

In 1848, Adelaïde Flore Duval, née Maressal, used a form that directed the widow according to whether or not her late husband had already retired and offered a blank place for services and the formula for determining the pension. It referred to a circular of April 4, 1831, asking the *procureur général* to give an opinion of the person's health. Remarking that her husband's pension had run out upon his death, she wrote about her own personal right that had consequently come into being. They had experienced forty-six years, eleven months, and twenty-four days of marriage, and he had received his pension for his thirty-one years, eight months, and twenty-seven days of service, enjoying it for eleven years. Now was her turn. One of the witnesses upon his death was a son-in-law with whom they were co-residing in Amiens. Another witness, friend, and neighbor was mayor of the city.[38] Perhaps he had encouraged the language of right.

The demand of Marie Thérèse Hamelin, née Kretz, revealed a widow's new awareness of and need to manage money in the mid-1840s. She was born

June 18, 1798, married in 1819, and widowed November 27, 1845. She wrote King Louis-Philippe, claiming she had been unaware of her husband's debts. Evidently her entire estate amounted to 993 francs, 70 centimes, upon which return at 5 percent yielded 49.68 francs, not enough for herself and two children, and she was getting some help from kin and friends. The dossier reveals the shame brought on by her economic condition. According to the *procureur général*, she had acted out of amour propre in initially disguising her state and overestimating her income at two hundred francs and, thus, receiving nothing on the first try. Both she and the *procureur général* spoke of the need to protect magistrates from becoming a public spectacle. The procureur reported that she had the "enjoyment of a small garden and two small rooms that she took care of while renting the rest of her house to cover taxes." All that remained was fifty francs of net revenue. According to his doctors, Stoebel and Brèche, Monsieur Hamelin, *juge au tribunal de Schlestadt*, had succumbed to "a disease of the liver and stomach" resulting from his hard work. That may have helped on the next try.[39]

It is evident from these early nineteenth-century sources that aging Frenchmen in one particular segment of society complained much more extensively than aging Frenchwomen. Perhaps men complained more often because their rights were more secure, while women's "rights" were more dependent upon the mercy of the bureaucracy and demonstration of need. Yet such demonstration grew less important as the system developed. The more essential point may be that while differences over rights resulted in different self-images and bases for comparison, the possession of rights was contested and the experience of making claims in writing itself led to different kinds of self-images.[40]

Historically widowhood was a much more important category than chronological age. It had a drama that aging itself did not. This is not to ignore the historical existence of women who never married but to recognize the moments of crisis in past and present and the limits of our sources. It was the fact of widowhood that made these women eligible for support, never age alone; however, they could mention their old age as contributing to their predicament. The historical literature on widowhood in the early modern period offers an ambiguous status. Abandonment and isolation were the lot of some, but for those with sufficient resources, widowhood might have brought important gains. Widows might have an unaccustomed sense of authority and agency, and thus have the status of "honorary men."[41] But it should be recognized that a significant amount of that authority came to those who could actually perform the work that their late husbands had done. Thus, businessmen and skilled artisans might leave widows able to act in their places. It was not so simple for widows of magistrates who had no opportunity to take over their husbands' functions. The best they could hope for was professional succession passed down to a son or economic security derived from family wealth. Or we might view widows' demands as assertions of mature senses of self.

When widows wrote, they discussed the deaths of husbands and their new needs, especially those of raising and educating children, as they tended to be younger than their late husbands. The presence of young children compounded the challenge, but established children might be in a position to help. Remarriage, as we have seen, could bring some security, but it was hardly routine, and it would involve sacrificing any pension that had been awarded.

Never-married women do not exist in my sample, except for a few daughters, who played a role in the care of retired fathers. Victoire-Catherine-Désirée Auber wrote in 1821 at age forty-three and complained of an incurable tumor on the stomach. Three brothers were scattered and unable to help. Her mother's death in 1787 left her caring for her infirm father, who had ended his working career in 1816 because of age and failing eyesight. In her fifties, she would arrive in the Hospice de Charenton, staying at least two years for mental illness, but no more is revealed.[42] Nevertheless, the challenge of aging confronted her as much as it did her father.

Olwen Hufton famously defined the eighteenth-century French economy as one of "makeshifts."[43] She was referring both to women and to laboring classes in general. Most families in the magistracy were obviously much better off, but they also found themselves having to improvise and make do. Revolutionary-era losses were real, and *juges de paix* and *employés* generally came from modest backgrounds. Moreover, some widows found themselves far from their places of origin and even belonged to what we might call sandwich generations, providing rather than receiving support both up and down.

The issue of residence tells us something about the functioning of the system and the vagaries of women's lives, including the consequences of following family across boundaries. Elisabeth Sophie Deubler, widow Rautenstrauch, found herself in the 1820s having to demonstrate that she was still French. Supposedly a resident of Strasbourg, she spent much time outside France. She claimed never having renounced French citizenship, but the ministry wanted to know where she paid taxes (*contribution personnelle*). According to the *procureur général près la cour royale de Colmar*, she had been living with her oldest son in Trèves, had not kept her lodging in Strasbourg, and did not pay taxes there. She had, however, retained a simple pied-à-terre and, thus, claimed part-time residence, but when she came she lodged with her niece or her sister. Her younger son was working in Cologne.[44]

Being caught in a challenging generational sandwich, Mme Bricaille, widow Delaroche, asked for help in 1832. Her husband died at sixty-eight. She was forty-eight, saddled with eleven children and an octogenarian mother, and she herself had lost her right eye. She died in 1839 at the age of fifty-five.[45] Similarly, Marie Anne Henry, widow Le Bretton, was caring for her infirm father, eighty-two. He was said to have been ruined in business because of the revolutionary maximum. She wrote the king that two of her three sons were killed in war: "mowed down ruthlessly in the field of carnage, and of the destruction of French youth. After these two sacrifices too painful for a tender Father, and for which he has never been consoled, he was forced successively to cede his fortune; such that upon his death, his wife found herself denuded of all type of resource and means of existence." The third son had served in "the Royal volunteers of Normandy" and counted on a post that would allow him to live in "honest mediocrity." She evoked the needs of her eighty-two-year-old father, the happy memory of a comfortable existence during her husband's life, and her "confidence in the paternal welfare of your Majesty." According to the Tribunal civil de Falaise, her late husband had helped families affected by the deportation of priests and émigrés.[46]

Sometimes a grandchild played a role aiding a grandmother. Thus, the grandson of Marie Catherine Roccofort, widow Riboud, wrote in 1835 to a friend in the ministry. She was already in her seventies when her husband, already pensioned, died.[47]

Two of the widows and one daughter referred to their own careers, thus creating subjects for dramatization independent of their husbands or father. Only the daughter, Ysabeau Delavergne, whose father was *ancien premier greffier de la grande chapitre du Parlement de Paris*, explicitly mentioned work, soliciting either a pension or a "Stamp Office with which I might subsist and end my career protected from need." She referred to two hundred years of service and to incarceration as a royalist.[48] In using the word *carrière* some widows seem to have referred more generally to their lifetimes. Marie-Pauline Poulliande, seen earlier appealing directly to the king in June 1816 and looking back at how her husband had been disgraced in 1806, sensed that her "career will be no longer." Claudine Perrin, widow Mottet, wrote of her desire to avoid ending "my career in sadness and misery."[49]

Referring to another form of work, Mme Sophie Wilhelmine Philippine Heyler, widow of a *juge de paix* in Strasbourg named Zeyss, mentioned having founded a school. But her case was complicated by her remarriage. The claim of need began in 1828, and in 1848 she tried to obtain an increase in her pension. Her letter gives a good sense of the impact of events (occupation) and career choices—especially in border regions. She had two sick children, and he had four others from his first marriage—this was his third. She was born in 1787, married in 1819, widowed at age thirty-nine in 1827. So her first pension was to help her in middle age. Her first marriage was to a pastor, the profession of her own father. Her life story took a turn from association with a religious calling to service in the lower ranks of the judiciary. And she had to reach back to a different sort of work earlier in her second husband's life. She reported in 1848 that her husband's service in the Republic was not counted in the Restoration. He was already *commissaire de police* in Strasbourg in 1793 (when she was only six). She was now sixty-one and wanted enough to live on. She compared herself with other widows and dreaded having to resort to begging. Her husband had said just before dying that the *patrie* would come to her aid based upon his service.[50]

Another way of glimpsing women's work is to look again at the men's dossiers and see what happened when magistrates themselves found themselves widowers having to fend for themselves. Seeking retirement at seventy in 1829–30, Demouchy, who had worked a total of thirty-six years, ten months, three days, and who would die at eighty-four in 1845, wrote, as we have already seen, about having lost his wife, who managed his properties, and how he anticipated a rapid decline in his moral and physical strength. When he was told that pension funds were not yet available, he concluded it would be better to continue serving but still wanted to be replaced at the start of the next year.[51]

Women's own dossiers reveal husbands' past plights as well as their own. The widow of Sr Beuzelin, a *piqueur* killed by a horse of the *grand juge*, had been granted a pension by Régnier, but it finished when he died. She mentioned having worked for the Prince de Conty for thirty-three years.[52] Anne Converset, widow Roullois, wrote, "In order to live I have worked but today I am 72 years old and my strength betrays my intention," but she did not specify what work she had done.[53] Her husband had received a pension in 1808 but died in 1810, so she was ineligible. Nonetheless, she referred to the king as a father, expressed shame at the prospect of beggary and despair, and recounted being a victim of robbery during the second invasion of France. She tried to argue that her husband's hard work had led to his infirmity and death. She was turned down in 1815. Her nephew wrote for her in 1819, and she tried again in 1831 (at seventy-two). Marie-Hyacinthe Duvillard, widow Garlan, was more specific about what she might do. When her husband died in 1815, she wrote that she wanted a portion of the *pension viagère* he had been awarded in 1810 or "a place as *femme de confiance*, or some help."[54] Three sons had been killed in military action at Wagram, in Prussia, and in Salamanca. In 1825 she tried again, referring to a "pension to which she thinks she has a right. She dares count on the character of goodness and the spirit of equity that animate and direct your Grandeur [garde des sceaux]." She touched upon right, kindness, and equity, but the answer remained no.

Widows' work ranged from different categories of remunerative work to unpaid but expected family duties. Historical scholarship on the Old Regime has described a wide range of women developing effective (and affective) networks of mutual support, friendship, and service.[55] Among aging women in general, images of friendship and sociability coexisted with those of isolation. Self-images presumably drew upon this range of possibilities.

Some of the widows described their labors at home, but of course it was the husbands' contributions that mattered to the ministry, whose rules made of assistance a form of recompense for public service as well as right. A key element was the attempt to present the husband's career in a coherent and meritorious way, but coherence was at a minimum in an era of revolution and war, and merit might take a variety of forms.

Several widows complained of a world in which the rules had changed. Personal ties to formerly powerful people no longer guaranteed support. Some complained about bureaucratic details. Widows of clerks protested their not being eligible for a pension, and widows of judges who had retired before the adoption of the ordinances or whose total years of service fell short of the required thirty demanded special consideration. They could try to claim that their husbands' service was as continuous as that of the exiled Louis XVIII.

Many letters began by describing the death of the husband. They praised his qualities, often indicating that he had emerged from public service poorer than when he had begun. This was a common trope of older public servants themselves. One sometimes wonders whether such a complaint in the voice of the widow provided a window into disappointment over lack of financial success, but more common was a united front in dealing with the twists and turns of the era.

After an initial delay in 1815 and a rejection in 1818, sixty-five-year-old Aimée-Gabrielle Chaillon, widow Letourneux, seventeen years a widow, was still describing to the Orleanist regime in 1831 her late husband's sacrifices.[56] She resented the policies of the anti-revolutionary Restoration and appealed to King Louis-Philippe. She contested her long-ago rejection, pointing out that her husband had died on September 16, 1814, one week before the issuing of the royal *ordonnance* of September 23. She called this a "frivolous pretext." Trying to find a silver lining, Romer pointed out in 1831 that she had revenues exceeding what she could have gotten as a pension anyway. She was not the only one to complain about the absurdity of adhering to the letter of the law. Marie Catherine Largentier, widow Baudoin, made demands from 1814 to 1824, when, at age seventy-two, she wrote exasperatedly, "As if women who have had the sorrow of becoming widows before this epoch did not have the same right to the grace of his Majesty."[57] She was blending the languages of favor and right but focusing on more intuitive notions of right and recompense.

Combining stories of revolutionary-era loss, generations of service, and more recent selflessness, Catherine-Elisabeth-Françoise Loyson told a tale of "prison, seizure of property, dispossession," and totaled 159 years of service of her husband, his ancestors, and hers. She turned his life into a heroic narrative of service to humanity after the Revolution had put a temporary halt to his judicial career. He directed military hospitals before returning to the judiciary from 1801 to 1813, when, still serving the sick and wounded from the Russian campaign, he came down with a nervous fever and died a premature death.[58] She mentioned that the family had been victimized by the Revolution and evoked their devotion and fidelity to God and king.

Widows were looking back at their own family histories as well as their husbands' and trying to communicate an appropriate standard of living after a period of remarkable change. One widow wrote that she and her daughter had no need for "a brilliant existence, but at least the assurance of not seeing themselves deprived of the things most indispensable for life."[59] Her own identity was tied to that of her husband, whose understanding of public service included values of probity and integrity. He had lived modestly, soberly, saving what he could, scorning luxury, and now it was not enough. Notions of integrity and responsibility for raising a child were part of her sense of self and of her overall case. For many, surviving awful events in the past contributed to the self-image. One Mme Rey recalled a house that also served as her husband's office of the Régie générale of Brignolles pillaged in March 1789 (with the guilty subsequently amnestied) and a daughter frightened out of her wits by the events of the Revolution, which led the family to flee Aix-en-Provence.[60] Descriptions of debts, losses, lawsuits, and living in a pension or furnished room contributed to portraits of victimization.

The biggest challenge for the widows was that of ensuring the education and settlement of children. Marie-Anne Picquart, widow Bourgeois, and two daughters described how revolutionary losses had put their family in "a precarious state . . . that rules out an education suitable for the grandson of a magistrate."[61] Augustine Gabrielle Collet, widow Rivoallon, widowed in 1812 with eight children, emphasized her children's education as having led her into debt, but her sons' early careers had not improved the situation. "The eldest of my children might still serve as protector and support of his mother . . . wounded and taken prisoner in Spain, he languishes today in the prisons of England! He implores my help, and I can offer him none!" Imprisoned in January 1812, he was released in May 1814, but he remained unemployed. The second son earned little in the naval administration in Brest, the third was a jurist, the fourth a medical student making slow progress.[62] She was being coached by *Conseillers de la Cour de Rennes*, her husband's former colleagues, who contended she had a *droit acquis*. She did not. When she wrote for the last time in 1822, she had been residing with a son in Brest, still claiming a right.

Neither the widows nor the bureaucrats seemed to think that adult children should be forced to support their elders, but the letters occasionally reveal such dependence or at least efforts of mutual support. Mme Bourgarel, widow Charlier, had two sons in public service in the *contributions indirectes* who had experienced reduction in pay and status.[63] Other widows reported adult children facing economic challenges themselves. A justice of the peace in Strasbourg wrote in favor of Catherine Marguerite Osterrieth, widow Spielmann:

> The eldest of her children was married to Mr. Beyer, businessman of Paris, who was obliged to cease his payments, to leave Paris and go to Le Havre, where he is seeking his fortune, the second was in business with his brother-in-law, but after the failure could no longer stay, came back here and finally left for Frankfurt in the hope of making a living there: the third is a young

man ... [The mother] wanted to retire to her daughter's in Paris, but the misfortune that has occurred to her son-in-law put an end to that idea.[64]

Some left the city to live in rural retirement; sometimes this permitted elderly women to live out a dream of returning home and completing a cycle of life.[65] Others continued to travel, dividing time between city and country. For example, Marie Etiennette Tournon, widow Riolz, alternated between a residence in Lyon and with her daughter and son-in-law in the commune of Charvieux, canton de Meyzieu, arrondissement de Vienne (Isère). Wherever she found herself, she was able to tell the story of her husband's work on jurisprudence, including a collaboration with Prost de Royer on a *Dictionnaire de Jurisprudence*. She wrote of her husband's refusal of positions until after the Terror, when he had an opportunity to re-establish order.[66] Widows' itineraries revealed choices as well as vulnerability.

Even as they presented themselves as vulnerable, widows asking for help sometimes presented an image of domestic authority and of responsibility for kinship networks. Marie Louise Ulrique Meunier, widow Vasse St Ouen, wrote in one letter of her eighteen grandchildren whose parents were far from being well off. A son, father of two, was missing in action in Russia; one son-in-law, also father of two, had been blinded, while another son-in-law, a notary and father of six, had been ruined by the war.[67] Her husband, whose career lasted fifty-five years, had been granted an Old Regime pension, but it was suppressed by the Revolution. She gave financial details and described how "the public and private life of Mr Vasse St Ouen was that of a perfect Magistrate." She went on about "his scrupulous equity, his attachment to morality, to religion and to his legitimate Princes." The losses were horrifying, but the very telling of the story indicated the central role of the old woman in her family. Weakness and strength, despair and courage coexisted.

The 1830s saw much more recourse to bureaucratic forms. For example, Catherine Agathe Jullien, widow Madier-Montjau, used a "bordereau des pièces à produire par les veuves de magistrats ou d'employés du Ministère de la Justice pour justifier de leurs droits à la pension (Imp. Royale, avril 1831)."[68]

Having to deal with the growing bureaucracy, however, may have alienated many of the widows. Seventy-seven-year-old Geneviève Adelaïde Bruxelle, widow of Justice of the Peace Dumont, lived in a *pension bourgeoise* on the Left Bank of the Seine in 1827, and told a tale of some confusion in dealing with the bureaucracy, perhaps even of dementia.[69] She had received a derisory pension in 1815. In 1819 she asked that it be raised to

350 francs, stated that the supplement was "necessary to her age and her infirmities," and requested that the increase be retroactive to 1815. The attempt failed. Later, in 1827, she wrote again, recalling encounters over twelve years with bureaucrats who sometimes asked her why she had not requested money owed her and at other times claimed to know nothing about it. She remembered noticing one bureaucrat telling another not to say anything, and she grew suspicious. Her story involved some mental wandering back and forth in time. The official interpretation, indicated in the margin of her dossier, was that the original pension was only a favor, as her husband had died before September 23, 1814, and that the old woman "does not possess all her intellectual faculties." Nonetheless, her letter seems more than rational. She had a couple of adult daughters. A twenty-two-year-old unmarried daughter resided with her, but sometimes she lived and boarded with another daughter, wife of a soldier, with two young children of their own. She knew the language to use for her husband's qualities, noting "that he distinguished himself by much zeal, enlightenment, equity, gentleness, impartiality and the most noble disinterest; that he made great sacrifices to raise his numerous family, and that his only wealth was the confidence and esteem of all his superiors and fellow citizens."

Bruxelle's death in October 1829 was reported by her grandson, a thirty-four-year-old bronze founder, and her son-in-law, a sixty-six-year-old locksmith, living at separate addresses on the Right Bank. Did the aged widow maintain independence in her *pension bourgeoise*, or was she abandoned? Was she declining into senility and imagining conversations or conspiracies? It is impossible to say, but the very effort of formulating a series of demands forced her to turn her life into a narrative.

Others also created narratives that interpreted their husbands' careers and described their own plights. Marguerite-Josephine Martin, widow Igonel, recounted how after twenty years of service in the ministry her husband was "forced" to take the advice of his doctors, and they moved south. He received a position in Marseille, but he died after two years of "continual suffering." The municipal authorities of Marseille supported her request for a pension, and she returned to Paris, but she had obtained nothing after twenty months.[70] Like so many other wives, she had been vulnerable to changes in her husband's career and health, and she found herself more vulnerable at his death, but she comes across as no mere victim. She had evidently headed the household and learned to deal with the appropriate authorities.

When Marie Françoise Simplet, widow of printer Jean-Joseph Puntis, found herself widowed in 1812, she faced the common challenge of having to raise three young children and the less common memory of the Egyptian campaign. By the time she wrote Napoleon on May 6, 1815, they were ages ten, eight, and four, and the time was hardly auspicious to be writing the emperor. The source of the family's financial difficulties was not only her husband's death but also a loss of property abandoned by him in Egypt, probably before their marriage.

[She wrote] that in the year 6 of the Republic, her husband was called by the Government to fill the place of overseer (*prote*) at the printer established in Cairo in Egypt . . . that he filled these functions until the moment when the French were forced to evacuate Egypt; that during his stay he had acquired for 53,000 Medins some national property, consisting of a garden called El-Matiaby; on which were planted 179 trees, as many dates as others; that he had built on this land for more than 36,000 Medins buildings that he had leased to Citizen Simon, *limonadier restaurateur* following the army; that the Commissaire ordonnateur des guerres Duprat, having found this land suitable to put the ambulance of the Army, had cut down the trees for palisades.

She offered to present a contract of sale for 30 Vendémiaire, Year IX, but pleaded ignorance of the value of Egyptian money and relied on "the justice and paternal goodness" of Bonaparte.[71]

We may be dealing with a case of frustration when the wife of Dutrone, seen by the ministry as a dangerous Bonapartist and enemy of the Restoration government, wrote also on April 12, 1816, while he was still alive, asking that he be reappointed to judicial functions, then on July 15 that he receive a retirement pension.[72] He claimed to have been persecuted in the Revolution, but his personnel report of June 10, 1817, was held against him. His wife came alone to Paris to plead his case.

The possibility of asking for help gave aging women in a privileged sector of French society the opportunity to present their lives, make use of available images, and develop new self-images. Letter-writing reveals images of the aging self that have something in common with what literary critics have found in autobiography, another kind of writing that combines formality of genre with the pose of authenticity. Autobiographical writing is always artificial.[73] Moreover, the literature on women's writing suggests an even more problematic cobbling together of identity and self-image.[74] If that is true for women who wrote for publication, it is probably also true for those who were moved to write only in time of emergency.[75]

It was through the development of a bureaucratic system designed to benefit men that widows gained the right to present themselves for support by the Ministry of Justice. They provided life stories that revealed a variety of self-images. The widows' self-images depended partly upon how they had viewed themselves earlier in life, when their identities were subordinated to the demands of their late husbands' careers, political commitments, and health as well as the needs of their children. They tried to retain a sense of where they stood in a changing society and to worry about establishing the next generation. The new challenges of widowhood and aging taught them how to make claims of an evolving state bureaucracy that tried to treat them equitably, but inevitably some women felt abandoned, while others were rewarded. As a result, aging women used a language of pathos—though this was not nearly as pathetic as the language of men—to present an image of both vulnerability and responsibility. They wrote out of need, but their writing also revealed strength and limited authority.

Widows' self-images, while sometimes expressing greater and greater isolation, often placed them within familial and neighborhood networks. To some extent, they aged among friends, but they also aged while their children were still maturing, and they tried to ensure continuity of the magistracy from one generation to another, even as the language of public service and meritocracy was imposing itself on their world. When they spoke of public service, they referred not only to their late husbands' careers but also to those of their own fathers and sons. Public service was a male activity, but a certain spirit of service flowed through the female line as well.

The widows called for help by projecting images ranging from vulnerability to self-confidence. Religious aging is conspicuous by its absence. Widows of judges and the officials they addressed had this-worldly issues on their minds. The widows were exploring new territory in the experience of women. Their concerns emphasized private life over the public sphere, but the opportunity to write about both spheres developed out of their redefinition across the revolutionary and Napoleonic divide and contributed to an apprenticeship in women's self-expression.

As we have seen, half of the women in the early period had politics on their minds. A somewhat smaller number referred to right. Many more discussed family. After 1830 the political became far less important, but right became increasingly common, a depoliticized sort of entitlement. The correspondence also became more routine, and demands were accompanied by printed forms. Overall we see a shift from seeking sympathy (for need, family, and political experience) to documenting right.

To apply the language of recent sociological investigation into gender and aging, women and men diverged in relying upon an ethic of need or an ethic of justice.[76] To some extent they relied upon both, but nineteenth-century widows resemble more recent populations of aging women in emphasizing the former. Their commitments in the private sphere were characterized by continuous availability to meet familial expectations. They operated according to social temporalities defined by their husbands' careers, their own reproductive schedules, and expectations concerning the establishment of their grown children. In some cases, opportunities for remarriage complicated their situations and altered the balance between need and justice.

Ethics of need and justice coexisted, and seekers of pensions deployed the language of both. Widows were always dependent upon the rules that were designed primarily to reward their husbands in the spirit of justice. Knowing something of widows' vulnerabilities clarifies not only their own experiences but also what had accrued to magistrates as a matter of right.

Conclusion

Right and Memory in the Shadow of Revolution

This book has woven together elements derived from multiple historiographical contexts. As a social history of the life course, old age, and retirement, it owes a debt to social and demographic studies of past populations as well as family-history studies of households and responsibilities for care; it builds upon labor-history studies of work, exit, and dependency, and policy histories connecting law and regulation to realities on the ground. As a cultural history of representations of the aging self against the backdrop of an evolving national historical narrative, it goes beyond simple illustration to a focus on deeper meanings and constructions of the aging self, including the gendered, aging self. As a political history of changing regimes and anticipations of welfare-state formulas for determining pension rights, it follows those who have tried to make sense of the interplay of state actors, generations, and interest groups. As an institutional history, it involves not just the creation of a bureaucracy but also appeals to that bureaucracy by individuals who understood themselves as deserving a reward and constituting a professional group.

The subjects of all those histories labored in the shadow of the immediate revolutionary and Napoleonic past. So it makes sense to consider briefly how treatment of their stories aligns with recent trends in studies of the French Revolution, especially those that have developed the idea of revolution as civil war.[1] While many of my characters were caught up in such conflict, they expended a great deal of energy trying to claim that they had risen above it, even ignoring or denying the evidence that implicated them. The permanence of the state and state service as well as shared political, familial, and professional memories enabled their efforts.

Another key trend has been to conceptualize the French Revolution as a war of independence.[2] To a large extent this reflects the influence of historical studies of the United States and the Caribbean, which loom large in Atlantic-world histories, but even parts of France have been seen as seeking independence from Versailles or Paris. To be sure, some individuals seeking pensions made arguments about their independence as magistrates, but in general they demanded to be seen as having played a role in the nation and state, whatever its form.

A third trend has been to globalize French revolutionary studies.[3] Those magistrates who had served in occupied and imperial territories told stories of hardship, displacement, heroism, and service; for them serving France involved serving a global state. We have seen individual cases of service in Italian and German territories and of family investments in Saint-Domingue and Egypt. Empire offered both opportunities and risks, and it linked individuals and families to far-reaching networks.

A fourth trend has been to examine family and community networks over generations in the construction of identities, an approach that makes the French Revolution one part of a longer story focused on property and family trajectories. For example, the families in Brittany studied by Christopher Johnson constitute a bourgeoisie establishing itself through kinship relations over two centuries, and the complex kinship, community, and property networks centered on Angoulême and explored by Emma Rothschild extend across five generations.[4] This work does not quite have their chronological reach, but it shares their presentation of the Revolution as a chapter in a much longer story.[5]

Historiographical contexts matter, but this study of career and retirement has identified its own set of issues. It has focused on claims of right as careers in public service came to an end, on uses of the state by individuals, on the development of bureaucracy and a kind of standardization of the life course, and on ways of presenting the self, making it visible to government officials but presumably also reproducing self-presentation that was simultaneously occurring in families and communities. And it was made possible by the survival of ministerial dossiers created upon receipt of requests for pensions. Aging magistrates and, in some cases, their widows presented documentation of a career, complete with proof of time served, letters from physicians and surgeons, and demands that took the form of life reviews that deployed a rhetoric of service, of need, and of right. Often it was an emotional language, but over time it grew more and more routine. A formula of thirty years of service and sixty years of age set the ground rules, but for those who had become infirm before those conditions had been met, a case could still be made if the infirmity had been caused by the work. Thus emerged a discourse of the maladies of the sedentary professional life.

Postulants painted verbal self-portraits and presented their own lives in letters and forms. The book has explored the rhetorical strategies of their letters and even their look when, for example, a neatly scribed narrative was accompanied by a scrawled plea for help. One concern in many such letters, as in parliamentary debates over pension policy, was the potential impact of the visibility of the aging magistrate on his reputation and on that of the magistracy in general. Letter-writers sought honor and recompense; they contributed to a cultural shift from favor to right. And they warned against letting the public see an aged *fonctionnaire* abandoned, in decline, and in need of charity. Such aging individuals pioneered a territory more and more people would occupy in the twentieth century and beyond.

At the simplest level, this book has been about the invention and implementation of a pension system in post-revolutionary France. It fits in a longer history of social policy that may be understood in French, European, or even global terms. This account pushes back the usual chronology, which tends to privilege the late nineteenth and twentieth centuries, but it also looks ahead to the democratization of retirement.[6] Whether we are looking at relatively privileged magistrates in the Restoration or miners and railroad workers in the later nineteenth century or citizens of all ranks in the twentieth, we recognize various ways that individuals assumed rights and imagined a reward after a period of labor.

Equally importantly, we have examined the intersecting histories of the life course, individual families, and politics. Lives were intertwined with local and national affairs. Individuals and cohorts looked back at careers across a turbulent period of French history and gave meaning to their lives in making claims built upon documentation, argument, memory, and emotion.

The search for supporting documents was a part of the process. Public entities, attempting to deal with individual demands, created and examined them, and public servants, anticipating the rest of the population, made use of them. In a country that maintained a relatively large public sector, the *fonctionnaire* became the model for the citizen, more so than the elusive bourgeois, although such categories might well have overlapped.[7] And bureaucracy became an essential element of society.

In the establishment of a working bureaucratic system, postulants themselves made arguments that were rooted in legislation, notions of both implicit and explicit right, and a sense of their careers' significance. They had probably learned not just from their education and broader culture, but also from a host of people who had justified themselves in their courtrooms. The back-and-forth between individual and ministry, and the evidence of colleagues' successes and failures, reached beyond particular cases to institutionalize norms.

That process grew out of historical experience mediated by memory. Individual and family memories jumbled Old Regime, Revolution, and the regimes that followed. Memories were adapted and marshaled in order to argue for pension rights. Stories and rules developed in tandem with each other. Before time in service could alone justify a reward—it would eventually do just that—individuals presented memories of past regimes, of dramatic political events, of military service or occupation, of the deaths of children, and of the loss of property. Putting such memories to work expressed a certain late-life personhood in a bureaucratizing world.

Emotion, linked to need, desire, and sense of self, played a role in that memory-work and in the exercises in self-presentation that made their way to the ministry. Even as politicians debating policy discussed the shame that might redound to retired magistrates who were refused support, individuals made claims that also warned about potential shame. They did so in an emotional register that came easily to a great number of them. The more bureaucratic the system became, the less individuals would have to display such emotion. Whether through individual demands or collective debate, French magistrates and politicians were seeking ways of avoiding shame and maintaining professional and personal dignity.

The history of retirement pensions in subsequent eras and other places involved some of the same principles. Documented lives and policy arguments resulted in rules that tried to lessen the importance of individual historical memories and emotions or of outliving one's ability or desire to work. But at critical moments, such memories, whether of the Great Depression or the Second World War, played a role in jump-starting the rational systems of the welfare state. In the story we have told, it was the *orage révolutionnaire*, administrative efforts under Napoleon, and formal changes in the Bourbon Restoration that contributed to a new logic of the life course and a sense of *droits acquis*.

Revolutionary and post-revolutionary conceptualization of the life course involved a shift from favor to right. The story is obviously more complicated, as postulants blended the language of favor and personal connection with the notion of right or entitlement. Even the idea of reward for service was open to modification in a society of citizens with growing expectations. Magistrates thought of themselves at least partly as still belonging to a corporate body, even as they adopted a broad language of human rights and put the emphasis as much on the physical and mental challenges of a medicalized late life as on the state's rewarding particular services.

Postulants presented themselves both as heroes and victims. They bragged and they complained. In making retrospective sense of history and their role in it, they described the passage of time, the construction and succession of generations, and how a career might appear from one or another terminus. Sometimes they second-guessed earlier decisions. Often they justified having been political weathervanes. And always they were experimenting with strategies for making claims of right and social debt in a presentation of self. They were making language work for them. They came to know what future generations and other social groups would also have to learn in making initial claims of right, that even social systems that were supposed to operate in machinelike fashion might require forceful argument, rhetorical support, and piles of documentation. Argument and rhetoric became less important in the period of widespread pension rights and the social-security era, while documentation remained central. But the late twentieth-century questioning of the welfare state made argument and rhetoric again essential in defense of social rights.

The final drafting of these pages was undertaken as President Macron and the French public debated the pension system, which had developed both out of individual arrangements with the state and national ideas of the rights of citizens. It was completed in the shadow of Covid-19, whose disruptive and deadly impact also prompted debates over the relation between state and society, individual reflections about life and death, and a historians' debate over the proper historical analogies (1930s, fourteenth century, French Revolution, 1918, First World War) for understanding how we pass from one period to another. In an era of dramatic change, the transition from period to period matters, but individual and collective lives have a way of connecting and transcending them and, in advanced age, making sense of them retrospectively. In this book we have had access to numerous people who found themselves in a position to recall their lives for government officials and anyone else who might listen. They deserve our attention.

When we do pay attention, we recognize that they were a diverse lot ideologically who could combine complaint about their bodily and financial situations with assertions of right based both in service and humanity.

What I've described as a step toward the logic of the welfare state, thus, came not from one particular regime or one particular ideological camp, not from a purely abstract notion of humanitarianism, but from people's lived experience of aging and history. To be sure, revolutionary-era and post-revolutionary-era notions of right were essential to this development, and subsequent generations would find arguments for extending retirement rights in more particular ideologies and periods of crisis, but individual arguments may have been most convincing when people recognized a shared experience of aging and accepted a shared language of humanity. To work that out would require another book. To achieve it more fully in this world would require even more.

Notes

Preface

1. Among the works on lawyers and magistrates are studies of judicial organization and functioning such as Robert Allen, *Les tribunaux criminels sous la Révolution et l'Empire, 1792–1811* (Rennes: Presses Universitaires de Rennes, 2005), Emmanuel Berger, *La justice pénale sous la Révolution: Les enjeux d'un modèle judiciaire libéral* (Rennes: Presses Universitaires de Rennes, 2008), and Hervé Leuwers, *L'invention du barreau français 1660–1830: La construction nationale d'un groupe professionnel* (Paris: Editions de l'Ecole des hautes études en sciences sociales, 2006); prosopographical studies such as Vincent Bernaudeau, *La justice en question: Histoire de la magistrature angevine au XIXe siècle* (Rennes: Presses Universitaires de Rennes, 2007), Pascal Plas, *Avocats et barreaux dans le ressort de la cour d'appel de Limoges, 1811–1939* (Limoges: Presses Universitaires de Limoges, 2007), and Didier Veillon, *Magistrats au XIXe siècle en Charente-Maritime, Vienne, Deux-Sèvres et Vendée* (La Crèche: Geste éditions, 2001); and the collection of articles on justices of the peace in Jacques-Guy Petit, ed., *Une justice de proximité: La justice de paix 1790–1958* (Paris: Presses Universitaires de France, 2003). On *fonctionnaires*, see Jean Le Bihan, *Au service de l'État: Les fonctionnaires intermédiaires au XIXe siècle* (Rennes: Presses Universitaires de Rennes, 2008), and Marc Bergère and Jean Le Bihan, eds., *Fonctionnaires dans la tourmente: Épurations administratives et transitions politiques à l'époque contemporaine* (Geneva: Georg, 2009). On the history of bureaucracy, see Ralph R. Kingston, *Bureaucrats and Bourgeois Society: Office Politics and Individual Credit in France, 1789–1848* (Houndmills, UK: Palgrave Macmillan, 2012). For my own contribution to the history of emotion, see David Troyansky, "Émotion et carrière: Demandes de pension et récits de vie de la magistrature française post-révolutionnaire," in *Émotions contemporaines: XIXe–XXIe siècles*, ed. Anne-Claude Ambroise-Rendu, Anne-Emmanuelle Demartini, Hélène Eck, and Nicole Edelman (Paris: Armand Colin, 2014), 233–241. On pension requests from writers and *savants*: Jean-Luc Chappey and Antoine Lilti, "L'écrivain face à l'État: Les demandes de pensions et de secours des hommes de lettres et savants (1780–1820)," *Revue d'histoire moderne et contemporaine* 57, no. 4 & 4bis (October–December 2010): 156–184.
2. For various approaches to exiting the period of "the Terror," see Roger Dupuy, ed., *1795, pour une république sans révolution* (Rennes: Presses Universitaires de Rennes, 1996; republished by OpenEdition Books in 2015); see also James Livesey, *Making Democracy in the French Revolution* (Cambridge, MA: Harvard University Press, 2001), and Andrew Jainchill, *Reimagining Politics after the Terror: The Republican Origins of French Liberalism* (Ithaca, NY: Cornell University Press, 2008). On overcoming trauma,

see Ronen Steinberg, *The Afterlives of the Terror: Facing the Legacies of Mass Violence in Post-revolutionary France* (Ithaca, NY: Cornell University Press, 2019); on literally burying the dead, see Erin-Marie Legacey, *Making Space for the Dead: Catacombs, Cemeteries, and the Reimagining of Paris, 1780–1830* (Ithaca, NY: Cornell University Press, 2019). For the politics of remembering and forgetting, see Sheryl Kroen, *Politics and Theater: The Crisis of Legitimacy in Restoration France, 1815–1830* (Berkeley: University of California Press, 2000); for reconstructing society, see Denise Davidson, *France after Revolution: Urban Life, Gender, and the New Social Order* (Cambridge, MA: Harvard University Press, 2007); for reconstruction in the religious sphere, see Carol Harrison, *Romantic Catholics: France's Post-revolutionary Generation in Search of a Modern Faith* (Ithaca, NY: Cornell University Press, 2014). For the ways in which a French revolutionary terrorist made a career as postrevolutionary liberal publisher and nobleman, see Jeff Horn, *The Making of a Terrorist: Alexandre Rousselin and the French Revolution* (New York: Oxford University Press, 2021). I heartily thank the author for sharing his manuscript with me before its publication.

3. Sarah Maza, *The Myth of the French Bourgeoisie: An Essay on the Social Imaginary, 1750–1850* (Cambridge, MA: Harvard University Press, 2003); Christopher H. Johnson, *Becoming Bourgeois: Love, Kinship, and Power in Provincial France, 1670–1880* (Ithaca, NY: Cornell University Press, 2015).

4. Emma Rothschild, *An Infinite History: The Story of a Family in France over Three Centuries* (Princeton, NJ: Princeton University Press, 2021).

Introduction

1. Karen Schniedewind, "Soziale Sicherung im Alter: Nationale Stereotypen und unterschieliche Lösungen in Deutschland und Frankreich in der ersten Hälfte des 20. Jahrhunderts," *Francia* 21, no. 3 (1994): 29–49.

2. David G. Troyansky, *Old Age in the Old Regime: Image and Experience in Eighteenth-Century France* (Ithaca, NY: Cornell University Press, 1989).

3. For important historical, philosophical, and sociological perspectives on the self, see Jerrold Seigel, *The Idea of the Self: Thought and Experience in Western Europe since the Seventeenth Century* (Cambridge: Cambridge University Press, 2005); Charles Taylor, *Sources of the Self: The Making of the Modern Identity* (Cambridge, MA: Harvard University Press, 1989); and Jean-Claude Kaufmann, *L'invention de soi: Une théorie de l'identité* (Paris: Armand Colin, 2004).

4. The 1990s saw the emergence of multidisciplinary studies of age as a category. Placing the emphasis on midlife, for example, Margaret Morganroth Gullette made a claim for the importance of "age studies" in *Declining to Decline: Cultural Combat and the Politics of the Midlife* (Charlottesville: University Press of Virginia, 1997). More recently, an *American Historical Review* forum on chronological age (vol. 125, no. 2, April 2020) and an issue of the *Radical History Review* devoted to old age (vol. 2021, no. 139, January 2021) demonstrated the timeliness of such study.

5. See, for example, Gilles Pollet, "Les retraites en France (1880–1914): La naissance d'une politique sociale," Université de Lyon 2 (1990), and Bruno Dumons, "Les retraités sous la Troisième République: Lyon et sa région (1880–1914). Population, modes de vie et comportements," Université de Lyon 2 (1990), remarkable *thèses* produced under the direction of Yves Lequin. They summarize some of the material in those nine volumes in Pollet and Dumons, "La naissance d'une politique sociale: Les retraites en France (1900–1914)," *Revue française de science politique* 41 (1991): 627–648, and in their book, *L'état et les retraites: Genèse d'une politique* (Paris: Belin, 1994). W. Andrew Achenbaum has discussed the difficulty of defining retirement and writing its history in a chapter called "U.S. Retirement in Historical Context," in *The Columbia Retirement Handbook*, ed. Abraham Monk (New York: Columbia University Press, 1994), 12–28.
6. Sudhir Hazareesingh, ed., *The Jacobin Legacy in Modern France: Essays in Honour of Vincent Wright* (Oxford: Oxford University Press, 2002); Michel Vovelle, *Les Jacobins, de Robespierre à Chevènement* (Paris: La Découverte, 1999).
7. Martin Kohli, "Ageing as a Challenge for Sociological Theory," *Ageing and Society* 8 (1988): 367–394; "The World We Forgot: A Historical Review of the Life Course," in *Later Life: The Social Psychology of Aging*, ed. V. W. Marshal (Beverly Hills, CA: Sage, 1986), 271–303.
8. Anne-Marie Guillemard, *La retraite: Une mort sociale* (Paris: Mouton, 1973); *Le déclin du social: Formation et crise des politiques de la vieillesse* (Paris: Presses Universitaires de France, 1986).
9. Peter Laslett, *A Fresh Map of Life: The Emergence of the Third Age* (London: Weidenfeld and Nicolson, 1989).
10. Anne-Marie Guillemard, "Emploi, protection sociale et cycle de vie: Résultats d'une comparaison internationale des dispositifs de sortie anticipée d'activité," in *Entre travail, retraite et vieillesse: Le grand écart*, ed. A.-M. Guillemard, J. Légaré, and P. Ansart (Paris: L'Harmattan, 1995), 43–71.
11. Paul B. Baltes and Margret M. Baltes, eds., *Successful Aging: Perspectives from the Behavioral Sciences* (Cambridge: Cambridge University Press, 1990). Even scholarship on dependency can have a positive spin, as in Margret M. Baltes, *The Many Faces of Dependency in Old Age* (Cambridge: Cambridge University Press, 1996).
12. Peter N. Stearns, "Review Article," in *History and Theory* 30 (1991): 261–270; Georges Minois, *Histoire de la vieillesse* (Paris: Fayard, 1987), translated by Sarah Hanbury Tenison as *History of Old Age* (Chicago: University of Chicago Press, 1989).
13. John A. Burrow, *The Ages of Man: A Study in Medieval Writing and Thought* (Oxford: Oxford University Press, 1986); Elizabeth Sears, *The Ages of Man: Medieval Interpretations of the Life Cycle* (Princeton, NJ: Princeton University Press, 1986). For an overview and remarks on greater variability in the postmodern life course, see Sherri Klassen, "The Life Cycle," in *Encyclopedia of European Social History from 1350 to 2000*, ed. Peter N. Stearns, vol. 2 (Detroit: Charles Scribner's Sons, 2001), 193–203.
14. Lynn Botelho, "Old Age and Menopause in Rural Women of Early Modern Suffolk," in *Women and Ageing in British Society since 1500*, ed. Lynn Botelho and Pat Thane (Harlow, Essex: Longman/Pearson Education, 2001), 43–65.

15. Annemarie de Wildt and Willem van der Ham, *Tijd van Leven: Ouder worden in Nederland vroeger en nu* (Amsterdam: Amsterdams Historisch Museum, 1993); Caroline Schuster Cardone, *Le crépuscule du corps: Images de la vieillesse féminine* (Gollion, Switzerland: Infolio, 2009).
16. Peter Borscheid, *Geschichte des Alters 16.–18. Jahrhundert* (Münster: Coppenrath, 1987).
17. Troyansky, *Old Age*; Jean-Pierre Bois, *Les vieux: De Montaigne aux premières retraites* (Paris: Fayard, 1989); Jean-Pierre Gutton, *Naissance du vieillard: Essai sur l'histoire des rapports entre les vieillards et la société en France* (Paris: Aubier, 1988) relies heavily on Troyansky's 1983 dissertation.
18. Vincent Gourdon, *Histoire des grands-parents* (Paris: Perrin, 2001).
19. See the introduction to Paul Johnson and Pat Thane, eds., *Old Age from Antiquity to Post-modernity* (London: Routledge, 1998). For an earlier assortment of social historical studies, see Margaret Pelling and Richard M. Smith, eds., *Life, Death, and the Elderly: Historical Perspectives* (London: Routledge, 1991).
20. See the articles in David I. Kertzer and Warner K. Schaie, eds., *Age Structuring in Comparative Perspective* (Hillsdale, NJ: Lawrence Erlbaum Associates, 1989); Jacques Dupâquier, ed., *Marriage and Remarriage in Populations of the Past* (London: Academic Press, 1981); *Annales de démographie historique* (1985): *Vieillir autrefois*; *Annales de démographie historique* (1991): *Grands-Parents, Aïeux*.
21. Pat Thane, *Old Age in English History: Past Experiences, Present Issues* (Oxford: Oxford University Press, 2000). See also David G. Troyansky, *Aging in World History* (New York: Routledge, 2016).
22. Patrice Bourdelais, *Le nouvel âge de la vieillesse: Histoire du vieillissement de la population* (Paris: Odile Jacob, 1993).
23. Josef Ehmer, *Sozialgeschichte des Alters* (Frankfurt am Main: Suhrkamp, 1990).
24. Christoph Conrad, *Vom Greis zum Rentner: Der Strukturwandel des Alters in Deutschland zwischen 1830 und 1930* (Göttingen: Vandenhoeck & Ruprecht, 1994).
25. See the review of the literature in Carole Haber and Brian Gratton, *Old Age and the Search for Security: An American Social History* (Bloomington: Indiana University Press, 1993).
26. Guy Thuillier, *Les pensions de retraite des fonctionnaires au XIXe siècle* (Paris: Comité d'Histoire de la Sécurité Sociale, 1994); Pollet, "Les retraites en France"; Dumons, "Les retraités sous la Troisième République."
27. Peter Baldwin, *The Politics of Social Solidarity: Class Bases of the European Welfare State, 1875–1975* (Cambridge: Cambridge University Press, 1990); Susan Pedersen, *Family, Dependence, and the Origins of the Welfare State: Britain and France, 1914–1945* (Cambridge: Cambridge University Press, 1993).
28. Theda Skocpol, *Protecting Solders and Mothers: The Political Origins of Social Policy in the United States* (Cambridge, MA: Harvard University Press, 1992); Seth Koven and Sonya Michel, eds., *Mothers of a New World: Maternalist Politics and the Origins of Welfare States* (New York: Routledge, 1993); Roger Ransom and Richard Sutch, "The Labor of Older Americans," *Journal of Economic History* 46 (1986): 1–30; J.

Moen, "The Labor of Older Men: A Comment," *Journal of Economic History* 47 (1987): 761–767.

29. Chris Phillipson, *Capitalism and the Construction of Old Age* (London: Macmillan, 1982); Jill Quadagno, *The Transformation of Old Age Security: Class and Politics in the American Welfare State* (Chicago: University of Chicago Press, 1988).
30. Ronald Melchers, "La vieillesse ouvrière," unpublished manuscript based upon a 1984 *Thèse de troisième cycle* in economics, Université d'Aix-Marseille II.
31. John Macnicol, *The Politics of Retirement in Britain, 1878–1948* (Cambridge: Cambridge University Press, 1998). See Thane, *Old Age in English History*, for a dissent from Macnicol's political-economy approach, but see also Macnicol's more recent treatment of age discrimination primarily in Britain and the United States, *Age Discrimination: An Historical and Contemporary Analysis* (Cambridge: Cambridge University Press, 2006).
32. For the last of those issues, see the articles in Paul Johnson, Christoph Conrad, and David Thomson, eds., *Workers versus Pensioners* (Manchester: Manchester University Press, 1989).
33. Among her publications, see Françoise Cribier, "Change in the Life Course and Retirement: The Example of Two Cohorts of Parisians," in Johnson, Conrad, and Thomson, *Workers versus Pensioners*, 181–201.
34. Elise Feller, "Vieillissement et société dans la France du premier XXe siècle, 1905–1953," thèse d'histoire, 3 vols., Université Denis Diderot-Paris 7, 1997, a work on whose jury I was honored to serve. Feller has even more to say about the shift from old person to retiree and about the role of gender. See book version: *Histoire de la vieillesse en France (1900–1960): Du vieillard au retraité* (Paris: Seli Arslan, 2005).
35. Thomas Sokoll, "Armut im Alter im Spiegel englischer Armenbriefe des ausgehenden 18. und frühen 19. Jahrhunderts," in *Zur Kulturgeschichte des Alterns: Towards a Cultural History of Aging*, ed. Christoph Conrad and Hans-Joachim von von Kondratowitz (Berlin: Deutsches Zentrum für Altersfragen, 1993), 39–76. See also his *Essex Pauper Letters, 1731–1837* (Oxford: Oxford University Press, 2001).
36. Ministry of Justice series (BB), Archives Nationales, Paris (AN), BB25 66, doss. 495, cited in David G. Troyansky, "Retraite, vieillesse, et contrat social: L'exemple des juges de la Haute-Vienne sous la Restauration," in Guillemard, Légaré, and Ansart, *Entre travail, retraite et vieillesse*, 85–101.
37. See the articles devoted to "Bureaux and Bureaucrats: Literature and Social Theory" of *L'Esprit Créateur* 34, no. 1 (Spring 1994).
38. See the various studies by Guy Thuillier, including *La bureaucratie en France aux XIXe et XXe siècles* (Paris: Economica, 1987). On the bureaucratic self, see Ralph R. Kingston, *Bureaucrats and Bourgeois Society: Office Politics and Individual Credit in France, 1789–1848* (Houndmills, UK: Palgrave Macmillan, 2012).
39. Annie Poinsot, "Inventaire des dossiers de pension des magistrats et des employés du Ministère de la Justice," Archives Nationales. The three volumes cover the periods 1814–15, 1825–40, and 1840–56. They are now available online. The archival series itself is BB25.

40. *Bulletin des lois de la République Française*, 5th series, vol. 2 (1814), no. 40, 225-229; vol. 3 (1815), no. 70, 1-3.
41. AN BB2 10 and BB25 1-20.
42. Natalie Zemon Davis, *Fiction in the Archives: Pardon Tales and Their Tellers in Sixteenth-Century France* (Stanford: Stanford University Press, 1987); Pierre Nora, *Les lieux de mémoire*, 7 vols. (Paris: Gallimard, 1984-1993); Philippe Lejeune, *Je est un autre: L'autobiographie de la littérature aux médias* (Paris: Seuil, 1980); Jaber Gubrium, *Speaking of Life: Horizons of Meaning for Nursing Home Residents* (Hawthorne, NY: Aldine de Gruyter, 1993). On narrative and identity, see James A. Holstein and Jaber F. Gubrium, *The Self We Live By: Narrative Identity in a Postmodern World* (New York: Oxford University Press, 2000).
43. David A. Bell, *Lawyers and Citizens: The Making of a Political Elite in Old Regime France* (New York: Oxford University Press, 1994); Lenard R. Berlanstein, *The Barristers of Toulouse in the Eighteenth Century (1740-1793)* (Baltimore: Johns Hopkins University Press, 1975); Michael P. Fitzsimmons, *The Parisian Order of Barristers and the French Revolution* (Cambridge, MA: Harvard University Press, 1987).
44. See, for example, Keith Michael Baker, *Inventing the French Revolution* (Cambridge: Cambridge University Press, 1990); Dale Van Kley, ed., *The French Idea of Freedom: The Old Regime and the Declaration of Rights of 1789* (Stanford: Stanford University Press, 1994); Keith M. Baker, Colin Lucas, François Furet, and Mona Ozouf, eds., *The French Revolution and the Creation of Modern Political Culture*, 4 vols. (Oxford: Pergamon Press, 1987-94).
45. Isser Woloch, one of the few historians to have presented the period from the Revolution into the first third of the nineteenth century, does so in terms of a new civic order; see *The New Regime: Transformations of the French Civic Order, 1789-1820s* (New York: Norton, 1994). In terms of politics, law, and family life, see Jennifer Heuer, *The Family and the Nation: Gender and Citizenship in Revolutionary France, 1789-1830* (Ithaca, NY: Cornell University Press, 2005); for an examination of the French economy that looks both backward and forward, see Jeff Horn, *Economic Development in Early Modern France: The Privilege of Liberty, 1650-1820* (Cambridge: Cambridge University Press, 2015).

Chapter 1

1. Greg Eghigian, *Making Security Social: Disability, Insurance, and the Birth of the Social Entitlement State in Germany* (Ann Arbor: University of Michigan Press, 2000).
2. Christoph Conrad, "The Emergence of Modern Retirement: Germany in an International Comparison (1850-1960)," *Population: An English Selection* 3 (1991): 171-200. See also his important monograph *Vom Greis zum Rentner*.
3. Baldwin, *Politics of Social Solidarity*.
4. Macnicol, *Politics of Retirement in Britain*.
5. Gilles Pollet, "Retraite et retraités (fin XIXème-début XXème siècle)," vol. 1, "Les retraites en France de 1880 à 1914," 21.

6. See Helena Rosenblatt, *The Lost History of Liberalism, from Ancient Rome to the Twenty-First Century* (Princeton, NJ: Princeton University Press, 2018), which explores the range of views among liberals and the importance of post-revolutionary France in the history of liberalism.
7. Feller, *Histoire de la vieillesse en France*
8. Bruno Dumons, "Retraite et retraités (fin XIXème–début XXème siècle)," vol. 2, "Les retraités sous la Troisième République: Lyon et sa région (1880–1914)," 90–92.
9. On retirement in particular, see Thuillier, *Les pensions de retraite*, and Bernd Wunder, "Die Einführung des staatlichen Pensionssystems in Frankreich (1760–1850)," *Francia* 11 (1983): 417–474. On the state more generally, see Pierre Rosanvallon, *L'état en France de 1789 à nos jours* (Paris: Seuil, 1990), and André Gueslin, *L'état, l'économie et la société française XIXe–XXe siècle* (Paris: Hachette, 1992).
10. Guy Thuillier, *Les retraites des fonctionnaires: Débats et doctrines (1790–1914)*, 2 vols. (Paris: Comité d'Histoire de la Sécurité Sociale, 1996).
11. Jean-Pierre Bois, *Les anciens soldats dans la société française au XVIIIe siècle* (Paris: Economica, 1990).
12. William Doyle, *Venality: The Sale of Offices in Eighteenth-Century France* (Oxford: Clarendon Press, 1996).
13. T. J. A. Le Goff cuts through the revolutionary rhetoric in his "Essai sur les pensions royales," in *Etat, marine et société*, ed. M. Acerra et al. (Paris: Presses de l'Université de Paris-Sorbonne, 1995), 251–281.
14. For the civic order of elections, schooling, and justice, see Woloch, *The New Regime*. One example of professionalization is found in John Merriman, *Police Stories: Building the French State, 1815–1851* (New York: Oxford University Press, 2006). For both family honor and the awarding of honors, see William Reddy, *The Invisible Code: Honor and Sentiment in Post-revolutionary France, 1814–1848* (Berkeley: University of California Press, 1997). On bureaucrats, see Catherine Kawa, *Les ronds-de-cuir en révolution: Les employés du ministère de l'Intérieur sous la Première République (1792–1800)* (Paris: Comité des travaux historiques et scientifiques, 1997), and Kingston, *Bureaucrats and Bourgeois Society*.
15. Pollet and Dumons, *L'état et les retraites*; Elise Feller, "La construction sociale de la vieillesse (au cours du premier XXe siècle)," in *Histoire sociale de l'Europe: Industrialisation et société en Europe occidentale, 1880–1970*, ed. François Guedj and Stéphane Sirot (Paris: Seli Arslan, 1997), 293–317.
16. Vida Azimi, "Les pensions de retraite sous l'Ancien Régime," *Mémoires de la Société pour l'Histoire du Droit et des Institutions des anciens pays bourguignons, comtois et romands* 43 (1986): 77–103. Gurvitch links the idea of "droit intuitif" to a proto-revolutionary bourgeoisie in the chapter "Problèmes de sociologie du droit," in his *Traité de sociologie*, vol. 2 (Paris: PUF, 1968), 202. "Revolutionary bourgeoisie" is a loaded term with a complicated history. For Sarah Maza, such a bourgeoisie is at best a myth. See *Myth of the French Bourgeoisie*. For Colin Jones and William Sewell, some sort of bourgeoisie of the era still has a role in the history of French capitalism. Colin Jones, "The Great Chain of Buying: Medical Advertisement, the Bourgeois Public Sphere, and the Origins of the French Revolution," *American Historical Review* 101,

no. 1 (February 1996): 13–40; William H. Sewell Jr., "The Empire of Fashion and the Rise of Capitalism in Eighteenth-Century France," *Past and Present*, no. 206 (February 2010): 81–120.

17. Thuillier, *Les pensions de retraite*, 3.
18. An exception is another article by Vida Azimi, "Les droits de l'homme-fonctionnaire," *Revue historique de droit français et étranger* 67 (1989): 27–46.
19. The notion of themistocracy is used in Richard Mowery Andrews, *Law, Magistracy, and Crime in Old Regime Paris, 1735–1789*, vol. 1 (Cambridge: Cambridge University Press, 1994). Among the works on French bureaucracy are Clive H. Church, *Revolution and Red Tape: The French Ministerial Bureaucracy, 1770–1850* (Oxford: Clarendon Press, 1981); Howard G. Brown, *War, Revolution, and the Bureaucratic State: Politics and Army Administration in France, 1791–1799* (Oxford: Clarendon Press, 1995); and Thuillier, *La bureaucratie en France*.
20. A social historian's treatment of the magistracy is found in Christophe Charle, "Les magistrats en France au XIXe siècle: Les fondements sociaux et politiques d'une crise prolongée," in *El tercer poder: Hacia una comprensión histórica de la justicia contemporánea en España*, ed. Johannes-Michael Scholz (Frankfurt am Main: Vittorio Klostermann, 1992), 119–135. For the perspective of historians of law, see Jean-Pierre Royer, *La société judiciaire depuis le XVIIIe siècle* (Paris: PUF, 1979); Jean-Pierre Royer, Renée Martinage, and Pierre Lecocq, *Juges et notables au XIXe siècle* (Paris: PUF, 1982); and Marcel Rousselet, *La magistrature sous la monarchie de juillet* (Paris: Sirey, 1937). The most ambitious treatment of the judiciary across the Revolution covers one department of France and avoids general conclusions: Jean-Claude Gégot, "Le personnel judiciaire de l'Hérault (1790–1830)," thesis, Université Paul Valéry de Montpellier, 1974. For a broader international approach to comparable figures, see Robert Descimon, Jean-Frédéric Schaub, and Bernard Vincent, *Les figures de l'administrateur: Institutions, réseaux, pouvoirs en Espagne, en France et au Portugal 16e–19e siècle* (Paris: EHESS, 1997).
21. Robert Allen, *Les tribunaux criminels sous la Révolution et l'Empire, 1792–1811* (Rennes: Presses Universitaires de Rennes, 2005); Emmanuel Berger, *La justice pénale sous la Révolution: Les enjeux d'un modèle judiciaire libéral* (Rennes: Presses Universitaires de Rennes, 2008); Hervé Leuwers, *L'invention du barreau français 1660–1830: La construction nationale d'un groupe professionnel* (Paris: Editions de l'Ecole des hautes études en sciences sociales, 2006), 277.
22. Pascal Plas, *Avocats et barreaux dans le ressort de la cour d'appel de Limoges, 1811–1939* (Limoges: Presses Universitaires de Limoges, 2007), 14; Didier Veillon, *Magistrats au XIXe siècle en Charente-Maritime, Vienne, Deux-Sèvres et Vendée* (La Crèche: Geste éditions, 2001); Vincent Bernaudeau, *La justice en question: Histoire de la magistrature angevine au XIXe siècle* (Rennes: Presses Universitaires de Rennes, 2007). The recent literature on magistrates parallels that on a somewhat larger set of professional categories, the different ranks of the magistracy falling roughly within those of high and intermediate *fonctionnaires*. See Jean Le Bihan, *Au service de l'état: Les fonctionnaires intermédiaires au XIXe siècle* (Rennes: Presses Universitaires de Rennes, 2008); Marc Bergère and Jean Le Bihan, eds., *Fonctionnaires*

dans la tourmente: Épurations administratives et transitions politiques à l'époque contemporaine (Geneva: Georg, 2009). For an extraordinarily thorough prosopographical approach to one group of public servants founded in the revolutionary era, see Gaïd Andro, *Une génération au service de l'état: Les procureurs généraux syndics de la Révolution française (1780–1830)* (Paris: Société des études robespierristes, 2015).
23. The role of the Enlightenment is featured more prominently in Bell, *Lawyers and Citizens*, than in Fitzsimmons, *Parisian Order of Barristers*.
24. Jean-Pierre Royer, *Histoire de la justice en France de la monarchie absolue à la République* (Paris: PUF, 1995), 107.
25. My thinking on the topic benefited from a year in the seminar of Robert Descimon at the École des hautes études en sciences sociales.
26. Royer, *Histoire de la justice*, 123.
27. Lucien Karpik, *French Lawyers: A Study in Collective Action, 1274 to 1994*, trans. Nora Scott (Oxford: Clarendon Press, 1999).
28. Karpik, *French Lawyers*, 74, as cited in Sarah Maza, "Le tribunal de la Nation: Les mémoires judiciaires et l'opinion publique à la fin de l'Ancien Régime," *Annales: E.S.C.* 1 (1987): 73–90. See also Bell, *Lawyers and Citizens*.
29. AN BB25 35, doss. 206. This paragraph and the next first appeared in Troyansky, "Personal and Institutional Narratives of Aging: A French Historical Case," *Journal of Aging Studies* 17 (2003): 40–41.

Chapter 2

1. Thouvenel's dossier is found in the AN BB2 10, doss. 533. Part of this chapter has appeared as Troyansky, "Personal and Institutional Narratives." An earlier draft was presented in 1999 at the Obermann Center Seminar on Late Life, University of Iowa, organized by Teresa Mangum and Kathleen Buckwalter. Other material appeared in Troyansky, "Aging and Memory in a Bureaucratizing World: A French Historical Experience," in *Power and Poverty: Old Age in the Pre-industrial Past*, ed. Susannah R. Ottaway, L.A. Botelho, and Katharine Kittredge (Westport, CT: Greenwood Press, 2002), 15–30, especially 20–27.
2. On the culture of French nobility, see Ellery Schalk, *From Valor to Pedigree: Ideas of Nobility in France in the Sixteenth and Seventeenth Centuries* (Princeton, NJ: Princeton University Press, 1986); Jay M. Smith, *The Culture of Merit: Nobility, Royal Service, and the Making of Absolute Monarchy in France, 1600–1789* (Ann Arbor: University of Michigan Press, 1996).
3. The classic article on the life review is Robert Butler, "The Life Review: An Interpretation of Reminiscence in the Aged," *Psychiatry* 26 (1963): 65–76.
4. See Barbara Myerhoff, "Life History among the Elderly: Performance, Visibility, and Re-membering," and Barbara Myerhoff and Virginia Tufte, "Life History as Integration: Personal Myth and Aging," in Barbara Myerhoff, *Remembered Lives: The Work of Ritual, Storytelling, and Growing Older* (Ann Arbor: University of Michigan Press, 1992), and the important introduction to the volume by Marc Kaminsky.

Kaminsky also discusses the life review in *The Uses of Reminiscence: New Ways of Working with Older Adults* (New York: Haworth Press, 1984). For a review of the literature, see David Haber, "Life Review: Implementation, Theory, Research, and Therapy," *International Journal of Aging and Human Development* 63, no. 2 (September 2006): 153–171. Practical implementation in gerontology programs has often paired student facilitators with aged subjects. See, for example, the Life Review Project at the University of Missouri–Saint Louis, which was directed by Tom Meuser until July 2018.

5. See, for example, Christian Lalive d'Epinay and Stefano Cavalli, *Le quatrième âge ou la dernière étape de la vie* (Lausanne: Presses Polytechniques et Universitaires Romandes, 2013), and several volumes by James Holstein and Jaber Gubrium, including *The Self We Live By*.
6. For precise career patterns in sample departments across the period, see chapter 4. For a discussion of the importance of transrevolutionary continuity well into the nineteenth century, see Royer, *La société judiciaire*.
7. *Bulletin des lois de la République Française*, 4th series, vol. 5e (Paris, 1807), 501–502.
8. *Bulletin des lois de la République Française*, 4th series, vol. 7e (Paris, 1808), 311.
9. AN BB2 10, doss. 325.
10. AN BB2 10, doss. 303 or 1768.
11. AN BB25 1, doss. 480.
12. *Abrégé des hommes illustres de Plutarque, à l'usage de la jeunesse*, vol. 1 (Beauvais-Oise: De L'Imprimerie de Desjardins, an v), in comparing Plutarch and his translator Jacques Amyot, recommends the teaching of music in every *école centrale* and singing a hymn to the Supreme Being (42) and includes the text for such a hymn. A later edition of vol. 2 (Paris, Amiens, Beauvais, an ix) begins by paying homage to Bonaparte. Thus, his intellectual work serves the cultural and political needs of the moment, but it also draws attention to the meanings of individual lives.
13. AN BB25 4, doss. 1333 (also 762, 649, 1961).
14. AN BB25 3, doss. 1034 or 3512.
15. AN BB25 6, doss. 6800 or 181. For his activities on 9 Thermidor, see Colin Jones, *The Fall of Robespierre: 24 Hours in Revolutionary Paris* (Oxford: Oxford University Press, 2021), 65, 67, 181, 193, 206. The dramatic metaphor in the second paragraph of the quotation calls to mind an important aspect of revolutionary rhetoric. See Paul Friedland, *Political Actors: Representative Bodies and Theatricality in the Age of the French Revolution* (Ithaca, NY: Cornell University Press, 2002).
16. Berthollet (1814), AN BB25 34, doss. 162.
17. Le Bois des Guays (1811), AN BB25 33, doss. 131.
18. Bérenger (1814), AN BB25 31, doss. 51.
19. Deligné's dossier is found in AN BB25 5. Most of the dossiers used in this study are cataloged in series BB25, but some Napoleonic-era correspondence is found in BB2 10. See my chapter in Johnson and Thane.
20. This paragraph is drawn from Troyansky, "Aging and Memory," 20.

21. I use the term "nostalgia" more loosely than does Thomas Dodman in *What Nostalgia Was: War, Empire, and the Time of a Deadly Emotion* (Chicago: University of Chicago Press, 2018).
22. He favors banishment over execution. "Mon opinion sur le jugement de Louis XVI" (1792), Bibliothèque nationale de France (BNF): 8-LB41-252.
23. AN BB25 31, doss. 38. He tells the same story in a printed "Réclamation d'un député de la Somme, patriote opprimé; Et compte moral de sa conduite pendant la Révolution" (1794), p. 2, n. 1, BNF: 8-LN27-6052.
24. AN BB25 36. For his role on 9 Thermidor, see Jones, *The Fall of Robespierre*.
25. AN BB25 33. On Gamon's role in espionage, see Jacques Godechot, *The Counter-revolution: Doctrine and Action, 1789–1804*, trans. Salvator Attanasio (Princeton, NJ: Princeton University Press, 1981), 190–192.
26. Jacques Godechot, *Le comte d'Antraigues: Un espion dans l'Europe des émigrés* (Paris: Fayard, 1986). And see the review by Jean-René Suratteau in *Annales historiques de la Révolution française*, no. 263 (1986): 110–113.
27. AN BB2 10.
28. AN BB2 10.
29. Briefly discussed in Troyansky, "Personal and Institutional Narratives," 35.
30. AN BB2 10, no. 506 or 520. This and the following paragraph appear in Troyansky, "Aging and Memory," 23.
31. AN BB25 31, no. 37. See Troyansky, "Aging and Memory," 26–27.
32. AN BB25 18. Troyansky, "Aging and Memory," 23.
33. Henri-François d'Aguesseau, "XV. Mercuriale. La Fermeté, Prononcée à la Saint-Martin, 1711," *Oeuvres de M. le chancelier d'Aguesseau*, vol. 1 (Paris: Les libraires associés, 1759), 172–181.
34. "Abus d'autorité; humanité outragée. Adresse de François-Anne-Louis Phelippes, connu sous le nom de Tronjolly" (Paris: Imprimerie nationale, 1789).
35. "Demande d'une indemnité et récompense pour M. François-Anne-Louis Phelippes de Coatgoureden de Tronjolly, et pour sa famille, demande répétée depuis plus de trente ans" (1814). BNF: Ln27 31363.
36. François-Anne-Louis Phelippes de Coatgoureden de Tronjolly, *Essais historiques et philosophiques sur l'éloquence judiciaire, depuis sa naissance jusqu'à nos jours, et depuis la renaissance des lettres, par rapport à la France seulement*, vol. 1 (Paris: Charles-Béchet, 1829).

Chapter 3

1. Alan Forrest, *The French Revolution and the Poor* (New York: St. Martin's Press, 1981); Colin Jones, *Charity and Bienfaisance: The Treatment of the Poor in the Montpellier Region, 1740–1815* (Cambridge: Cambridge University Press, 1983). For the evolution of attitudes and practices of social welfare and the importance of gender and social identity across the Revolution, see Lisa DiCaprio, *The Origins of the Welfare State: Women, Work, and the French Revolution* (Urbana: University of Illinois Press,

2007); Catherine Duprat, *"Pour l'amour de l'humanité": Le temps des philanthropes. La philanthropie parisienne des Lumières à la monarchie de juillet* (Paris: CTHS, 1993), and *Usages et pratiques de la philanthropie: pauvreté, action sociale et lien social, à Paris, au cours du premier XIXe siècle*, 2 vols. (Paris: Comité pour l'étude de l'histoire de la sécurité sociale, 1996–97). More generally on social policy, see Jean-Pierre Gross, *Fair Shares for All: Jacobin Egalitarianism in Practice* (New York: Cambridge University Press, 1997).

2. AN BB25 27. Much useful information concerning the working out of pensions can be found in that carton, but particularly in that manuscript, which is the basis for what follows.
3. Emmanuel-Auguste-Dieudonné Las Cases, *Mémorial de Sainte-Hélène* (Paris: L'Auteur, 1823–24), cited in Jean Tulard, *Dictionnaire Napoléon* (Paris: Fayard, 1987), 1455.
4. AN BB25 21.
5. AN BB25 22.
6. AN BB25 23.
7. AN BB25 22.
8. AN BB25 23.
9. AN BB25 24.
10. For an example of the conflicts that occurred under imperial rule, with deep roots in local conditions, see Michael Broers, "Revolution as Vendetta: Napoleonic Piedmont, 1801–1814," *Historical Journal* 33, no. 4 (December 1990): 787–809. The article follows up on "Revolution as Vendetta: Patriotism in Piedmont, 1794–1821," *Historical Journal* 33, no. 3 (September 1990): 573–597.
11. Broers, "Revolution as Vendetta: Napoleonic Piedmont."
12. *Archives Parlementaires*, edited by J. Mavidal and E. Laurent, 2nd series, vol. 12, *du 31 mars 1814 au 1er octobre 1814* (Paris, 1868), 491.
13. The total grew as follows: 15,750.25 in 1814, 64,438.25 in 1815, 144,810.86 in 1816, 372,595.86 in 1817, and 477,075.36 in 1818.
14. *Archives Parlementaires*, 2nd series, vol. 40 (Paris, 1878), 7.
15. *Archives Parlementaires*, 40:48.
16. *Archives Parlementaires*, 40:400–404.
17. *Archives Parlementaires*, 40:529.
18. *Esprit des lois*, book 13, chap. 20.
19. *Archives Parlementaires*, 2nd series, vol. 41 (Paris, 1878), 351.
20. *Archives Parlementaires*, 41:364.
21. *Archives Parlementaires*, 41:368.
22. *Archives Parlementaires*, 41:369.
23. *Archives Parlementaires*, 41:370.
24. *Archives Parlementaires*, 41:371–373.
25. *Archives Parlementaires*, 41:375.
26. *Archives Parlementaires*, 41:396.
27. *Archives Parlementaires*, 41:398.

28. If he died in office having served fewer than thirty years but more than ten in the judiciary, she would be able to receive a pension based upon the withholding fund if she could demonstrate that the pension was necessary. So too for the widow of a magistrate who died in retirement and who received a pension for less than thirty years before the publication of the *ordonnance*. The pension would be considered necessary if the income of the widow at the time of her husband's death was less than two-thirds of the pension that he was receiving or which he could have obtained.

    The process for revealing income came in an *ordonnance* of October 16, 1822. If the widow's income did not exceed one-third of the pension her husband received or could have received, the pension would be one-third the husband's, but not less than one hundred francs. If her income were greater than one-third his pension, her combined income would not exceed two-thirds of the husband's pension. If she received income equal to or greater than two-thirds of the pension, she would receive no pension. She had to have been married five years before the husband stopped working and could not have been separated from him at his demand. Widows' pensions ended upon remarriage. Financial aid given orphans would be one-twentieth of the pension the father would have had for each child but not below fifty francs. Guardians or major orphaned children would document lack of income in conformity with the *ordonnance* of October 16, 1822.

29. See Fabian Rausch, "The Impossible *Gouvernement Représentatif*: Constitutional Culture in Restoration France, 1814–1830," *French History* 27, no. 2 (2013): 223–248; Andrew J. Counter, guest editor, *French History*'s virtual issue on the Bourbon Restoration: https://academic.oup.com/fh/pages/restoration_virtual_issue_introduction. Most influential has been the work of Pierre Rosanvallon, for example, *La monarchie impossible: Les chartes de 1814 et de 1830* (Paris: Fayard, 1994).

30. For one of the best treatments of the politics of forgetting (*l'oubli*), see Sheryl Kroen, *Politics and Theater: The Crisis of Legitimacy in Restoration France, 1815–1830* (Berkeley: University of California Press, 2000).

31. *Bulletin des lois de la République Française*, 10th series, vol. 9e (Paris, 1852), no. 495, p. 438.

32. That ineffectiveness is confirmed by Didier Veillon, who claims that it wasn't applied at all (*Magistrats au XIXe siècle*, 115).

33. *Bulletin des lois*, 441.

Chapter 4

1. Louis-Ferdinand Bonnet, "Les trois âges de l'avocat" (1786), in *Annales du Barreau Français*, vol. 8, ed. MM De Sèze et Bonnet (Paris: Warée, 1822), 175–210. See Bell, *Lawyers and Citizens*, 30–31.
2. Bonnet, "Les trois âges," 201.
3. Bonnet, "Les trois âges," 202.
4. On the "natural proximity" and "rapprochement symbolique" between *avocats* and *juges*, see Leuwers, *L'invention du barreau français*.

5. Lynn Hunt, *The Family Romance of the French Revolution* (Berkeley: University of California Press, 1992).
6. David G. Troyansky, "Generational Discourse in the French Revolution," in *The French Revolution in Culture and Society*, ed. David G. Troyansky, Alfred Cismaru, and Norwood Andrews Jr. (New York: Greenwood Press, 1991), 23–31.
7. The first cartons of series BB25 include many such dossiers. It is worth noting that, in *L'âge de la vieillesse: Histoire du vieillissement de la population* (Paris: Odile Jacob, 1993), Patrice Bourdelais's discussion of divisions of populations into age groups finds the earliest examples in French Canada before they were taken up in France itself.
8. See, for example, Barli, AN BB2 10.
9. The printed *circulaire*, dated May 14, 1819, is found, for example, in Archives Départementales, Calvados, Sous-Série 3U4 6047(1), Tribunal Civil de Lisieux.
10. Romer was born in 1780, worked as *employé à l'administration générale des Eaux et forêts*, 1801–4, served as *secrétaire particulier du Ministre de la Justice*, 1804–9, and headed the accounting department from February 1809 until his death in July 1832. He was *chevalier* and *capitaine* of the Légion d'honneur and officer in the National Guard. For his *inventaire après décès*, see AN MC/RE/XVIII/28. For the Légion d'honneur: AN LH/2377/36. His widow's pension demand refers to his death from the *maladie régnante* (presumably cholera), AN BB25 140, doss. 2377.
11. AN BB25 33.
12. AN BB25 36.
13. AN BB25 252.
14. See Marc Kaminsky, "The Uses of Reminiscence: A Discussion of the Formative Literature," in Kaminsky, *The Uses of Reminiscence*, 156. One use of the term "subjectivity" refers to the stance of the historian. See Susan Crane, "Historical Subjectivity: A Review Essay," *Journal of Modern History* 78 (June 2006): 434–456. Another, which is intended here, places the emphasis on the perspectives of historical actors. Such an approach was pioneered by historians of *mentalités*, or attitudes. See, for example, various works of Michel Vovelle, Carlo Ginzburg, and Robert Darnton as well as Gérard Noiriel, "Pour une approche subjectiviste du social," *Annales* 44 (November–December 1989): 1435–1459.
15. See, for example, Donald R. Kelley, *Historians and the Law in Post-revolutionary France* (Princeton, NJ: Princeton University Press, 1984).
16. For particular examples, see David G. Troyansky, "Old Age, Retirement, and the Social Contract in 18th- and 19th-Century France," in *Zur Kulturgeschichte des Alterns. Towards a Cultural History of Aging*, ed. Christoph Conrad and Hans-Joachim von Kondratowitz (Berlin: Deutsches Zentrum für Altersfragen, 1993), 77–95, and Troyansky, "Retraite, vieillesse, et contrat social."
17. Andrew Abbot, "The Historicality of Individuals," *Social Science History* 29, no. 1 (2005): 3. See Ronen Steinberg's use of Abbot's idea in *The Afterlives of the Terror: Facing the Legacies of Mass Violence in Post-revolutionary France* (Ithaca, NJ: Cornell University Press, 2019), 82. Steinberg focuses on memories of one major

event rather than emphasizing career and life course over several decades, as this book does.
18. Abbot, "Historicality of Individuals," 9.
19. See Royer, *La société judiciaire*; and Royer, Martinage, and Lecocq, *Juges et notables*.
20. Rousselot, *La magistrature*.
21. Gégot, "Le personnel judiciaire de l'Hérault." For his examination of a critical period, see "Les magistrates héraultais et la restauration (1814–1815)," in *Droite et gauche de 1789 à nos jours* (Montpellier: Centre d'histoire contemporaine du Languedoc méditerranéen et du Roussillon, 1975), 91–103.
22. See, for example, Veillon, *Magistrats au XIXe siècle*; Bernaudeau, *La justice en question*.
23. AN BB25 41, doss. 499.
24. AN BB25 51(8), doss. 1174 and 1175.
25. AN BB25 66, doss. 495.
26. AN BB25 35, doss. 237.
27. Nonetheless, he continued to participate periodically (and perhaps out of a defensive strategy) in meetings of the Jacobin Club of Limoges. See A. Fray-Fournier, *Le Club des Jacobins de Limoges (1790–1795), d'après ses délibérations, sa correspondance et ses journaux* (Limoges: Charles-Lavauzelle, 1903). On the purchase of *biens nationaux*, see Jean Levet, "La destruction du couvent des Grandes Carmes à Limoges," *Bulletin de la Société Archéologique et Historique du Limousin* 113 (1986): 53–57.
28. Philippe Grandcoing, *Les demeures de la distinction: Châteaux et châtelains au XIXe siècle en Haute-Vienne* (Limoges: Presses Universitaires de Limoges, 2000), 136. Grandcoing names seventy-four-year-old Jean-Baptiste Sireys at Aigueperse and eighty-two-year-old François Talabot at Maury; he discusses Juge Saint-Martin more fully on pp. 132–134. Besides his works in agriculture, Juge Saint-Martin is probably best known for his *Changements survenus dans les moeurs des habitants de Limoges depuis une cinquantaine d'années*, 2nd ed. (1808; Limoges, 1817).
29. AN BB25 49, doss. 802.
30. AN BB25 103, doss. 1398.
31. AN BB25 35, doss. 219.
32. AN BB25 44, doss. 638.
33. That summer was characterized by violence between Jacobins and anti-Jacobins a year before the 1793 Toulon revolt. See Malcolm Crook, *Toulon in War and Revolution: From the* Ancien Régime *to the Restoration, 1750–1820* (Manchester: Manchester University Press, 1991).
34. AN BB25 51(3), doss. 942.
35. AN BB25 55, doss. 51.
36. AN BB25 67, doss. 512. Jean-Pierre-Antoine Bouteille, *juge de paix à Aix*, made brief mention of emigration in 1793–94 but presented continuous service from 1791 to 1827. It does not appear that he was gone long enough to have been replaced at all (AN BB25 106, doss. 1469).

204 NOTES TO PAGES 109–120

37. AN BB25 48, doss. 756. This Joseph Lombard is not to be confused with another, a judge in Tarascon who was accused of falling asleep in court at age seventy-seven and carousing in cafés with the younger people of the area. See AN BB6 (II) 267.
38. AN BB25 84, doss. 949.
39. AN BB25 32, doss. 86.
40. AN BB25 46, doss. 680.
41. AN BB25 41, doss. 519.
42. AN BB25 51(5), doss. 1063.
43. AN BB25 51(3), doss. 958.
44. AN BB25 274, doss. 2117.
45. AN BB25 88, doss. 1055.
46. AN BB25 90, doss. 1099.
47. AN BB25 111, doss. 1606.
48. AN BB25 110, doss. 1585.
49. AN BB25 125, doss. 1969.
50. AN BB25 173, doss. 3207.
51. AN BB25 198, doss. 3862.
52. AN BB25 218, doss. 4400. Similarly, Charles-Guillaume Roger de la Chouquais began a career of three successive positions in 1812, holding on until 1853. His family was seen as ridiculously pretentious, but he was, after all, a man of a far different era. And he managed to have his son appointed to a post before dying in 1865 (AN BB25 244, doss. 5133; see also BB6 (II) 372).
53. See Hazareesingh, *Jacobin Legacy*, and Vovelle, *Les Jacobins*.
54. AN BB25 174, doss. 3221.
55. AN BB25 250, doss. 122.
56. AN BB25 250, doss. 123.
57. AN BB25 250, doss. 123.
58. AN BB25 134, doss. 2200.

Chapter 5

1. "Etat de situation du travail relative au remplacement des juges compris dans les Décrets du 24 Mars sur l'éxécution du Senatus Consulte du 12 octobre 1807", AN BB2 10. Pension demands and other personnel matters are found here. The 110 dossiers found in this carton indicate more generally the concerns of the Napoleonic era.
2. In addition to the 110 dossiers found in series BB2 10, the first twenty cartons in series BB25 constitute the rest of the evidentiary basis for this chapter.
3. Among fathers hoping to be replaced by sons, see Delangle, Conseiller à Caen (born 1737, dossier begun 1813), AN BB25 34, doss. 188; Claude-Joseph Rabusson Devaure, Juge à Gannat (1742, 1814), AN BB25 34, doss. 198; and Honoré-Sauveur Fabri Borrilly, Vice-Président à Marseille (1739, 1814), AN BB25 35, doss. 219. Among uncles hoping to be replaced by nephews, see Théodoric-Jacques Pressac, Procureur à Civray (1759, 1815), AN BB25 35, doss. 258. For a father-in-law hoping

to have his work performed by his son-in-law, see Jacques Fouache, Greffier à Caen (1742, 1814) AN BB25 32, doss. 98. *Greffiers*, however, were ineligible and systematically refused.

4. Alexandre Berrutti, Juge à San Remo (1814), AN BB25 30, doss. 4. Adelaïde-Victoire-Denise Leblanc de Chatauvillard, veuve de Chaillon de Joinville, Conseiller d'Etat (1814), AN BB25 31, doss. 62. Bouly de Lesdain, Procureur Impérial à Assen (1815), AN BB25 35, doss. 233. François-Georges Bourguin, Employé (1774, 1814), AN BB25 30, doss. 8. Marc-Marie Doudard de Lagrée, Conseiller à Riom (1759, 1814), AN BB25 30, doss. 24. Anne-Thérèse-Louise de Bruges, veuve Jaiguelius, Conseiller au Conseil Souverain d'Alsace (1814), AN BB25 32, doss. 75. François-Marie Perret, Président à Rennes (1756, 1815), AN BB25 33, doss. 123. Julien-Pierre Couteille, Employé aux Droits Réunis (1750, 1814), AN BB25 34, doss. 177.
5. François Corhumel, Substitut à Sélestat (1814), AN BB25 32, doss. 70.
6. Joseph-Henry Combettes de la Fajole, Juge Suppléant à Villefranche (1759, 1815), AN BB25 35, doss. 242. Marie-Joseph Milscent, Président à la Cour d'Angers (1752, 1815), AN BB25 35, doss. 255. Thomas, Président à Lure (1814) AN BB25 34, doss. 190. Veuve Rey, Ancien Directeur de la Régie Générale de Brignolles, AN BB25 31, doss. 61.
7. Jean-Jacques-Antoine Moll, Procureur du Gouvernement à Délémont (1763, 1815), AN BB25 35, doss. 241.
8. Berthollet, Huissier au Conseil d'Etat (1752, 1814), AN BB25 34, doss. 162.
9. Anne-Guillaume-Claude Arbrinet, Greffier à Brie-Comte-Robert (1741, 1814), AN BB25 32, doss. 88.
10. Jacques-François Le Bois des Guays, Ancien Procureur-Général de la Cour Criminelle de l'Yonne (1740, 1811), AN BB25 33, doss. 131.
11. Jean-Jacques Gros, Conseiller à la Cour Prévôtale à Hambourg (1765, 1815), AN BB25 35, doss. 222.
12. Louis-René Crespin, Procureur-Général à l'Isle de France (1768, 1814), AN BB25 30, doss. 7.
13. AN BB25 1, doss. 1518 and 916.
14. AN BB25 1, doss. 5027.
15. AN BB25 1, doss. 1176 and 6707 and 1048.
16. AN BB25 1, doss. 36.
17. AN BB25 1, doss. 1187.
18. Anthoine, AN BB25 1, doss. 7155.
19. AN BB2 10, doss. 550.
20. AN BB2 10, doss. 636.
21. Aansorgh, Utrecht, 1811, AN BB25 1, doss. 1467.
22. AN BB25 5, doss. 228.
23. AN BB25 1, doss. 790.
24. AN BB25 25, doss. 7036.
25. Joseph Delorne and Joseph Louis Lafarge, doss. 454.
26. Lambelin, Ancien Magistrat à Montreuil-sur-Mer, AN BB25 28.
27. Bérenger, Président à Valence (1814), AN BB25 31, doss. 51.

28. Jean-Baptiste Goulard, Juge de Paix à Beaumont (1814), AN BB25 33, doss. 142.
29. AN BB25 26, doss. 7055 and 313.
30. Raymond d'Aiguy, *Ma vie*, vol. 1 (Lyon, 1858), 338–339.
31. Jean Delage, Président à Montron (1749, 1814), AN BB25 34, doss. 156.
32. Marsucco, ancien fonctionnaire public et ex-greffier du tribunal civil de Port Maurice (Montenotte), AN BB2 10, doss. 659. Balthazard Berard, juge civil à Suze (Po), AN BB25 1, doss. 1145 and 61D. Alexis Parguez, juge au tribunal de première instance à St-Hypolite (Doubs), AN BB2 10, doss. 4030.
33. Jacques François Le Fossier Grandprey, président du tribunal d'Argentan (Orne) as described by his son, AN BB2 10, doss. 718; see also Charles Maurice Boutier, juge à la cour d'appel de Trèves, AN BB25 2, doss. 1410.
34. AN BB25 1, doss. 480.
35. AN BB2 10, doss. 504 and 444.
36. AN BB2 10, doss. 571.
37. AN BB2 10, doss. 712.
38. AN BB2 10, doss. 675.
39. AN BB2 10, doss. 604.
40. AN BB25 18, doss. 18.
41. AN BB25 18, doss. 3756, 709.
42. AN BB2 10, doss. 536.
43. AN BB2 10, doss. 557 and 1535.
44. BB2 10, doss. 714. For a report on three other ailing judges in the region of Turin, see Roatis, Reggio, and Tobon, AN BB2 10, doss. 569.
45. AN BB25 5, doss. 7522.
46. AN BB25 1, doss. 1062.
47. AN BB25 8, doss. 3452.
48. AN BB25 2, doss. 17.
49. The debates can be followed from April 17 to June 12 in *Archives Parlementaires*, vols. 40 and 41.
50. AN BB25 1, doss. 244.
51. AN BB25 272, doss. 1972.
52. AN BB25 10, doss. 411.
53. AN BB25 4, doss. 671.
54. AN BB25 4, doss. 257 and 7429.
55. AN BB25 4, no number.
56. On grandparents and grandchildren, see *Annales de démographie historique*, 1991: *Grands-parents, aïeux*. Also Gourdon, *Histoire des grands-parents*.
57. On precise changes that resulted from the Revolution, see Margaret Darrow, *Revolution in the House: Family, Class, and Inheritance in Southern France, 1775–1825* (Princeton, NJ: Princeton University Press, 1989); Suzanne Desan, *The Family on Trial in Revolutionary France* (Berkeley: University of California Press, 2004); Heuer, *Family and the Nation*; Roderick Phillips, *Family Breakdown in Late Eighteenth-Century France: Divorces in Rouen, 1792–1803* (Oxford: Clarendon Press, 1980); Francis Ronsin, *Le contrat sentimental: Débats sur le mariage, l'amour, le divorce, de*

l'Ancien Régime à la Restauration (Paris: Aubier, 1990). At a high level of generality, Hunt, *Family Romance*. Career dossiers permit a look at family romance at a lower level of abstraction.

58. On such use of the royal family in another national context, see the discussion of the "Queen Caroline Affair" in Catherine Hall's chapter, "The Sweet Delights of Home," in *History of Private Life*, vol. 4, pp. 47–50; while not going to that extreme, postrevolutionary France had at least gone a long way from the pornographic image of the royal family in the late eighteenth century. Louis XVIII is often referred to as Louis le désiré.
59. AN BB2 10, doss. 13.
60. AN BB2 10, doss. 115.
61. AN BB25 1, doss. 597.
62. AN BB25 1, doss. 480.
63. AN BB25 1, doss. 3883.
64. AN BB25 7, doss. 524.
65. AN BB25 1, doss. 891.
66. AN BB25 3, doss. 787.
67. AN BB25 11, doss. 23.
68. AN BB25 9, doss. 901.
69. AN BB25 5, doss. 249.
70. Jean-François-Guillaume Dol, président honoraire du tribunal de première instance séant à Draguignan (Var), AN BB2 10, doss. 514; Nicolas Acher, AN BB25 1, doss. 480.
71. AN BB2 10, doss. 630.
72. AN BB2 10, doss. 3.
73. AN BB25 8, doss. 1131.
74. AN BB2 10, doss. 14.
75. AN BB2 10, doss. 1542.
76. AN BB25 46, doss. 698.
77. AN BB25 49, doss. 802.
78. AN BB25 50, doss. 854.
79. AN BB25 51(1), doss. 904.
80. AN BB25 51(2), doss. 922.
81. AN BB25 2, doss. 2373. On calumny more generally, see Charles Walton, *Policing Public Opinion in the French Revolution: The Culture of Calumny and the Problem of Free Speech* (Oxford: Oxford University Press, 2009).
82. AN BB25 2, doss. 773. Similarly Joseph Antoine Comaschi, vice-président du tribunal de première instance de Plaisance (Taro), AN BB25 4, doss. 916, and Jean Baptiste Copin, ex-juge civil au tribunal civil de Vouzières (Ardennes), AN BB25 4, doss. 1126, spoke of the machinations, intrigues, and calumny of rivals.
83. AN BB25 7, doss. 792.
84. AN BB25 3, doss. 5020.
85. AN BB25 4, doss. 575.
86. AN BB2 10, doss. 115.
87. AN BB2 10, doss. 1441.

88. AN BB25 1, doss. 753.
89. AN BB25 1, doss. 729.
90. AN BB25 14, doss. 770.
91. AN BB2 10, doss. 439.
92. AN BB2 10, doss. 143. Similarly, Jean Antoine Vignali, ancien greffier en chef du suprême conseil de Parme, wrote from Plaisance on June 6, 1810, of "l'heureux circonstance de son auguste mariage" (AN BB2 10, doss. 303 and 1768).
93. AN BB25 1, doss. 729.
94. Letter of April 26, 1808, AN BB25 8, doss. 322.
95. Letter of April 29, 1808, AN BB25 8, doss. 322.
96. AN BB25 12, doss. 127.
97. AN BB25 1, doss. 7170.
98. AN BB25 7, doss. 532.
99. AN BB25 9, doss. 472.
100. AN BB25 7, doss. 348.
101. The most important work on political "weathervanes" is Pierre Serna, *La république des girouettes, 1789–1815 et au-delà: Une anomalie politique. La France de l'extrême centre* (Paris: Champ Vallon, 2005), but see also Jean-Luc Chappey, "Nouveaux regards sur les 'girouettes': Ecritures et stratégies intellectuelles en Révolution," in *On ne peut pas tout réduire à des stratégies: Pratiques d'écritures et trajectoires sociales*, ed. Dinah Ribard and Nicolas Schapira (Paris: Presses Universitaires de France, 2013), 43–69.
102. AN BB25 14, doss. 80.
103. AN BB25 25, doss. 133.
104. Procureur Impérial à Gand (1757, 1814), AN BB25 30, doss. 11.
105. See, for example, Paul-Nicolas Stourm, Procureur-Général à Trèves (1755, 1814), AN BB25 31, doss. 54.
106. On continuity from the Napoleonic judiciary through the Restoration, see Pascal Durand-Barthez, *Histoire des structures du Ministère de la Justice, 1789–1945* (Paris: PUF, 1973), 37.
107. AN BB25 25, doss. 497.
108. The computer simulations of family and kinship dimensions by Hervé Le Bras, "Evolution des liens de famille au cours de l'existence," in *Les âges de la vie*, ed. Ivan Darrault-Harris and Jacques Fontanille, vol. 1 (Paris: PUF, 1982), 27–39, and "Parents, grands-parents, bisaïeux," *Population* 28 (1973): 9–38, are still useful, most recently borrowed by Bourdelais, *L'âge de la vieillesse*.
109. Méaulle, AN BB25 30, doss. 11; Eléonore Plessis, Vice-Président à Metz (1740, 1814), AN BB25 33, doss. 149; Claude-Joseph Gros, Procureur-Général à Besançon (1753, 1814), AN BB25 34, doss. 171.
110. Guillaume Joseph Liévin Durand, Juge de Première Instance à Neufchâtel, AN BB25 28.
111. Marc-Antoine Guilleman, Juge à Dunkerque (1747, 1814), AN BB25 33, doss. 108.
112. Richard-François Chaix d'Estange, Procureur-Général à Reims (1814), AN BB25 31, doss. 37. On the marriage of priests, see Claire Cage, *Unnatural Frenchmen: The*

Politics of Priestly Celibacy and Marriage, 1720-1815 (Charlottesville: University of Virginia Press, 2015), and Xavier Maréchaux, *Les noces révolutionnaires: Le mariage des prêtres en France (1789-1815)* (Paris: Editions Vendémiaire, 2017).

113. Scellier, AN BB25 28.
114. Joseph-Clément Poullain de Grandprey, Président à Trèves (1744, 1814), AN BB25 30, doss. 26.
115. Jacques-Alexis Thuriot, Avocat Général à la Cour de Cassation (1753, 1815), AN BB25 36, doss. 270.
116. AN BB25 11, doss. 4499 and 1046.
117. AN BB25 11, doss. 3923 and 693.
118. AN BB25 1, doss. 422 and 443.
119. AN BB25 1, doss. 1507.
120. AN BB25 15, doss. 723.
121. AN BB25 14, doss. 748. On *la bande d'Orgères*, see chapter 5 of Richard Cobb, *Reactions to the French Revolution* (Oxford: Oxford University Press, 1972), 180–215 (notes on pp. 283–294); also André Zysberg, *L'affaire d'Orgères 1790–1800* (Chartres: Société archéologique d'Eure et Loir, 1985).
122. AN BB25 13, doss. 693.
123. AN BB25 13, doss. 1004.
124. AN BB25 13, doss. 916.
125. AN BB25 13, doss. 3578.

Chapter 6

1. Lidonne, ancien employé du Ministère de la Police, AN BB25 30, doss. 27; Leprince, Pierre Claude Mathurin, ancien juge au tribunal de première instance séant à Chartres, AN BB25 30, doss. 32.
2. Vidard la Boujonnière, AN BB25 51(8), doss. 1176.
3. Parmentier, AN BB25 34, doss. 176.
4. Louis Furey Vincent Rabache, conseiller à Amiens (1840), AN BB25 173, doss. 3198.
5. Thuriot, who had voted the execution of the king, served for a time on the Comité de Salut Public, and presided over the session of 9 Thermidor in the Convention, not allowing Robespierre to speak (AN BB25 36, doss. 270); Pierre Nicolas Geffroy, juge de paix du canton d'Acheux (Somme), AN BB25 185, doss. 3517.
6. AN BB25 169, doss. 3109.
7. AN BB25 123, doss. 1894.
8. Bernat (1826), AN BB25 100, doss. 1340.
9. Hémart (1827), AN BB25 108, doss. 1530.
10. Plonquet (1829), AN BB25 117, doss. 1761.
11. Mollin, AN BB25 122, doss. 1891.
12. Hubert Lahuberdière, AN BB25 51(1), doss. 868.
13. AN BB25 134, doss. 2200. This dossier contains much discussion of right.
14. AN BB25 77, doss. 796.

15. AN BB25 51(8), doss. 1189.
16. AN BB25 111, doss. 1606.
17. AN BB25 32, doss. 75.
18. AN BB25 35, doss. 246.
19. AN BB25 48, doss. 756.
20. AN BB25 129, doss. 2079.
21. AN BB25 115, doss. 1703.
22. AN BB25 51(4), doss. 992.
23. AN BB25 73, doss. 679.
24. AN BB25 51(7), doss. 1129. On the *fédérés* as comprising a heterogeneous mix of people, see Robert Alexander, *Bonapartism and Revolutionary Tradition in France: The Fédérés of 1815* (Cambridge: Cambridge University Press, 1991).
25. AN BB25 41, doss. 503.
26. Jacques Denis Laporte, prosecutor in the Hautes Pyrénées, AN BB25 38, doss. 367 and 715.
27. AN BB25 87, doss. 1033.
28. AN BB25 51(5), doss. 1063.
29. François Dieudonné Thibaut de Monbois, ancien conseiller en la Chambre des Comptes de Lorraine. AN BB25 32, doss. 78.
30. AN BB25 49, doss. 791.
31. Alexandre Berrutti, AN BB25 30, doss. 4; Jean Louis Henry, AN BB25 30, doss. 6; Claude André Baudin, AN BB25 30, doss. 20; Jacques André Devals, AN BB25 30, doss. 22; Nicolas Cottenet (also thrown twice from *voiture*), AN BB25 32, doss. 71; Nicolas Rozières: "Je crois cependant avoir au moins autant de droits qu'eux," AN BB25 37, doss. 339; Besson is humiliated because others in the same category received aid: "Pourquoy donc n'aurois-je pas le même droit?" AN BB25 38, doss. 362; Dame Lesouef, veuve d'un ancien juge de paix du canton de Picquigny (Somme) complains that another widow received half of what her husband was due, not a third (AN BB25 212, doss. 4256). That woman is exceptional because comparisons are much more common among men.
32. AN BB25 44, doss. 614. The father first recounted what he had accomplished in Saint-Domingue, then tried generalizing to the needs of the country. Guillaume-Pierre-François Delamardelle, *Réforme judiciaire en France; par Gme. Delamardelle, Avant 1789 Conseiller d'Etat, Procureur général au Conseil supérieur de Saint-Domingue* (Paris: Cellot, 1806).
33. AN BB25 51(2), doss. 906 and 335.
34. AN BB25 104, doss. 1429.
35. AN BB25 41, doss. 520.
36. AN BB25 42, doss. 526.
37. AN BB25 44, doss. 635.
38. M. C.-M.-F. Puthod, *Coup d'oeil sur les moyens les plus praticables de procéder à la liquidation de l'indemnité affectée aux colons français réfugiés de Saint-Domingue, par M. C.-M.-F. Puthod*... (Paris: J. G. Dentu, 1825),) available on Gallica: http://gallica.bnf.fr/ark:/12148/bpt6k5774098k.

39. Puthod de Maison-Rouge, *Le nouveau Louis IX, sur le Trône* (Paris: n.p., 1816).
40. AN BB25 46, doss. 680.
41. AN BB25 51(3), doss. 958.
42. AN BB25 51(3), doss. 968.
43. AN BB25 30, doss. 33.
44. AN BB25 33, doss. 136.
45. Le Follet explicitly referred to "fonctionnaires publics" (AN BB25 41, doss. 519). Le Baron de L'Horme asserted his identity as "fonctionnaire" (AN BB25 125, doss. 1969).
46. AN BB25 35, doss. 222.
47. AN BB25 41, doss. 479.
48. AN BB25 44, doss. 623. Navière des Goutes, writing in 1818 about having been imprisoned during the Revolution, used the analogy of the Bourbons never ceasing to possess the Crown to support the contention that his time in prison should count as time of service (AN BB25 59, doss. 223).
49. AN BB25 118, doss. 1775.
50. AN BB25 31, doss. 38.
51. Jean-Louis Daigremont refers to three generations of magistrates (AN BB25 32, doss. 86). See also Pierre Jean Olivier Bonaventure Leminihy, AN BB25 37, doss. 358.
52. AN BB25 76, doss. 780.
53. AN BB25 48, doss. 763.
54. AN BB25 107, doss. 1505.
55. AN BB25 75, doss. 751.
56. AN BB25 103, doss. 1398.
57. AN BB25 51, doss. 1009.
58. AN BB25 116, doss. 1722.
59. AN BB25 70, doss. 597. For a rich treatment of Morand de Jouffrey's marriage and family life, see Anne Verjus and Denise Davidson, *Le roman conjugal: Chroniques de la vie familiale à l'époque de la Révolution et de l'Empire* (Seyssel: Champ Vallon, 2011).
60. AN BB25 41, doss. 499.
61. AN BB25 69, doss. 563.
62. AN BB25 100, doss. 1335.
63. AN BB25 151, doss. 2654.
64. AN BB25 219, doss. 4428.
65. AN BB25 36, doss. 277. Trie, *Tables générales et absolument nouvelles de tous les titres qui composent le corps du droit romain et français, suivant l'édition de Contius, comparée avec celle de Denys Godefroi* (Marseille: impr. de Mme Mine, 1811). See on Gallica: http://gallica.bnf.fr/ark:/12148/bpt6k6439353z.
66. Papon (l'abbé), *Histoire de la revolution française, depuis l'ouverture des Etats-Généraux (mai 1789) jusqu'au 18 Brumaire (Novembre 1799), ouvrage posthume de l'abbé Papon, Historiographe de Provence, publié par M. Papon le jeune, Juge au Tribunal Civil de Marseille* (Paris: Poulet, 1815).
67. AN BB25 51, doss. 1008.
68. AN BB25 182, doss. 3420.
69. AN BB25 51(5), doss. 1034.

70. AN BB25 51(5), doss. 1052.
71. AN BB25 54, doss. 6.
72. AN BB25 57, doss. 130.
73. AN BB25 58, doss. 169.
74. AN BB25 90, doss. 1099.
75. AN BB25 95, doss. 1219.
76. AN BB25 107, doss. 1493.
77. AN BB25 112, doss. 1626.
78. AN BB25 117, doss. 1749.
79. AN BB25 144, doss. 2484. On the Parlement de Provence: *Essais historiques sur le Parlement de Provence depuis son origine jusqu'à sa suppression, 1501-1790* (Paris: A. Pihan Delaforest, 1826). See also *Réquisitoire de M. Prosper Cabasse, procureur général du Roi, dans l'affaire des trois hommes de couleur de la Martinique* (Basse-Terre, 1827). It's cited in Françoise Thésée, *Le général Donzelot à la Martinique* (Paris: Karthala, 1997).
80. AN BB25 153, doss. 2704.
81. AN BB25 173, doss. 3207.
82. AN BB25 174, doss. 3221.
83. AN BB25 189, doss. 3605.
84. AN BB25 192, doss. 3713.
85. AN BB25 193, doss. 3723.
86. AN BB25 201, doss. 3978.
87. AN BB25 204, doss. 4063.
88. AN BB25 217, doss. 4391.
89. AN BB25 218, doss. 4392.

Chapter 7

1. Veuve Mianné, AN BB25 38, doss. 366.
2. *Bulletin des lois de la République Française*, 5th series, vol. 2 (Paris, 1814), no. 40, pp. 225–229; vol. 3 (Paris, 1815), no. 70, pp. 1–3.
3. On the importance of kinship to the careers of an emerging "national" bourgeois elite, see Christopher H. Johnson, *Becoming Bourgeois: Love, Kinship, and Power in Provincial France, 1670–1880* (Ithaca, NY: Cornell University Press, 2015).
4. AN BB25 34, doss. 186.
5. AN BB25 35, doss. 232.
6. AN BB25 36, doss. 298.
7. AN BB25 37, doss. 318.
8. AN BB25 36, doss. 263.
9. AN BB25 33, doss. 113.
10. AN BB25 194, doss. 3759.
11. This first sample is taken from AN BB25 27, 28, 30–36, first presented in "Retired Judges and Their Families in Restoration France," a paper given at the Second

Carleton Conference on the History of the Family in Ottawa, Canada, May 1994. The next two paragraphs are drawn from that paper.
12. AN BB25 87, doss. 1035.
13. AN BB25 30, doss. 18: Bavelaër—he is ill at sixty-four; AN BB25 36, doss. 264: Marraud du Tolza—he is paralyzed.
14. Dena Goodman makes the case more generally in the context of the Enlightenment, but here we're dealing with institutional demands. Goodman, *Becoming a Woman in the Age of Letters* (Ithaca, NY: Cornell University Press, 2009).
15. Catherine Rosalie Joseph Hardy veuve Le Boeuf, AN BB25 36, doss. 292. Her husband had died in 1811, so the nephew's mention of *droit* and *dette* was to no avail.
16. AN BB25 33, doss. 152.
17. AN BB25 51(6), doss. 1071.
18. AN BB25 73, doss. 702.
19. AN BB25 98, doss. 1300.
20. AN BB25 31, doss. 62.
21. AN BB25 32, doss. 75.
22. AN BB25 33, doss. 132.
23. AN BB25 34, doss. 169.
24. AN BB25 91, doss. 1126. Jean-François Vitet was a cousin of Pierre Vitet, one of the figures in Verjus and Davidson, *Le roman conjugal*, 38.
25. AN BB25 92, doss. 1146.
26. AN BB25 99, doss. 1307.
27. AN BB25 189, doss. 3619.
28. AN BB25 192, doss. 3700.
29. AN BB25 165, doss. 2984.
30. AN BB25 195, doss. 3769.
31. AN BB25 212, doss. 4256.
32. AN BB25 35, doss. 202.
33. AN BB25 38, doss. 390.
34. AN BB25 148, doss. 2590.
35. AN BB25 167, doss. 3042.
36. AN BB25 141, doss. 2394. It's even less likely that Françoise Augustine Sombret, née Lefebvre, wrote her letter, as the signature was barely literate: AN BB25 149, doss. 2591.
37. See Angélique Charlotte Louise Duhamel, née Duchâtel, AN BB25 150, doss. 2626; Louise Françoise Bosquillon du Fay, veuve Hanocq, AN BB25 171, doss. 3137; Adelaide Madeleine Creton, veuve Malot, AN BB25 172, doss. 3183; Catherine Séraphine Charlet, veuve Denamps, AN BB25 200 doss. 3943; Mme de Vouges de Chanteclair, née Collonel, AN BB25 202, doss. 3952.
38. AN BB25 210, doss. 4197.
39. AN BB25 198, doss. 3855.
40. On images and self-images of old women in a range of historical settings, see Monique Stavenuiter, Karin Bijsterveld, and Saskia Jansens, eds., *Lange levens, stille getuigen: Oudere vrouwen in het verleden* (Zutphen: Walburg Pers, 1995). English

translations of some of the contents appeared in the *Journal of Family History* 25, no. 2 (2000).

41. On the idea of widows as honorary men, see Janine Lanza, *Wife to Widow in Early Modern Paris: Gender, Economy, and Law* (Aldershot: Ashgate, 2007). Among other relevant works on the history of widowhood, see Jan Bremmer and Lourens van den Bosch, eds., *Between Poverty and the Pyre: Moments in the History of Widowhood* (London: Routledge, 1995); Sandra Cavallo and Lyndan Warner, eds., *Widowhood in Medieval and Early Modern Europe* (New York: Longman, 1999); Josette Brun, *Vie et mort du couple en Nouvelle-France: Québec et Louisbourg au XVIIIe siècle* (Montreal: McGill-Queen's University Press, 2006); Scarlett Beauvalet-Boutouyrie, *Être veuve sous l'ancien régime* (Paris: Belin, 2001).
42. AN BB25 67, doss. 511.
43. AN Olwen Hufton, *The Poor of Eighteenth-Century France, 1750–1789* (Oxford: Clarendon Press, 1974).
44. AN BB25 42, doss. 552 and 409.
45. AN BB25 142, doss. 2423.
46. AN BB25 51(7), doss. 1126.
47. AN BB25 156, doss. 2764.
48. AN BB25 30, doss. 19.
49. Marie-Pauline-Domitille Poulliande veuve de Laistre, AN BB25 36, doss. 263; Claudine Perrin veuve Mottet, AN BB25 36, doss. 267.
50. AN BB25 113, doss. 1646.
51. AN BB25 117, doss. 1749.
52. AN BB25 35, doss. 209.
53. AN BB25 33, doss. 129.
54. AN BB25 37, doss. 311 and 341.
55. Sherri Klassen, "Old and Cared For: Place of Residence for Elderly Women in Eighteenth-Century Toulouse," *Journal of Family History* 24, no. 1 (1999): 35–52.
56. AN BB25 33, doss. 136.
57. AN BB25 34, doss. 160.
58. AN BB25 36, doss. 235 and 269.
59. Marie Anne Catherine Wimpffen veuve Albert, AN BB25 35, doss. 203.
60. AN BB25 31, doss. 61.
61. AN BB25 33, doss. 118.
62. AN BB25 35, doss. 210.
63. AN BB25 31, doss. 48, for example.
64. AN BB25 51(10), doss. 1260.
65. For example, the above-mentioned Converset left Paris to retire to her hometown in the Côte d'Or (AN BB25 33, doss. 129).
66. AN BB25 42, doss. 549.
67. AN BB25 36, doss. 282.
68. AN BB25 148, doss. 2585.
69. AN BB25 31, doss. 64.
70. AN BB25 31, doss. 44.

71. AN BB25 37, doss. 334.
72. AN BB25 46, doss. 680.
73. John Sturrock, *The Language of Autobiography: Studies in the First Person Singular* (Cambridge: Cambridge University Press, 1993).
74. Shari Benstock, ed., *The Private Self: Theory and Practice of Women's Autobiographical Writings* (Chapel Hill: University of North Carolina Press, 1988); Leigh Gilmore, *Autobiographics: A Feminist Theory of Women's Self-Representation* (Ithaca, NJ: Cornell University Press, 1994).
75. See the comment on differences between women's voices in autobiography and in letters or diaries in Carolyn G. Heilbrun, *Writing a Woman's Life* (New York: W.W. Norton, 1988), 24–25. On women's memoirs from the period in question, see Marilyn Yalom, *Blood Sisters: The French Revolution in Women's Memory* (New York: Basic Books, 1993).
76. Temporalities differed as well. Marc Bessin et Corinne Gaudart, "Les temps sexués de l'activité: La temporalité au principe du genre?," *Temporalités* 9 (2009); Marc Bessin, "Présences sociales: Une approche phénoménologique des temporalités sexuées du care," *Temporalités* 20 (2014). On gender differences in aging after retirement, see Vincent Caradec, "Vieillir après la retraite, une expérience genrée, *SociologieS*, Dossiers, Genre et vieillissement, posted November 15, 2012, accessed January 11, 2018, http://journals.openedition.org/sociologies/4125.

Conclusion

1. See, for example, David Armitage, "Every Great Revolution Is a Civil War," in *Scripting Revolution: A Historical Approach to the Comparative History of Revolutions*, ed. Keith Michael Baker and Dan Edelstein (Stanford, CA: Stanford University Press, 2015), 57–68, but other chapters in that volume also take up the theme.
2. Pierre Serna, "Every Revolution Is a War of Independence," in Suzanne Desan, Lynn Hunt, and William Max Nelson, *The French Revolution in Global Perspective* (Ithaca, NY: Cornell University Press, 2013), 165–182.
3. The literature on the global context of the French Revolution is growing quickly. In addition to the Desan, Hunt, and Nelson volume, exemplary works are Janet Polasky, *Revolutions without Borders: The Call to Liberty in the Atlantic World* (New Haven: Yale University Press, 2015) and "Forum: The French Revolution as an Imperial Revolution," edited by Manuel Covo and Megan Maruschke, *French Historical Studies* 44, no. 3 (2021). For a judicious and skeptical take, see David Bell, "Questioning the Global Turn: The Case of the French Revolution, *French Historical Studies* 37, no. 1 (2014): 1–24.
4. Johnson, *Becoming Bourgeois*; Emma Rothschild, *An Infinite History: The Story of a Family in France over Three Centuries* (Princeton, NJ: Princeton University Press, 2021). Louis Bergeron, Adeline Daumard, and other historians of earlier generations anticipated this trend to some extent, but without the rich cultural detail of recent works.

5. Biographies of individual French Revolutionaries, for understandable reasons, don't often go much past the Revolution itself. A notable exception is Horn, *Making of a Terrorist*, the subject of which lived until 1847.
6. A global convergence around patterns of demographic aging and gerontological thought is a theme of the later chapters of my *Aging in World History*. For an important insight into the awkward application of Western ideas to a global context, see Kavita Sivaramakrishnan, *As the World Ages: Rethinking a Demographic Crisis* (Cambridge, MA: Harvard University Press, 2018).
7. On the difficulty of finding the bourgeoisie as any sort of norm, see Maza, *Myth of the French Bourgeoisie*.

Bibliography

Primary Sources

Archives Nationales
BB2 10. Napoleonic-era pension demands
Série BB25 Cartons 1–282. Pension demands from Bourbon Restoration to midcentury.
Minutier Central: Romer *inventaire après décès*, MC/RE/XVIII/28. Légion d'honneur: LH/2377/36.
For comparisons with pensions in other areas of the state:
F7. Police générale. 12278. Pensions de retraite et secours, 1814–1828.
F12. Commerce et industrie. 4812–4827. Sociétés de secours mutuels, caisses de retraite, 1810–1877.
F17. Instruction publique. 3245–3248. Pensions de retraite, 1813–1855.
Relevant materials in the departmental archives of the six departments in the sample (Bas Rhin, Bouches-du-Rhône, Calvados, Rhône, Somme, Haute-Vienne) were consulted, but they added little to what the national materials yielded. Nonetheless, it is worth mentioning the following:
A.D. Calvados: Sous-série 3U4.
A.D. Rhône. U 708. Discours de rentrées, recueil et feuillets, 1823–1839.
A.D. Somme. 2 U 914–999. Cour d'appel, an 9–1938. Especially 2 U 914 on retirement of *juge de paix* and 2 U 915. Registre, 1834–1835.

Printed Primary Sources

Acher, Nicolas. *Abrégé des hommes illustres de Plutarque, à l'usage de la jeunesse*. Vol. 1, Beauvais-Oise: De L'Imprimerie de Desjardins, Year V (1796–97). Vol. 2, Paris, Amiens, Beauvais, Year IX (1800–01).
Aguesseau, Henri-François d'. "XV. Mercuriale. La Fermeté, Prononcée à la Saint-Martin, 1711." In *Oeuvres de M. le chancelier d'Aguesseau*, vol. 1, 172–181. Paris: Les libraires associés, 1759.
Aiguy, Raymond d'. *Ma vie*. Vol. 1. Lyon, 1858.
Archives Parlementaires. Edited by J. Mavidal and E. Laurent. Paris: Librairie administrative de P. Dupont, 1868–84.
Bonnet, Louis-Ferdinand. "Les trois âges de l'avocat" (1786). In *Annales du Barreau Français*, vol. 8, edited by MM De Sèze et Bonnet, 175–210. Paris: Warée, 1822.
Bulletin des lois. 4th series, vols. 5 and 7. 5th series, vols. 2 and 3. 10th series, vol. 9. Paris, 1807, 1814, 1815, 1852.
Cabasse, Prosper. *Essais historiques sur le Parlement de Provence depuis son origine jusqu'à sa suppression, 1501–1790*. Paris: A. Pihan Delaforest, 1826.

Cabasse, Prosper. *Réquisitoire de M. Prosper Cabasse, procureur général du Roi, dans l'affaire des trois hommes de couleur de la Martinique.* Basse-Terre, 1827.
Delamardelle, Guillaume-Pierre-François. *Réforme judiciaire en France.* Paris: Cellot, 1806.
Devérité, Louis-Alexandre. "Mon opinion sur le jugement de Louis XVI" (1792). BNF: Lb41 252 A.
Devérité, Louis-Alexandre. "Réclamation d'un député de la Somme, patriote opprimé; Et compte moral de sa conduite pendant la Révolution" (1794). BNF: 8-LN27 6052.
Juge Saint-Martin, Jacques-Joseph. *Changements survenus dans les moeurs des habitants de Limoges depuis une cinquantaine d'années.* Limoges, 1st ed. 1808, 2nd ed. 1817.
La Chapelle, Salomon de. *Histoire judiciaire de Lyon et les départements de Rhône-et-Loire et du Rhône depuis 1790. Documents relatifs aux tribunaux de district de département et d'arrondissement.* Vol. 1. Lyon, 1880.
Las Cases, Emmanuel-Auguste-Dieudonné. *Mémorial de Sainte-Hélène.* Paris: L'Auteur, 1823–24.
Oudot, C-F. *Théorie du jury ou Observations sur le jury et sur les institutions judiciaires criminelles anciennes et modernes.* Paris: Joubert, 1845.
Papon (l'abbé). *Histoire de la révolution française, depuis l'ouverture des États-Généraux (mai 1789) jusqu'au 18 Brumaire (Novembre 1799), ouvrage posthume de l'abbé Papon, Historiographe de Provence, publié par M. Papon le jeune, Juge au Tribunal Civil de Marseille.* Paris: Poulet, 1815.
Puthod, C.-M.-F. *Coup d'oeil sur les moyens les plus praticables de procéder à la liquidation de l'indemnité affectée aux colons français réfugiés de Saint-Domingue.* Paris: J. G. Dentu, 1825.
Puthod de Maison-Rouge. *Le nouveau Louis IX, sur le Trône.* Paris, 1816.
Trie. *Tables générales et absolument nouvelles de tous les titres qui composent le corps du droit romain et français, suivant l'édition de Contius, comparée avec celle de Denys Godefroi.* Marseille: impr. de Mme Mine, 1811.
Tronjolly, François-Anne-Louis-Phelippes. *Abus d'autorité.* Paris: Imprimerie nationale, 1789.
Tronjolly, François-Anne-Louis-Phelippes. "Demande d'une indemnité et récompense" (1814). BNF: Ln27 31363.
Tronjolly, François-Anne-Louis Phelippes de Coatgoureden de. *Essais historiques et philosophiques sur l'éloquence judiciaire, depuis sa naissance jusqu'à nos jours, et depuis la renaissance des lettres, par rapport à la France seulement.* Vol. 1. Paris: Charles-Béchet, 1829.

Secondary Sources

Abbot, Andrew. "The Historicality of Individuals." *Social Science History* 29, no. 1 (2005): 1–13.
Achenbaum, W. Andrew. "U.S. Retirement in Historical Context." In *The Columbia Retirement Handbook*, edited by Abraham Monk, 12–28. New York: Columbia University Press, 1994.
Alexander, Robert. *Bonapartism and Revolutionary Tradition in France: The Fédérés of 1815.* Cambridge: Cambridge University Press, 1991.

Allen, Robert. *Les tribunaux criminels sous la Révolution et l'Empire, 1792–1811.* Rennes: Presses Universitaires de Rennes, 2005.
Andrews, Richard Mowery. *Law, Magistracy, and Crime in Old Regime Paris, 1735–1789.* Vol. 1. Cambridge: Cambridge University Press, 1994.
Andro, Gaïd. *Une génération au service de l'État: Les procureurs généraux syndics de la Révolution française (1780–1830).* Paris: Société des études robespierristes, 2015.
Annales de démographie historique (1985): *Vieillir autrefois.*
Annales de démographie historique (1991): *Grands-Parents, Aïeux.*
Armitage, David. "Every Great Revolution Is a Civil War." In *Scripting Revolution: A Historical Approach to the Comparative History of Revolutions*, edited by Keith Michael Baker and Dan Edelstein, 57–68. Stanford, CA: Stanford University Press, 2015.
Azimi, Vida. "Les droits de l'homme-fonctionnaire." *Revue historique de droit français et étranger* 67 (1989): 27–46.
Azimi, Vida. "Les pensions de retraite sous l'Ancien Régime." *Mémoires de la Société pour l'Histoire du Droit et des Institutions des anciens pays bourguignons, comtois et romands* 43 (1986): 77–103.
Baker, Keith Michael. *Inventing the French Revolution.* Cambridge: Cambridge University Press, 1990.
Baker, Keith Michael, Colin Lucas, François Furet, and Mona Ozouf, eds. *The French Revolution and the Creation of Modern Political Culture.* 4 vols. Oxford: Pergamon Press, 1987–94.
Baldwin, Peter. *The Politics of Social Solidarity: Class Bases of the European Welfare State, 1875–1975.* Cambridge: Cambridge University Press, 1990.
Baltes, Margret M. *The Many Faces of Dependency in Old Age.* Cambridge: Cambridge University Press, 1996.
Baltes, Paul B., and Margret M. Baltes, eds. *Successful Aging: Perspectives from the Behavioral Sciences.* Cambridge: Cambridge University Press, 1990.
Beauvalet-Boutouyrie, Scarlett. *Être veuve sous l'ancien régime.* Paris: Belin, 2001.
Bell, David A. *Lawyers and Citizens: The Making of a Political Elite in Old Regime France.* New York: Oxford University Press, 1994.
Benstock, Shari, ed. *The Private Self: Theory and Practice of Women's Autobiographical Writings.* Chapel Hill: University of North Carolina Press, 1988.
Berger, Emmanuel. *La justice pénale sous la Révolution: Les enjeux d'un modèle judiciaire libéral.* Rennes: Presses Universitaires de Rennes, 2008.
Bergère, Marc, and Jean Le Bihan, eds. *Fonctionnaires dans la tourmente: Épurations administratives et transitions politiques à l'époque contemporaine.* Geneva: Georg, 2009.
Berlanstein, Lenard R. *The Barristers of Toulouse in the Eighteenth Century (1740–1793).* Baltimore: Johns Hopkins University Press, 1975.
Bernaudeau, Vincent. *La justice en question: Histoire de la magistrature angevine au XIXe siècle.* Rennes: Presses Universitaires de Rennes, 2007.
Bessin, Marc. "Présences sociales: Une approche phénoménologique des temporalités sexuées du care." *Temporalités* 20 (2014). https://journals.openedition.org/temporalites/2944.
Bessin, Marc, and Corinne Gaudart. "Les temps sexués de l'activité: La temporalité au principe du genre?" *Temporalités* 9 (2009). https://journals.openedition.org/temporalites/979.
Bois, Jean-Pierre. *Les anciens soldats dans la société française au XVIIIe siècle.* Paris: Economica, 1990.

Bois, Jean-Pierre, *Les vieux: De Montaigne aux premières retraites*. Paris: Fayard, 1989.
Borscheid, Peter. *Geschichte des Alters 16.-18. Jahrhundert*. Münster: Coppenrath, 1987.
Botelho, Lynn. "Old Age and Menopause in Rural Women of Early Modern Suffolk." In *Women and Ageing in British Society since 1500*, edited by Lynn Botelho and Pat Thane, 43-65. Harlow, Essex: Longman/Pearson Education, 2001.
Bourdelais, Patrice. *Le nouvel âge de la vieillesse: Histoire du vieillissement de la population*. Paris: Odile Jacob, 1993.
Bremmer, Jan, and Lourens van den Bosch, eds. *Between Poverty and the Pyre: Moments in the History of Widowhood*. London: Routledge, 1995.
Broers, Michael. "Revolution as Vendetta: Napoleonic Piedmont, 1801-1814." *Historical Journal* 33, no. 4 (December 1990): 787-809.
Broers, Michael. "Revolution as Vendetta: Patriotism in Piedmont, 1794-1821." *Historical Journal* 33, no. 3 (September 1990): 573-597.
Brown, Howard G. *War, Revolution, and the Bureaucratic State: Politics and Army Administration in France, 1791-1799*. Oxford: Clarendon Press, 1995.
Brun, Josette. *Vie et mort du couple en Nouvelle-France: Québec et Louisbourg au XVIIIe siècle*. Montreal: McGill-Queen's University Press, 2006.
"Bureaux and Bureaucrats: Literature and Social Theory." *L'Esprit Créateur* 34, no. 1 (Spring 1994).
Burrow, John A. *The Ages of Man: A Study in Medieval Writing and Thought*. Oxford: Oxford University Press, 1986.
Butler, Robert. "The Life Review: An Interpretation of Reminiscence in the Aged." *Psychiatry* 26 (1963): 65-76.
Cage, Claire. *Unnatural Frenchmen: The Politics of Priestly Celibacy and Marriage, 1720-1815*. Charlottesville: University of Virginia Press, 2015.
Caradec, Vincent. "Vieillir après la retraite, une expérience genrée." *SociologieS*. Dossiers, Genre et vieillissement. Posted November 15 2012, accessed January 11, 2018. http://journals.openedition.org/sociologies/4125.
Cardone, Caroline Schuster. *Le crépuscule du corps: Images de la vieillesse féminine*. Gollion, Switzerland: Infolio, 2009.
Cavallo, Sandra, and Lyndan Warner, eds. *Widowhood in Medieval and Early Modern Europe*. New York: Longman, 1999.
Chappey, Jean-Luc. "Nouveaux regards sur les 'girouettes': Ecritures et stratégies intellectuelles en Révolution." In *On ne peut pas tout réduire à des stratégies: Pratiques d'écritures et trajectoires sociales*, edited by Dinah Ribard and Nicolas Schapira, 43-69. Paris: PUF, 2013.
Chappey, Jean-Luc, and Antoine Lilti. "L'écrivain face à l'État: Les demandes de pensions et de secours des hommes de lettres et savants (1780-1820)." *Revue d'histoire moderne et contemporaine* 57, nos. 4-4bis (October-December 2010): 156-184.
Charle, Christophe. "Les magistrats en France au XIXe siècle: Les fondements sociaux et politiques d'une crise prolongée." In *El tercer poder: Hacia una comprensión histórica de la justicia contemporánea en España*, edited by Johannes-Michael Scholz, 119-135. Frankfurt am Main: Vittorio Klostermann, 1992.
Church, Clive H. *Revolution and Red Tape: The French Ministerial Bureaucracy, 1770-1850*. Oxford: Clarendon Press, 1981.
Cobb, Richard. *Reactions to the French Revolution*. Oxford: Oxford University Press, 1972.
Conrad, Christoph. "The Emergence of Modern Retirement: Germany in an International Comparison (1850-1960)." *Population: An English Selection* 3 (1991): 171-200.

Conrad, Christoph. *Vom Greis zum Rentner: Der Strukturwandel des Alters in Deutschland zwischen 1830 und 1930*. Göttingen: Vandenhoeck & Ruprecht, 1994.

Crane, Susan. "Historical Subjectivity: A Review Essay." *Journal of Modern History* 78 (June 2006): 434–456.

Cribier, Françoise. "Change in the Life Course and Retirement: the Example of Two Cohorts of Parisians." In *Workers versus Pensioners*, edited by Paul Johnson, Christoph Conrad, and David Thomson, 181–201. Manchester: Manchester University Press, 1989.

Crook, Malcolm. *Toulon in War and Revolution: From the Ancien Régime to the Restoration, 1750–1820*. Manchester: Manchester University Press, 1991.

Darrow, Margaret. *Revolution in the House: Family, Class, and Inheritance in Southern France, 1775–1825*. Princeton, NJ: Princeton University Press, 1989.

Davis, Natalie Zemon. *Fiction in the Archives: Pardon Tales and Their Tellers in Sixteenth-Century France*. Stanford, CA: Stanford University Press, 1987.

Desan, Suzanne. *The Family on Trial in Revolutionary France*. Berkeley: University of California Press, 2004.

Descimon, Robert, Jean-Frédéric Schaub, and Bernard Vincent. *Les figures de l'administrateur: Institutions, réseaux, pouvoirs en Espagne, en France et au Portugal 16e–19e siècle*. Paris: EHESS, 1997.

DiCaprio, Lisa. *The Origins of the Welfare State: Women, Work, and the French Revolution*. Urbana: University of Illinois Press, 2007.

Dodman, Thomas. *What Nostalgia Was: War, Empire, and the Time of a Deadly Emotion*. Chicago: University of Chicago Press, 2018.

Doyle, William. *Venality: The Sale of Offices in Eighteenth-Century France*. Oxford: Clarendon Press, 1996.

Dumons, Bruno. "Les retraités sous la Troisième République: Lyon et sa région (1880–1914). Population, modes de vie et comportements." Doctoral thesis, Université de Lyon 2, 1990.

Dupâquier, Jacques, ed. *Marriage and Remarriage in Populations of the Past*. London: Academic Press, 1981.

Duprat, Catherine. *"Pour l'amour de l'humanité": Le temps des philanthropes. La philanthropie parisienne des Lumières à la monarchie de juillet*. Paris: CTHS, 1993.

Duprat, Catherine. *Usages et pratiques de la philanthropie: Pauvreté, action sociale et lien social, à Paris, au cours du premier XIXe siècle*. 2 vols. Paris: Comité pour l'étude de l'histoire de la sécurité sociale, 1996–97.

Durand-Barthez, Pascal. *Histoire des structures du Ministère de la Justice, 1789–1945*. Paris: PUF, 1973.

Eghigian, Greg. *Making Security Social: Disability, Insurance, and the Birth of the Social Entitlement State in Germany*. Ann Arbor: University of Michigan Press, 2000.

Ehmer, Josef. *Sozialgeschichte des Alters*. Frankfurt am Main: Suhrkamp, 1990.

Feller, Elise. "La construction sociale de la vieillesse (au cours du premier XXe siècle)." In *Histoire sociale de l'Europe: Industrialisation et société en Europe occidentale, 1880–1970*, edited by François Guedj and Stéphane Sirot, 293–317. Paris: Seli Arslan, 1997.

Feller, Elise. "Vieillissement et société dans la France du premier XXe siècle, 1905–1953." Thesis, Université Denis Diderot–Paris 7, 1997. Book version: *Histoire de la vieillesse en France (1900–1960): Du vieillard au retraité*. Paris: Seli Arslan, 2005.

Fitzsimmons, Michael P. *The Parisian Order of Barristers and the French Revolution*. Cambridge, MA: Harvard University Press, 1987.

Forrest, Alan. *The French Revolution and the Poor*. New York: St. Martin's Press, 1981.
Fray-Fournier, A. *Le Club des Jacobins de Limoges (1790–1795), d'après ses délibérations, sa correspondance et ses journaux*. Limoges: Charles-Lavauzelle, 1903.
Friedland, Paul. *Political Actors: Representative Bodies and Theatricality in the Age of the French Revolution*. Ithaca, NY: Cornell University Press, 2002.
Gégot, Jean-Claude. "Le personnel judiciaire de l'Hérault (1790–1830)." Thesis, Université Paul Valéry de Montpellier, 1974.
Gégot, Jean-Claude. "Les magistrats héraultais et la restauration (1814–1815)." In *Droite et gauche de 1789 à nos jours*, 91–103. Montpellier: Centre d'histoire contemporaine du Languedoc méditerranéen et du Roussillon, 1975.
Gilmore, Leigh. *Autobiographics: A Feminist Theory of Women's Self-Representation*. Ithaca, NY: Cornell University Press, 1994.
Godechot, Jacques. *Le comte d'Antraigues: Un espion dans l'Europe des émigrés*. Paris: Fayard, 1986.
Godechot, Jacques. *The Counter-revolution: Doctrine and Action, 1789–1804*. Translated by Salvator Attanasio. Princeton, NJ: Princeton University Press, 1986.
Goodman, Dena. *Becoming a Woman in the Age of Letters*. Ithaca, NY: Cornell University Press, 2009.
Gourdon, Vincent. *Histoire des grands-parents*. Paris: Perrin, 2001.
Grandcoing, Philippe. *Les demeures de la distinction: Châteaux et châtelains au XIXe siècle en Haute-Vienne*. Limoges: Presses Universitaires de Limoges, 2000.
Gross, Jean-Pierre. *Fair Shares for All: Jacobin Egalitarianism in Practice*. New York: Cambridge University Press, 1997.
Gubrium, Jaber. *Speaking of Life: Horizons of Meaning for Nursing Home Residents*. Hawthorne, NY: Aldine de Gruyter, 1993.
Gueslin, André. *L'état, l'économie et la société française XIXe–XXe siècle*. Paris: Hachette, 1992.
Guillemard, Anne-Marie. *Le déclin du social: Formation et crise des politiques de la vieillesse*. Paris: PUF, 1986.
Guillemard, Anne-Marie. "Emploi, protection sociale et cycle de vie: Résultats d'une comparaison internationale des dispositifs de sortie anticipée d'activité." In *Entre travail, retraite et vieillesse: Le grand écart*, edited by A.-M. Guillemard, J. Légaré, and P. Ansart, 43–71. Paris: L'Harmattan, 1995.
Guillemard, Anne-Marie. *La retraite: Une mort sociale*. Paris: Mouton, 1973.
Gullette, Margaret Morganroth. *Declining to Decline: Cultural Combat and the Politics of the Midlife*. Charlottesville: University Press of Virginia, 1997.
Gurvitch, Georges. "Problèmes de sociologie du droit." In *Traité de sociologie*, vol. 2, 173–206. Paris: PUF, 1968.
Gutton, Jean-Pierre. *Naissance du vieillard: Essai sur l'histoire des rapports entre les vieillards et la société en France*. Paris: Aubier, 1988.
Haber, Carole, and Brian Gratton. *Old Age and the Search for Security: An American Social History*. Bloomington: Indiana University Press, 1993.
Haber, David. "Life Review: Implementation, Theory, Research, and Therapy." *International Journal of Aging and Human Development* 63, no. 2 (September 2006): 153–171.
Hall, Catherine. "The Sweet Delights of Home." In *A History of Private Life*, vol. 4, edited by Michelle Perrot, 47–93. Cambridge, MA: Harvard University Press, 1990.

Hazareesingh, Sudhir, ed. *The Jacobin Legacy in Modern France: Essays in Honour of Vincent Wright*. Oxford: Oxford University Press, 2002.
Heilbrun, Carolyn G. *Writing a Woman's Life*. New York: W.W. Norton, 1988.
Heuer, Jennifer. *The Family and the Nation: Gender and Citizenship in Revolutionary France, 1789–1830*. Ithaca, NY: Cornell University Press, 2005.
Holstein, James A., and Jaber F. Gubrium. *The Self We Live By: Narrative Identity in a Postmodern World*. New York: Oxford University Press, 2000.
Horn, Jeff. *Economic Development in Early Modern France: The Privilege of Liberty, 1650–1820*. Cambridge: Cambridge University Press, 2015.
Horn, Jeff. *The Making of a Terrorist: Alexandre Rousselin and the French Revolution*. New York: Oxford University Press, 2021.
Hufton, Olwen. *The Poor of Eighteenth-Century France, 1750–1789*. Oxford: Clarendon Press, 1974.
Hunt, Lynn. *The Family Romance of the French Revolution*. Berkeley: University of California Press, 1992.
Johnson, Christopher H. *Becoming Bourgeois: Love, Kinship, and Power in Provincial France, 1670–1880*. Ithaca, NY: Cornell University Press, 2015.
Johnson, Paul, Christoph Conrad, and David Thomson, eds. *Workers versus Pensioners*. Manchester: Manchester University Press, 1989.
Johnson, Paul, and Pat Thane, eds. *Old Age from Antiquity to Post-modernity*. London: Routledge, 1998.
Jones, Colin. *Charity and Bienfaisance: The Treatment of the Poor in the Montpellier Region, 1740–1815*. Cambridge: Cambridge University Press, 1983.
Jones, Colin. *The Fall of Robespierre: 24 Hours in Revolutionary Paris*. Oxford: Oxford University Press, 2021.
Jones, Colin. "The Great Chain of Buying: Medical Advertisement, the Bourgeois Public Sphere, and the Origins of the French Revolution." *American Historical Review* 101, no. 1 (February 1996): 13–40.
Kaminsky, Marc. *The Uses of Reminiscence*. New York: Haworth Press, 1984.
Karpik, Lucien. *French Lawyers: A Study in Collective Action, 1274 to 1994*. Translated by Nora Scott. Oxford: Clarendon Press, 1999.
Kaufmann, Jean-Claude. *L'invention de soi: Une théorie de l'identité*. Paris: Armand Colin, 2004.
Kawa, Catherine. *Les ronds-de-cuir en révolution: Les employés du ministère de l'Intérieur sous la Première République (1792–1800)*. Paris: Comité des travaux historiques et scientifiques, 1997.
Kelley, Donald R. *Historians and the Law in Post-revolutionary France*. Princeton, NJ: Princeton University Press, 1984.
Kertzer, David I., and Warner K. Schaie, eds. *Age Structuring in Comparative Perspective*. Hillsdale, NJ: Lawrence Erlbaum Associates, 1989.
Kingston, Ralph R. *Bureaucrats and Bourgeois Society: Office Politics and Individual Credit in France, 1789–1848*. Houndmills, UK: Palgrave Macmillan, 2012.
Klassen, Sherri. "The Life Cycle." In *Encyclopedia of European Social History from 1350 to 2000*, edited by Peter N. Stearns, vol. 2, 193–203. Detroit: Charles Scribner's Sons, 2001.
Klassen, Sherri. "Old and Cared For: Place of Residence for Elderly Women in Eighteenth-Century Toulouse." *Journal of Family History* 24, no. 1 (1999): 35–52.
Kohli, Martin. "Ageing as a Challenge for Sociological Theory." *Ageing and Society* 8 (1988): 367–394.

Kohli, Martin. "The World We Forgot: A Historical Review of the Life Course." In *Later Life: The Social Psychology of Aging*, edited by V.W. Marshall, 271–303. Beverly Hills: Sage, 1986.

Koven, Seth, and Sonya Michel, eds. *Mothers of a New World: Maternalist Politics and the Origins of Welfare States*. New York: Routledge, 1993.

Kroen, Sheryl. *Politics and Theater: The Crisis of Legitimacy in Restoration France, 1815–1830*. Berkeley: University of California Press, 2000.

Lalive d'Epinay, Christian, and Stefano Cavalli. *Le quatrième âge ou la dernière étape de la vie*. Lausanne: Presses Polytechniques et Universitaires Romandes, 2013.

Lanza, Janine. *Wife to Widow in Early Modern Paris: Gender, Economy, and Law*. Aldershot: Ashgate, 2007.

Laslett, Peter. *A Fresh Map of Life: The Emergence of the Third Age*. London: Weidenfeld and Nicolson, 1989.

Le Bihan, Jean. *Au service de l'État: Les fonctionnaires intermédiaires au XIXe siècle*. Rennes: Presses Universitaires de Rennes, 2008.

Le Bras, Hervé. "Evolution des liens de famille au cours de l'existence." In *Les âges de la vie*, vol. 1, 27–39. Paris: PUF, 1982.

Le Bras, Hervé. "Parents, grands-parents, bisaïeux." *Population* 28 (1973): 9–38.

Le Goff, T. J. A. "Essai sur les pensions royales." In *État, marine et société*, edited by M. Acerra et al., 251–281. Paris: Presses de l'Université de Paris-Sorbonne, 1995.

Lejeune, Philippe. *Je est un autre: L'autobiographie de la littérature aux médias*. Paris: Seuil, 1980.

Leuwers, Hervé. *L'invention du barreau français 1660–1830: La construction nationale d'un groupe professionnel*. Paris: Editions de l'Ecole des hautes études en sciences sociales, 2006.

Levet, Jean. "La destruction du couvent des Grandes Carmes à Limoges." *Bulletin de la Société Archéologique et Historique du Limousin* 113 (1986): 53–57.

Macnicol, John. *Age Discrimination: An Historical and Contemporary Analysis*. Cambridge: Cambridge University Press, 2006.

Macnicol, John. *The Politics of Retirement in Britain, 1878–1948*. Cambridge: Cambridge University Press, 1998.

Maréchaux, Xavier. *Les noces révolutionnaires: Le mariage des prêtres en France (1789–1815)*. Paris: Editions Vendémiaire, 2017.

Maza, Sarah. *The Myth of the French Bourgeoisie: An Essay on the Social Imaginary, 1750–1850*. Cambridge, MA: Harvard University Press, 2003.

Maza, Sarah. "Le tribunal de la Nation: Les mémoires judiciaires et l'opinion publique à la fin de l'Ancien Régime." *Annales: E.S.C.* 1 (1987): 73–90.

Melchers, Ronald. "La vieillesse ouvrière." Unpublished manuscript based upon a 1984 *Thèse de troisième cycle* in economics, Université d'Aix-Marseille II.

Merriman, John. *Police Stories: Building the French State, 1815–1851*. New York: Oxford University Press, 2006.

Minois, Georges. *Histoire de la vieillesse*. Paris: Fayard, 1987. Translated as *History of Old Age* by Sarah Hanbury Tenison. Chicago: University of Chicago Press, 1989.

Moen, Jon. "The Labor of Older Men: A Comment." *Journal of Economic History* 47 (1987): 761–767.

Myerhoff, Barbara. *Remembered Lives: The Work of Ritual, Storytelling, and Growing Older*. Ann Arbor: University of Michigan Press, 1992.

Noiriel, Gérard. "Pour une approche subjectiviste du social." *Annales* 44 (November–December 1989): 1435–1459.
Nora, Pierre. *Les lieux de mémoire*. 7 vols. Paris: Gallimard, 1984–93.
Pedersen, Susan. *Family, Dependence, and the Origins of the Welfare State: Britain and France, 1914–1945*. Cambridge: Cambridge University Press, 1993.
Pelling, Margaret, and Richard M. Smith, eds. *Life, Death, and the Elderly: Historical Perspectives*. London: Routledge, 1991.
Petit, Jacques-Guy, ed. *Une justice de proximité: La justice de paix 1790–1958*. Paris: PUF, 2003.
Phillips, Roderick. *Family Breakdown in Late Eighteenth-Century France: Divorces in Rouen, 1792–1803*. Oxford: Clarendon Press, 1980.
Phillipson, Chris. *Capitalism and the Construction of Old Age*. London: Macmillan, 1982.
Plas, Pascal. *Avocats et barreaux dans le ressort de la cour d'appel de Limoges, 1811–1939*. Limoges: Presses Universitaires de Limoges, 2007.
Poinsot, Annie. "Inventaire des dossiers de pension des magistrats et des employés du Ministère de la Justice." Archives Nationales. 3 vols. 1814–25, 1825–40, and 1840–56.
Pollet, Gilles. "Les retraites en France (1880–1914): La naissance d'une politique sociale." Doctoral thesis, Université de Lyon 2, 1990.
Pollet, Gilles, and Bruno Dumons. "La naissance d'une politique sociale: Les retraites en France (1900–1914)." *Revue française de science politique* 41 (1991): 627–648.
Pollet, Gilles, and Bruno Dumons. *L'état et les retraites: Genèse d'une politique*. Paris: Belin, 1994.
Quadagno, Jill. *The Transformation of Old Age Security: Class and Politics in the American Welfare State*. Chicago: University of Chicago Press, 1988.
Ransom, Roger, and Richard Sutch. "The Labor of Older Americans." *Journal of Economic History* 46 (1986): 1–30.
Rausch, Fabian. "The Impossible *Gouvernement Représentatif*: Constitutional Culture in Restoration France, 1814–1830." *French History* 27, no. 2 (2013): 223–248.
Reddy, William. *The Invisible Code: Honor and Sentiment in Post-revolutionary France, 1814–1848*. Berkeley: University of California Press, 1997.
Ronsin, Francis. *Le contrat sentimental: Débats sur le mariage, l'amour, le divorce, de l'Ancien Régime à la Restauration*. Paris: Aubier, 1990.
Rosanvallon, Pierre. *L'état en France de 1789 à nos jours*. Paris: Seuil, 1990.
Rosanvallon, Pierre. *La monarchie impossible: Les chartes de 1814 et de 1830*. Paris: Fayard, 1994.
Rosenblatt, Helena. *The Lost History of Liberalism, from Ancient Rome to the Twenty-First Century*. Princeton, NJ: Princeton University Press, 2018.
Rothschild, Emma. *An Infinite History: The Story of a Family in France over Three Centuries*. Princeton, NJ: Princeton University Press, 2021.
Rousselet, Marcel. *La magistrature sous la monarchie de juillet*. Paris: Sirey, 1937.
Royer, Jean-Pierre. *Histoire de la justice en France de la monarchie absolue à la République*. Paris: PUF, 1995.
Royer, Jean-Pierre. *La société judiciaire depuis le XVIIIe siècle*. Paris: PUF, 1979.
Royer, Jean-Pierre, Renée Martinage, and Pierre Lecocq. *Juges et notables au XIXe siècle*. Paris: PUF, 1982.
Schalk, Ellery. *From Valor to Pedigree: Ideas of Nobility in France in the Sixteenth and Seventeenth Centuries*. Princeton, NJ: Princeton University Press, 1986.

Schniedewind, Karen. "Soziale Sicherung im Alter: Nationale Stereotypen und unterschieliche Lösungen in Deutschland und Frankreich in der ersten Hälfte des Jahrhunderts." *Francia* 21, no. 3 (1994): 29–49.

Sears, Elizabeth. *The Ages of Man: Medieval Interpretations of the Life Cycle.* Princeton, NJ: Princeton University Press, 1986.

Seigel, Jerrold. *The Idea of the Self: Thought and Experience in Western Europe since the Seventeenth Century.* Cambridge: Cambridge University Press, 2005.

Serna, Pierre. *La république des girouettes, 1789–1815 et au-delà. Une anomalie politique: La France de l'extrême centre.* Paris: Champ Vallon, 2005.

Sewell, William H., Jr. "The Empire of Fashion and the Rise of Capitalism in Eighteenth-Century France." *Past and Present*, no. 206 (February 2010): 81–120.

Sivaramakrishnan, Kavita. *As the World Ages: Rethinking a Demographic Crisis.* Cambridge: Harvard University Press, 2018.

Skocpol, Theda. *Protecting Solders and Mothers: The Political Origins of Social Policy in the United States.* Cambridge, MA: Harvard University Press, 1992.

Smith, Jay M. *The Culture of Merit: Nobility, Royal Service, and the Making of Absolute Monarchy in France, 1600–1789.* Ann Arbor: University of Michigan Press, 1996.

Sokoll, Thomas. "Armut im Alter im Spiegel englischer Armenbriefe des ausgehenden 18. und frühen 19. Jahrhunderts." In *Zur Kulturgeschichte des Alterns. Towards a Cultural History of Aging*, edited by Christoph Conrad and Hans-Joachim von Kondratowitz, 39–76. Berlin: Deutsches Zentrum ür Altersfragen, 1993.

Sokoll, Thomas. *Essex Pauper Letters, 1731–1837.* Oxford: Oxford University Press, 2001.

Stavenuiter, Monique, Karin Bijsterveld, and Saskia Jansens, eds. *Lange levens, stille getuigen: Oudere vrouwen in het verleden.* Zutphen: Walburg Pers, 1995. English translations of some of the contents appeared in the *Journal of Family History* 25, no. 2 (2000).

Stearns, Peter N. "Review Article." *History and Theory* 30 (1991): 261–270.

Steinberg, Ronen. *The Afterlives of the Terror: Facing the Legacies of Mass Violence in Post-revolutionary France.* Ithaca, NY: Cornell University Press, 2019.

Sturrock, John. *The Language of Autobiography: Studies in the First Person Singular.* Cambridge: Cambridge University Press, 1993.

Taylor, Charles. *Sources of the Self: The Making of the Modern Identity.* Cambridge, MA: Harvard University Press, 1989.

Thane, Pat. *Old Age in English History: Past Experiences, Present Issues.* Oxford: Oxford University Press, 2000.

Thésée, Françoise. *Le général Donzelot à la Martinique.* Paris: Karthala, 1997.

Thuillier, Guy. *La bureaucratie en France aux XIXe et XXe siècles.* Paris: Economica, 1987.

Thuillier, Guy. *Les pensions de retraite des fonctionnaires au XIXe siècle.* Paris: Comité d'Histoire de la Sécurité Sociale, 1994.

Thuillier, Guy. *Les retraites des fonctionnaires: Débats et doctrines (1790–1914).* 2 vols. Paris: Comité d'Histoire de la Sécurité Sociale, 1996.

Troyansky, David G. "Aging and Memory in a Bureaucratizing World: A French Historical Experience." In *Power and Poverty: Old Age in the Pre-industrial Past*, edited by Susannah R. Ottaway, L. A. Botelho, and Katharine Kittredge, 15–30. Westport, CT: Greenwood Press, 2002.

Troyansky, David G. *Aging in World History.* New York: Routledge, 2016.

Troyansky, David G. "Émotion et carrière: Demandes de pension et récits de vie de la magistrature française post-révolutionnaire." In *Émotions contemporaines: XIXe–XXIe siècles*, edited by Anne-Claude Ambroise-Rendu, Anne-Emmanuelle Demartini, Hélène Eck, and Nicole Edelman, 233–241. Paris: Armand Colin, 2014.

Troyansky, David G. "Generational Discourse in the French Revolution." In *The French Revolution in Culture and Society*, edited by David G. Troyansky, Alfred Cismaru, and Norwood Andrews Jr., 23–31. New York: Greenwood Press, 1991.

Troyansky, David G. *Old Age in the Old Regime: Image and Experience in Eighteenth-Century France*. Ithaca, NY: Cornell University Press, 1989.

Troyansky, David G. "Old Age, Retirement, and the Social Contract in 18th- and 19th-Century France." In *Zur Kulturgeschichte des Alterns. Towards a Cultural History of Aging*, edited by Christoph Conrad and Hans-Joachim von Kondratowitz, 77–95. Berlin: Deutsches Zentrum ür Altersfragen, 1993.

Troyansky, David G. "Personal and Institutional Narratives of Aging: A French Historical Case." *Journal of Aging Studies* 17 (2003): 31–42.

Troyansky, David G. "Retraite, vieillesse, et contrat social: L'exemple des juges de la Haute-Vienne sous la Restauration." In *Entre travail, retraite et vieillesse: Le grand écart*, edited by A.-M. Guillemard, J. Légaré, and P. Ansart, 85–101. Paris: L'Harmattan, 1995.

Tulard, Jean. *Dictionnaire Napoléon*. Paris: Fayard, 1987.

Van Kley, Dale, ed. *The French Idea of Freedom: The Old Regime and the Declaration of Rights of 1789*. Stanford, CA: Stanford University Press, 1994.

Veillon, Didier. *Magistrats au XIXe siècle en Charente-Maritime, Vienne, Deux-Sèvres et Vendée*. La Crèche: Geste éditions, 2001.

Verjus, Anne, and Denise Davidson. *Le roman conjugal: Chroniques de la vie familiale à l'époque de la Révolution et de l'Empire*. Seyssel: Champ Vallon, 2011.

Vovelle, Michel. *Les Jacobins, de Robespierre à Chevènement*. Paris: La Découverte, 1999.

Walton, Charles. *Policing Public Opinion in the French Revolution: The Culture of Calumny and the Problem of Free Speech*. Oxford: Oxford University Press, 2009.

Wildt, Annemarie de, and Willem van der Ham. *Tijd van Leven: Ouder worden in Nederland vroeger en nu*. Amsterdam: Amsterdams Historisch Museum, 1993.

Woloch, Isser. *The New Regime: Transformations of the French Civic Order, 1789–1820s*. New York: W.W. Norton, 1994.

Wunder, Bernd. "Die Einführung des staatlichen Pensionssystems in Frankreich (1760–1850)." *Francia* 11 (1983): 417–474.

Yalom, Marilyn. *Blood Sisters: The French Revolution in Women's Memory*. New York: Basic Books, 1993.

Zysberg, André. *L'affaire d'Orgères 1790–1800*. Chartres: Société archéologique d'Eure et Loir, 1985.

Index

For the benefit of digital users, indexed terms that span two pages (e.g., 52–53) may, on occasion, appear on only one of those pages.

Figures are indicated by *f* following the page number

Abadie, Jean Joseph, 139–40
Abbot, Andrew, 83
Acher, Nicolas, 32, 123, 129
acte additionnel, 110–11, 135–36, 149–50, 151, 155
age, 3, 76–77
    at death, 94, 166
    fourth, 4
    at retirement, 88, 92, 94–95
    third, 75–76
aging, 3–4, 5–6, 9, 140, 187–88
Aguesseau, Henri-Cardin-Jean-Baptiste, marquis d', 65
Aguesseau, Henri-François, chancelier d', 51–52, 130–31
Aguillon, Pierre-Gabriel, 103–4, 108
Aix-en-Provence, 36, 84, 107–9, 121, 156–57, 166–67, 169
Alba (Chalon-sur-Saône), 134
Allen, Robert, 24
almanac, 31, 39, 83
Altanic Saint Ougal (Île de France and Vannes), 122
Amiens, 32, 60, 84, 137, 158, 170
    Treaty of (1802), 33
Anfrye, Pierre-François, 82
Antiboul, Claude-Honoré, 141–42
Antraigues, Louis-Alexandre de Launay, comte d', 47
Archives Nationales, 1–2, 9–10, 27
Arnaud de Puimoisson, Jean-Baptiste, 109
Auber, Victoire-Catherine-Désirée, 172
autobiography, 9, 13, 115, 180–81
Azimi, Vida, 22

Babeuf, Gracchus, 140

Baffier, François, 109
Baldwin, Peter, 7, 18
Barbier, Pierre, 113–14, 157–58
Barges, Jean André, 126
Barli, Antoine Joseph Louis Marie, 78*f*, 121, 123
Bas-Rhin, 10, 84, 85, 86, 94–95, 104. *See also* Strasbourg
Bell, David A., 75
Berger, Emmanuel, 24
Besançon, 60
Bessejon de la Chassagne, Antoine, 26–27
Besson, Jacques, 122
Bezard, François-Siméon, 137
Bichat, Xavier, 65
biens nationaux, 107, 111
Bismarck, Otto von, 2, 6–7, 17–18
Bladviel (Figeac), 125
Boissy d'Anglas, François Antoine, comte de, 69
Bonaparte, Napoléon, 25–26, 38–39
    administrative reorganization under, 20–21, 30–31, 55–60, 119
    appeal to, 28–29, 32, 34–35, 51–53, 122, 132–34, 139, 180
    criticism of, 149
    serving, 168–69
Bonnet, Louis-Ferdinand, 75–76
Borscheid, Peter, 5–6
Bouches-du-Rhône, 10, 84, 86, 94–95, 103–4, 157–58. *See also* Aix-en-Provence; Marseille
Bourbon dynasty, 109, 134–35, 156
Brenot, Jeanne, widow Vitet, 168
brigandage, 140, 141–42, 167–68
Brigands d'Orgères, 140

230 INDEX

Brittany, 51–52, 184
Brussels, 60, 132
Bruxelle, Geneviève Adelaïde, widow Dumont, 178–79
bureaucracy, 9, 27, 74
  appeals to, 183
  continuity of, 81, 158
  correspondence with, 2–3, 115, 170–71, 175
  development of, 4–5, 13, 17, 22, 60, 123, 137–38, 146
  failure of, 135–36
  functioning of, 154, 181

Cabasse, François Jean Alexandre Prosper, 156–57
Caen, 84, 110–13, 151, 157
cahiers de doléances, 24–25
Callamard, Jean-André, 114
calumny, 132
Calvados, 10, 84, 86, 94, 104, 109–13
  See also Caen
career(s), 4–5, 8, 26–27, 161, 168
  across regimes, 25
  imagining, 22, 28
  narrating, 32–35
  normalization of, 81, 115, 184–85
  patterns, 11–12, 75–76, 95–105, 109, 149
  retrospective construction of, 74
  women's, 162, 173–75
careerism, 3–4, 115
Caribbean, 183–84. *See also* Guadeloupe *and* Saint Domingue
Carpentier, Jean-Baptiste Le, 32–33
Carrier, Jean-Baptiste, 51, 133
Cartault (Fontainebleau), 35–36
Cetty, François-Louis, 129, 131
Chaillon, Aimée-Gabrielle, widow Letourneux, 176
Chaix d'Estanges, Richard François, 51
Chalopin, Gilles-Jacques-Charles, 109–10
Chamber of Deputies, 60, 69–71, 138
Chamber of Peers, 65–69
Chamber of Representatives, 110–11, 149–50
Charles X, 71–72, 150–51
Charter of 1830, 114–15

children, 34, 138, 172, 177–78
  orphaned, 10, 20–21, 56, 62, 71, 161
Chiniac, Pierre, 48–49, 50*f*
Chouans, 131
Cicero, 38, 39–40, 41*f*, 54, 75, 83
  De Senectute, 39–40, 41*f*
citizenship, 2, 13, 22
civic order, 13, 22–23, 26
civil servants, 3–4, 7, 11, 20, 22, 28–29, 55
Collet, Augustine Gabrielle, widow Rivoallon, 177
Collignon (Dinant), 31
commissions of judges, 64–65, 69–70
Committee of Public Safety, 44, 45, 112–13, 138
comparison and emulation, 130, 150
complaint, 2, 10–11, 13–14, 35, 169, 171, 187–88
  about rules, 72, 175–76
Conrad, Christoph, 6–7, 8, 18
Constitution of the Year VIII, 25
Constitutional Charter of 1814, 60–62, 65, 114
Converset, Anne, widow Roullois, 174–75
corps, 12–13, 24
Courmes, Antoine-Paul-Joseph, 114–15, 147–48, 170
Crespin, Louis-René, 120–21
Cribier, Françoise, 8
Cudenet, Jean-Antoine, 32–35

Daigremont, Jean-Baptiste-Augustin, 110
Dambray, Charles Henri, chancelier, 62
Dandrimont (Liège), 31
Danthine (Liège), 31
David, François, 8–9, 105–7, 158
David, Pierre Jean Baptiste, 158
Davis, Natalie Zemon, 11
de-Christianization, 5–6
Decree of March 1, 1852 on obligatory retirement, 73
Decree of March 24, 1808 on organization of justice, 119
Decree of October 2, 1807 on disability, 30, 31, 58, 125
Decree of September 13, 1806 on eligibility for retirement, 30, 57, 135
De Lautremange (Liège), 31

INDEX   231

Deligné, Gilles Joseph, 39–43
De L'Horme, Barthélemy-Fleury, 112–13
Demetz (Nancy), 30–31
Denizot (Paris), 130
Derivaux, Charles Joseph, 121–22
Descombles (Nantes), 133
Devérité, Louis-Alexandre, 44, 152
dignity, 73, 143, 186
Diverneresse-Lamarche, Léonard, 105, 154
documentation, 56, 57, 72, 84, 122–23, 139, 184–85
  and gender differences, 169
droits acquis, 122, 147, 156, 177, 186
Dumolard, Joseph Vincent, 60–62
Dumons, Bruno, 7, 19–20
Duplessis de Grénédan, Louis-Joseph, 70
Durand-Maillane, Pierre-Toussaint, 36–39
Dutrone (Caen), 110, 151, 180
Duval, Adelaïde Flore, née Maressal, 170
Duvillard, Marie-Hyacinthe, widow Garlan, 174–75

Eghigian, Greg, 17–18
Egypt, 180
Ehmer, Josef, 6–7
emigration, 107, 108, 122, 148, 167, 172–73
emotion, 184–85, 186
empire, 32, 60, 108, 120–21, 184
employees, 59, 170
emulation, 26–27
Enlightenment, 5–6, 7, 24–25, 54–55
entitlement(s), 3–4, 13, 22–23, 26, 119
  claims of, 10–11
  modern politics of, 1
  recognition of, 28–29
equity, 12–13, 26, 72, 140–41, 174–75
Espagnet, Augustin-Honoré-Louis d', 103–4, 107, 132
ethic of justice, 182
ethic of need, 182

Fabre, Baron Jean Marie Noël, 135–36
Fabri-Borrilly, Honoré-Sauveur, 103–4, 108
Falconnet, Ambroise, 26
family, 36, 83, 120, 128, 160–82

service, 32, 48, 111, 113, 130–31, 152–53
favor, 8–9, 12–13, 22–23
  language of, 28–29, 130–31, 146, 147
Federalist Revolt, 157
fédérés, 110, 113, 131, 149
Feller, Elise, 8, 19–20
fermiers-généraux (tax farmers), 22, 53, 54
First World War, 18
Foncez, Charles, 132
fonctionnaires, 20–21, 43, 112–13, 128–29, 144, 152, 159
  historical literature on, 24
  as models for citizens, 185
  under Napoleon, 134, 142–43
  outside France, 121–22
  reputation of, 185
Fontainebleau, 35
forms (bureaucratic), 72, 77–79, 78f, 170, 178, 185
fraternity, 138, 141–42
French Revolution (1789-99), 22–24, 28–29, 32–33, 76–77, 120. *See also* Terror
  events of, 36–38, 42, 44–45, 140, 152, 155, 166–67
  historiography of, 183–84
  human rights and, 2
  justice and, 25
  law and, 24–25
  legacy of, 1, 136
  legislation of, 21, 54–57, 173
  losses during, 166–67
  memory of, 42–45, 48–49, 82–83, 128–29, 132–33, 138–39, 148–52, 168
  social policy during, 2

Gamon, François Joseph, 45–47
Gaudin, Jacques, 134
Gégot, Jean-Claude, 83–84
gender, 13–14, 144–46, 160–82
generations. *See also* intergenerational relations
  construction of identity and, 184, 187
  households and, 172–73
  of public service, 43–44, 108–9, 134, 152–53, 176
Genoa, 60, 121
Germany, 6–7, 17–18, 20, 120–21
gerontocracy, 103–4

gerontology, 3–4, 13–14, 29, 82, 128, 142, 182
Girondins, 45–47
girouette (political weathervane), 136, 150–51, 187
Giscard, Antoine, 124–25
Gispert Dulçat, Joseph Honoré François, 130–31
Gonet, Héloise Rose Honorine, née Schaub, 163
grandchildren, 34, 128, 138, 173, 178, 179
Grandcoing, Philippe, 107
Grand Juge, Minister of Justice, 28, 58
grandparents, 5–6
Great Britain, 18, 20
Guadeloupe, 122, 156–57
Gubrium, Jaber, 11
Guérin, Charles-Antoine, 108–9
Guerrier, François, 135
Guillemard, Anne-Marie, 4
Gurvitch, Georges, 22
Guyot, Nicolas-Joseph, 122

Hamelin, Marie Thérèse, née Kretz, 170–71
Haute-Vienne, 10, 84, 86, 94–95, 104–5. *See also* Limoges
Hellouin, Jean-Baptiste, 111, 155
Henri IV, 110, 111–12, 148
Heyler, Sophie Wilhelmine Philippine, widow Zeyss, 174
history
  cultural, 5–6, 119, 183
  political, 183
  social, 3–5, 6–8, 24, 183
honor, 13–14, 26–27, 36–38, 39–40, 58, 185
honorary title, 58, 83, 159
Hufton, Olwen, 172
humanism, 39–40
Humbourg, Marie Jeanne Henriette, widow Besson, 168
Hundred Days, 12, 26, 59, 110–11, 137, 149, 155

Île de France (Mauritius), 120–21, 122
inamovibilité (life tenure), 13, 25–26, 27, 58, 60, 65–73, 114
infirmities, 123–28, 153, 158–59, 169, 172
  describing, 34, 82
  mental, 178–79
  public revelation of, 67
  reporting, 58, 64–65
intergenerational relations, 1–2, 3–4, 11–12, 29–30, 129, 171–72

Jacobinism, 4, 55, 113, 114
Johnson, Christopher, xi, 184
Johnson, Paul, 6
Juge Saint Martin, Jacques-Joseph, 105, 107
juges de paix (justices of the peace), 12, 35–36, 105, 113–14, 155, 174
July Monarchy, 83–84, 109, 112–14, 148, 150–51, 157–58
justice
  access to, 24–25
  distributive, 9, 109, 140–41
  independence of, 26, 27
  language of, 25, 72, 140–41
Justy, Magdeleine Cécile Delphine, widow Fossé, 161–62

Karpik, Lucien, 25, 26
Kohli, Martin, 4

Lally-Tolendal, Gérard, marquis de, 69
Lamoignon de Malesherbes, Chrétien-Guillaume, 130–31
Lanoailles-Lachèze, Jean-Joseph, 105
Lanoailles-Lachèze, Léonard, 105
Lapouyade, Françoise Pétrouille Bonhomme de, widow Senamand de Beaufort, 165
La Rochefoucauld, François, duc de, 139
Laslett, Peter, 4
Lauxerrois, Claude, 139
law codes, 28
Law of 8 Messidor, Year II, 54–55
Law of 15 Germinal, Year XI, 56–57, 129
Law of June 8, 1853, 20
Law of 1910, 19
lawyers, 11, 23–26, 75–76
leaves of absence, 39, 64
Leclerc de Beaulieu, François, 71
Lecouturier, Louis-François-Salomon, 111

Le Follet (Caen), 110–11
Legion of Honor, 36
Legislative Assembly, 44
letter-writing, 166, 180–81
Leuwers, Hervé, 24
liberalism, 19, 20
life course, 4, 5, 8, 13–14, 17, 19–20, 120, 184–85
life review, 3–4, 12–13, 29, 72, 74, 128, 184–85
life story, 82, 134–35, 152
Limoges, 60, 84, 105–7, 121, 149, 156–57, 158, 169
literary work, 32, 134, 139, 141–42, 154–55, 178
Lombard, Joseph, 109, 148
Long, Louis, 114
Loubers (de Cordes), Augustin, 47–48
Louis IX, 111–12, 148, 151
Louis XIV, 111–12, 148
Louis XVI, 44, 67, 82, 136–37, 138
Louis XVIII, 44, 46f, 71–72, 110, 140–41, 151, 175
Louis-Philippe, 148, 170–71, 176
loyalty, 43
Loyson, Catherine-Elisabeth-Françoise, 176
Lyon, 19–20, 84, 123, 129, 152, 168, 169, 178

Macnicol, John, 7, 18
Macron, Emmanuel, 2, 187
Madier de Montjau, Noel-Joseph, 152, 178
magistrates, 2–3, 10–11, 23–27, 43–44, 54, 159
    honor of, 53
    image of, 53
Malfillatre, Augustine, widow Dobignié, 161–62
Marat, Jean-Paul, 45–47
Marbois, François, marquis de Barbé-, 67, 112–13
marriage, 138, 172, 174
Marseille, 84, 114–15, 147–48, 154–55, 179
Martin, Marguerite-Josephine, widow Igonel, 179
Massena, André, Maréchal, 108–9

Maubant, Pierre-Adrien, 113, 157
Maupeou, René Nicolas Charles Augustin de, 25
Mayence (Mainz), 121
Maza, Sarah, xi, 26
medical certification, 125–26, 153
medicalization, 6, 13–14, 125–28, 186–87
melodrama, 13–14, 139, 169
Melun, 35–36
memory, 140, 186
merit, 12–14, 22, 28–29, 175
Meunier, Marie Louise Ulrique, widow Vasse St Ouen, 178
Ministry of Justice, 2, 9–10, 54, 56–58, 63–65, 84
Minois, Georges, 5
moderation, 53, 109, 134, 136–37
monarchists, 12, 108–9, 148, 151–52
Montesquieu, Charles de Secondat, Baron de la Brède et de, 67
Montpellier, 60, 121, 124–25
Morand de Jouffrey, Antoine, 154, 156–57
Morel, Philippe-Martin-Antoine, 111
Mousnier-Buisson, Jacques, 69–70
mutual aid societies, 18

Nantes, 51, 133
narcissism, 26–27, 142
narrative, 32–39, 43–44, 51, 176
    of careers and history, 27, 29–30
    "return to," 11
    revolutionary, 131, 140
National Convention, 44, 45–47, 136–37, 157
national guard, 48
national history, 12–13
Netherlands, 59–60, 77
Nîmes, 60
nobility, 26, 28–29
norms, 13, 81, 185–86
nostalgia, 43–44

old age, historiography of, 2, 3–8
Old Regime, 8–9, 12–13, 23–24, 25, 28–29, 43–44, 49, 151
Olivier, Elisabeth Toinette Emilie, née Barbier, 169

ordonnance royale of October 2, 1822 on temporary indemnities, 64
ordonnance royale of September 23, 1814 on retirement, 10, 13, 60, 62, 77–79, 119, 135, 161–62, 176
ordonnance royale of January 9, 1815 on retirement, 10, 13, 77–79, 119, 135
ordonnance royale of June 16, 1824 on infirmity forcing retirement, 64–65, 73
ordonnance royale of August 17, 1824 on widows and orphans of magistrates, 71, 161
ordonnance royale of November 24, 1824 on counting Old Regime service, 71–72
Orvilliers, Jean-Louis Tourteau, marquis d', 65
Osterrieth, Catherine Marguerite, widow Spielmann, 177–78
otium cum dignitate (leisure with dignity), 107
Oudot, Charles François, 81–82

Papon, Sylvestre-Antoine, 154–55
Paris, 8, 32, 51, 59, 140, 167–68, 177–79
Parlement de Bretagne, 39–40, 133
Parlement de Metz, 135
Parlement de Paris, 44, 48, 75, 167–68, 173–74
Parlement de Provence, 107, 156–57
parliamentary debate, 65–71, 126
Pasquier, Etienne, 69
pathos, 13–14, 139, 181
Pau, 60
Pazery de Thorame, François-Pierre-Joseph, 103–4, 107–8, 153
Pedersen, Susan, 7
pension(s), 9–10, 17–23, 28–29, 30–31, 55–65
    funds, 20–21, 64
    historiography of, 2, 7, 185, 186
    Old Regime, 21–23, 178
    reform, 2, 156
Pepin, Silvain, 136–37
Périgueux, 48
Perret, François Marie, 81
personnel, 26, 119, 154
Peyronnet, Pierre-Denis, comte de, 65, 66f, 67–70

Philippe-Delleville, Jean-François, 112
Piedmont, 124
Plutarch, 32, 134
Poitiers, 60
political culture, 12
Pollet, Gilles, 7, 19–20
Portalis, Joseph-Marie, comte, 152, 155
Poullain de Grandprey, Joseph-Clément, 138
Poulliande, Marie Pauline, widow de Laistre, 162
poverty, old-age, 5–6, 54–55
priests, 114, 122, 136, 141
privilege, 4–5, 10–11, 12–13, 28–29
professionalization, 22, 24–26, 83–84
public, 2–3
public utility, 55–56
purge, 26, 38–39, 76
Puthod, Claude-Marie-François, 150–51
Puthod de Maison Rouge, François-Marie, 151

Reck, Frédérique Marie Madeleine de, widow Leroy, 168–69
Régnier, Claude-Ambroise, Duc de Massa, 41f, 50f, 59–60, 61f, 130, 132, 133, 142, 174–75
Rennes, 39–40, 51, 177
Restoration, 8–9, 30, 44, 60–72, 80f, 81–82, 114, 139–40
    career transitions in, 134–35, 151
    judicial purge in, 26
    retirement in, 86
retirement
    and aging, 3
    dossiers, 12, 79–81, 84
    in early Restoration, 107
    forced or mandatory, 13, 31, 64–65, 72–74, 115
    as gendered, 14
    historiography of, 2, 7–8, 18–23
    humanist, 5–6, 83, 141
    as managing old age, 18, 77, 153
    model, 83, 141, 178
    planning, 12, 30–31, 154, 159
    prerevolutionary, 54
    procedure, 62–65, 129–30
    reactions to, 142
    seeking, 12
retraité, 19–20

retreat, 3–4
Revolution of 1830, 72, 81, 114, 137, 151–52, 156–57, 169
Revolution of 1848, 72–73, 115, 151–52, 158–59
Rhône, 10, 84, 86, 94–95, 104. *See also* Lyon
right(s), 1, 10–11, 12–13, 17
　human, 1, 23–24, 186–87
　intuitive, 22, 71, 176
　to retirement, 10–11, 19–20, 23, 27, 28–29, 57–58
Rivals de Lacombe, Jean-Pierre, 111–12, 148
Robespierre, Augustin, 108–9
Robespierre, Maximilien, 32–33, 44, 45–47, 138
Romer, Nicolas-Joseph, 59, 79, 80*f*, 111, 147, 154, 161–62, 168, 176
Rothschild, Emma, xi, 184
Rousseau, Jean-Jacques, 139
Roussel-Bouret, Joseph-François-Ignace, 49–51
Rousselet, Marcel, 83–84
Rousselin, Adrien-Pierre, 113
Rousselin, Pierre-François, 111, 151
Rousselin, Pierre-Marcel, 113
Royer, Jean-Pierre, 25, 83–84

Saint-Domingue, 122, 133, 150–51, 168
Saint-Malo, 32–33
Salm, 121–22
Sauty (Limoges), 149
Scandinavia, 18
self, 3, 9, 115
self-fashioning, 23–24, 77–79, 163
self-image, 71, 144, 171, 175, 176–77, 180–81
self-presentation, 8–9, 39, 77–79, 166
Sénatus-Consulte of October 12, 1807, 58, 119
Sèze, Casimir de, 158
Sèze, Jean Casimir de, 126, 127*f*
Sèze, Raymond, comte de, 67, 68*f*, 127*f*
Sieyès, Joseph-Barthelemy, 141–42
Simplet, Marie Françoise, widow Puntis, 180
social contract, 3–4, 20–21
socialism, 19
social security, 18–19, 22

society of orders, 4–5
Sokoll, Thomas, 8
Somme, 10, 84, 86, 94–95, 104. *See also* Amiens
Spitzer, Alan, 140
Stearns, Peter, 5
Strasbourg, 84, 148, 167, 168, 174

Talleyrand-Périgord, Charles Maurice de, 76–77
Tattegrain, Marie Claire Julie, 161
temporalities, 14, 182
Terror
　and break in careers, 130–31
　experiences of the, 131, 132–33, 152
　imprisonment during the, 51, 81, 110, 112–13
　and political enmity, 48
　and revolutionary justice, 25
　service in time of, 35–36
Thane, Pat, 18
"themistocracy," 23–24
Thermidor, 32–33, 44, 138
Third Republic, 19–20
Thouvenel (Sarrebourg and Nancy), 28–31
Thuillier, Guy, 7, 20–22
Thuriot de la Rosière, Jacques Alexis, 44–47, 138
Tocqueville, Alexis de, 3–4, 22
Toulouse, 47–48, 49
Tournon, Marie Etiennette, widow Riolz, 178
Tronjolly, François Anne Louis-Phelippes de, 51–53, 124
Turin, 60
Tuscany, 77, 121–22, 123

Uzerches, 48

Vannes, 122
Vatimesnil, Antoine-Lefebvre de, 71
venality of office, 3–4, 12–13
Vergennes, Charles Gravier, comte de, 130–31
veterans, 21
victimization, 130–32
　in self-presentation, 147–48, 150–52, 161–62, 176–77, 187
Vignali, Jean-Antoine, 32

Voltaire, 139

welfare state, 1–2, 3–4, 7, 17–19, 128–29
widows, 160–82
    demands by, 14
    limited benefits for, 55, 56, 59, 62
    rights of, 10, 20–21, 71
    support for, 56
    of veterans, 21
withholding (from salaries), 20–21, 22, 57–58, 63–64, 71, 137